I0329925

The Art of Crisis Management: The Howard Government Experience, 1996-2007

Andrew Blyth, Editor

Connor Court Publishing

Published in 2024 by Connor Court Publishing Pty Ltd.

Connor Court Publishing Pty Ltd.
PO Box 7257
Redland Bay QLD 4165
sales@connorcourt.com
www.connorcourt.com

ISBN: 9781923224261

Cover Design by Ian James

Front cover image supplied by Department of Defence.

Cover image: Australian Prime Minister, John Howard, the Indonesian Minister of Foreign Affairs, Dr Hassan Wirajuda (right), and the Vice Governor of Aceh Province, Mr Azwar Abubakar (left), discuss tsunami disaster relief work on site in the devastated provincial capital of Banda Aceh, 2 February 2005.

Printed in Australia.

Contents

Foreword

Sir Peter Cosgrove

"Events, dear boy, events" – said by Harold Macmillan, quoted herein by Richard Alston to illustrate one source of crisis to descend on governments.

Of course, the nature of an 'event' meant by Macmillan and assumed by all of us, is that it is unexpected, serious and unwelcomed and thus a crisis. There are of course those planned matters that government undertakes which with gritted teeth it must then manage through to acceptance, success or failure. This marvellous work by Andrew Blyth and his essayists canvasses the Howard years with fascinating accounts and insights into political leadership, management and outcomes. In doing so it is not just a most interesting read for all of us but a virtual primer for modern Australian governments.

I mentioned 'essayists'. Not only are all of them eminent in their field but they are diverse and persuasive. Andrew has avoided 'hagiography' and in John Howard's conclusion you will find that he tips his hat to that approach. I think that like me, you will conclude that makes this work, stronger and more valuable.

I was thrilled to be invited to pen this foreword – for a start I got a very early read! Part of the thrill though was that it was my fate to be closely involved in six years of the Howard Government's tenure and as a senior military officer, a keenly interested onlooker of the rest of that government's political life.

So, Andrew, essayists and readers, please forgive some brief observations on a crisis which 'didn't make the cut' – the Asian Tsunami of 26 December 2004. Australians were caught up in the tragedy but our homeland itself was unscathed. To our north it was a different story. Hundreds of thousands of people within and on the fringes of the Indian Ocean were displaced and at very high risk.

Vast numbers were killed in those terrifying waves, particularly in Indonesia. In the hours of that Boxing Day afternoon, at John Howard's direction, we dispatched an air armada full of people and life-supporting stores to Sumatra, mobilised ships and people to follow and crucially the government provided firm commitment of many hundreds of millions of dollars in relief aid.

Australia became the first of Indonesia's friends and neighbours to provide such major practical and financial aid and it showed immediately in not only the restoration of but significant improvement in, the bilateral relationship. In my view it was not only John Howard's immediate grasp of the public's sense of horror and compassion but his sense that a timely overriding of contemporary ill feelings between our two nations was possible. By any standards, his decisiveness, his balance of need and opportunity, showed a leader at the top of his game.

Dear readers, you will find abundant references throughout many of these accounts to the stability of the Howard Government (with some irony about a certain revolving door syndrome in its early years!). Such stability was indeed my experience as a close onlooker. It is fascinating to ponder whether it was 'the times' (viz the subsequent rise of social media, the notion of a more partisan legacy media); perhaps it was the innate discipline of the government parties; or was it from the top, the prime minister and his very senior colleagues.

Perhaps those days of relative stability and resolve are gone, which would be a great pity. Perhaps it would take a great tectonic shock to restore them, which would be again a great pity. Governments of today in many places around the world can seem to be irretrievably 'retail', can sometimes seem to engage in the weird sport of log-rolling: furiously running on top of a log floating in a river, to keep it rotating but essentially going nowhere.

In closing, I must congratulate Connor Court Publishing for their part in bringing it to what I know will be a most avid readership.

We are much endowed by this book, inspired, curated and edited by Andrew Blyth. We are indebted to the essayists for their eloquent and compelling observations of a very significant political and historical period, straddling the change of millennia in our nation. We the readership thank and congratulate them all.

General The Honourable Sir Peter Cosgrove AK AC (Mil) CVO MC (RETD)

26th Governor-General of Australia (2014-2019) and former Chief of the Defence Force (2002-2005)

Preface

Andrew Blyth

From 2 March 1996, to 24 November 2007, Australia experienced a profound transformation under the leadership of its 25th and second-longest serving prime minister, John Howard OM, AC.

The Art of Crisis Management: The Howard Government Experience, 1996-2007 delves deep into this transformative era, chronicling the strategic decisions, policy shifts, and political manoeuvrings that defined the Howard Government's approach to crisis management.

The following chapters are based on contributions delivered at the sixth annual Howard Government retrospective conference, held at the National Press Club of Australia in Canberra on 23-24 June 2022. This event brought together prominent scholars, policy makers, and political figures to reflect on and analyse the achievements, challenges, and legacy of the Howard Government. The insights and discussions from this conference form the foundation of the content presented in these chapters.

Like all political leaders, Howard faced both acclaim and criticism (more the latter) in his handling of events. This book offers a balanced exploration, shedding light on the successes and failures, the calculated risks, the unexpected challenges, and the lessons learned that continue to influence Australian political discourse.

Drawing on firsthand accounts from key political figures such as John Howard, Richard Alston, Mal Brough, Labor's Stephen Martin, leading political commentators Paul Kelly and Shaun Carney, academic professors David W. Lovell, Zarah Ghazarian, Pene Mathew, and James Walter, strategic analyst Peter Jennings, scholar-warrior David Kilcullen, and communications experts David Marshall and Fiona Wade, this comprehensive account provides insights into the art of political leadership during turbulent times. It also paints a vivid portrait of a nation's journey through an eventful eleven and a half years.

For scholars, policymakers, and curious readers alike, this book offers a front-row seat to the complex interplay of politics, public sentiment, and global events that shaped Australia at the turn of the millennium. Dive in to explore an era that, in many ways, set the stage for the challenges and opportunities the nation faces today.

Introduction

Managing crises:
The Howard Government in retrospect

David W. Lovell

Dealing with adversity is the default position of contemporary government. Unexpected, unwanted and unanticipated events are almost daily occurrences.

The reach of government now extends so far into our lives that citizens expect it not just to create a framework for individual flourishing (their traditional role of ensuring order and security), but to anticipate and defend against disasters great and small, natural, social and economic, and clean up and make right when the 'unthinkable' happens, as it so often does.

Indeed, popular expectations are such that government responses are rarely deemed either timely or adequate.

Blaming governments of the day for not living up to expectations they themselves have created is understandable, if simplistic.

The language of crisis has become the staple of day-to-day partisan posturing, whatever the issue. Yet adversity, despite media headlines and the insistence of oppositions, does not equal crisis.

Real crises are always unique, and usually unexpected, even if their portents and general shape might be discernable. Real crises happen when governments mishandle adversity.

Maladroit government responses are caused variously by inexperience, secrecy, arrogance (and its cousin, denial), inattention and, at worse, incompetence.

The record of the Howard Government (1996-2007) is instructive in separating real from imagined crises. Adversity aplenty; crises not so much.

That John Howard had been a minister in the Fraser Government meant that despite the relative inexperience of his Cabinet at the beginning of his prime ministership he had a feel for the tempests of office. His sure-footedness increased along with his tenure.

The Howard Government faced a number of acute challenges, from the beginning of the 'war on terror', through the (almost simultaneous) collapse of Australia's second airline, Ansett, through the threats to border control, to the scandal of the Australian Wheat Board's dealings with Iraq's leader, Saddam Hussein, and the waterfront struggles of Australia's stevedoring companies against union control. Few of them festered into crises.

The first test came just eight weeks after Howard won government. The Port Arthur massacre in April 1996 crystalised sentiments around the availability of firearms across Australia. Howard acted quickly, decisively and with clear intent. He coordinated with the Nationals, his Coalition partners, and the states. He spoke directly with the people.

Sending Australian troops to East Timor as part of INTERFET in September 1999 to protect the local population who had decided on independence from Indonesia was a decision fraught with danger for our forces and damaged Australia's relations with our largest neighbour.

September 11, 2001 was another such inflection point, when the terrorist attacks on the United States led Howard to invoke the ANZUS pact for the first time ever. This was uncharted territory that had the potential for a civilisational split between Christianity and Islam, which the Islamists had hoped to engineer. The Bali bombings in October 2002, killing 202 (including 88 Australians), was part of that terrorist offensive, but Howard's measured responses helped bring Australia and Indonesia closer again.

Apart from the Millenium Drought (2001-9), natural disasters were episodic and localised: the Thredbo landslide in July 1997; the Sydney hailstorm in April 1999; the Canberra fires in January 2003;

Cyclone Larry in north Queensland in March 2006; the Newcastle floods in June 2007, and floods in Gippsland the next month. While each of them revealed serious shortcomings, especially in equipment and communications, none called into fundamental question the structure of emergency responses, or government policy settings. The Drought, by contrast, led to the 2007 National Plan for Water Security.

Adversity, however, comes in different forms, from the contingent, acute challenges we readily dub crises, to the the systemic social, economic and other processes that lead to a catastrophic event and where the term crisis is also fitting.

The deep-seated crises facing the Howard Government, which erupt in episodic disasters still today, have for decades been the subject of growing concern and makeshift policy 'solutions'. They are notable in Indigenous affairs (which led, *inter alia*, to the Northern Territory intervention in 2007), in aged care (marked by the kerosene baths affair in 2000), and in the regulation of corporate governance (brought into focus by the collapse of HIH Insurance in 2001, perhaps the largest corporate collapse in Australia's history).

The challenge in these areas was, and remains, less about making a rapid response to an emergency than about addressing policymakers' own long-term perspectives and assumptions. As Howard himself said in October 2007, for example, Indigenous disadvantage was something he struggled with during his entire time as prime minister, and his way of looking at, and responding to, the crisis was 'an artefact of who I am and the time in which I grew up'.

Good government is about managing adversity well. It is about understanding the capabilities available, and about being nimble, open, direct and effectual. It is about more than being simply reactive. Sometimes it means looking at underlying problems with new lenses. Crises can help to re-set a debate, or re-frame a policy.

Governments must learn from managing crisis events: not so much establishing high-profile inquiries that often divert attention and delay action, but incorporating lessons into everyday practice. In more than eleven years in government, Howard called only three Royal Commissions and two Commissions of Inquiry.

The Howard Government has a deserved reputation for competence, for avoiding crises, real and manufactured. It dealt with the Chicken Littles soberly. The high political drama and the passionate debates that we associate with periods of crisis were not absent, but were not allowed the fuel to disable public life and decision making.

In managing the adversity that came its way, the Howard Government combined experience with a steady hand at the helm. But its shortcomings are also instructive. It is a record worth exploring today.

Contributors

Richard Alston is now on his fourth career. He commenced his working life as a barrister practising in crime and personal injuries and later in commercial and administrative law. In 1986 he was appointed to the Australian Senate and was on the front bench of the Coalition parties for 15 years. From 1996 until 2003 he was the Minister for Communications, Information Technology and the Arts and served as the deputy leader in the Senate for ten years. In 2005 he was nominated by Prime Minister John Howard as Australia's High Commissioner to London, where he served until 2008. Since that time, he has been involved in various aspects of commerce, having chaired three ASX listed companies and served for seven years on the international advisory board of one of the world's largest hedge funds as well as a director of a UK public listed company. From 2014–2017 he was the Federal President of the Liberal Party of Australia. He retains an abiding interest in the Arts and has published a memoir, *More to Life than Politics?* as well several essays on political themes.

Andrew Blyth is the inaugural John Howard Fellow at the Centre for Independent Studies. Previously, he held senior positions at University of New South Wales Canberra, including overseeing the establishment of the John Howard Prime Ministerial Library at Old Parliament House. Andrew has also served as a chief of staff and senior adviser in the Howard Government. He has an undergraduate degree in government and two postgraduate qualifications in business and international relations. In 2012, he was awarded a Fulbright Professional Scholarship in Australia-US Alliance Studies, where he conducted research into off-grid energy solutions at the University of Texas at Austin. Andrew has contributed to various publications analysing the four Howard governments and has edited *John Howard: From the Pavilion – Shaping the Ascent to Power* (Connor Court, 2023) and co-edited *The Art of Coalition: The*

Howard Government Experience, 1996-2007 (UNSW Press, 2022) with Professor David W. Lovell. Currently, Andrew is researching the role and effectiveness of think tanks through a professional doctorate at the University of New South Wales (UNSW) Canberra.

Jacqueline Laughland Booÿ is Senior Advisor, Impact Priorities at Australian Catholic University. She is also an Affiliate at Monash University. She holds a PhD in Sociology. As a qualitative researcher, her interests are in the fields of life-course studies and political sociology. She has a strong track record of publications that explore the behaviours and attitudes of young people as they transition from adolescence into adulthood.

Mal Brough was raised in the small semi-rural community of Slacks Creek in South-East Queensland. His family owned and operated the local community store. At 17 he joined the regular army and in December 1981 graduated from the Officer Cadet School, Portsea. He served with the infantry corps for 8 years. He entered parliament in 1996 and held various ministerial posts including Revenue Minister, Assistant Defence Minister, Employment Services Minister and Minister for Families, Communities and Indigenous Affairs. Mal was defeated in 2007 and returned to parliament as the member for the Sunshine Coast seat of Fisher for one term in 2013. Mal is married to Sue and has three children and 3 grandchildren.

Shaun Carney is a visiting fellow at the School of Humanities and Social Sciences at UNSW Canberra who has written extensively about leadership, politics and industrial relations since the Melbourne afternoon newspaper *The Herald* first sent him to work in the Canberra Press Gallery in 1979. He is a political columnist with *The Age* and the *Sydney Morning Herald*, and is a former associate editor of *The Age* and columnist at the *Herald Sun*. The author and editor of several books, including *Australia in Accord – Politics and Industrial Relations Under the Hawke Government* (1988), *Peter Costello – the New Liberal* (2001), *The Change Mak-*

ers – 25 Leaders in Their Own Words (2019) and a memoir, *Press Escape* (2016), he is also a Vice-Chancellor's Professorial Fellow at Monash University.

Peter Collignon is an Infectious Diseases physician and microbiologist at the Canberra Hospital. He is also a Professor at the Australian National University Medical School. He is active in many research and public health advocacy issues. Particular interests are antibiotic resistance (especially in Staph), hospital acquired infections (especially blood stream and intravascular catheter infections) and resistance that develops through the use of antibiotics in animals. He is extensively involved in Infection Control projects looking at procedures and current practices in medicine. He has been and continues to be an active member of many national and international committees, including those of the Australian Quality and Safety Commission. He has been appointed to many of the expert committees of the World Health Organization (WHO) on the issue of antibiotic resistance and the use of antibiotics in food animals. In June 2010 he was made a Member of the Order of Australia (AM) for services to Medicine in Infectious Diseases, Microbiology and Infection Control.

Zareh Ghazarian is currently the Head of Politics and International Relations in School of Social Sciences at Monash University. Zareh holds a PhD in Political Science from Monash University. Zareh is an award-winning educator and is a leading commentator on politics and public policy and is regularly called upon by national and international media to provide analysis. Zareh has published widely in Australian politics and recently co-edited *Australian Politics and Policy 2024*, *Gender Politics: Navigating Political Leadership in Australia*, and co-authored *Australian Politics for Dummies* (2nd edition).

Peter Jennings is Director of Strategic Analysis Australia and was the executive director of the Australian Strategic Policy Institute

(ASPI) from May 2012 to May 2022. He has worked in senior roles in the Australian Public Service on defence and national security. He was Deputy Secretary for Strategy in the Defence Department (2009-12); Chief of Staff to the Minister for Defence (1996-98) and Senior Adviser for Strategic Policy to the Prime Minister (2002-03). He has been a member of the Advisory Group on Australia-Africa Relations advising the Department of Foreign Affairs and Trade. Peter studied at the London Business School in 2000-01 as a Sloan Fellow and was awarded a Masters of Science (Management) with Distinction. He has a Master of Arts Degree in International Relations from the Australian National University (1987) and a BA (Honours) in History from the University of Tasmania (1980-84). He has been a Fulbright Fellow at the Massachusetts Institute of Technology (1985). Peter was awarded the Public Service Medal in the Australia Day 2013 Honours list, and Officer of the Order of Australia (AO) in the 2023 honours list.

Paul Kelly is Editor-at-Large on *The Australian*. He was previously Editor-in-Chief of the paper, and he writes on Australian politics, public policy and international affairs. Paul has covered Australian governments from Gough Whitlam to Anthony Albanese. He is a regular television commentator on *Sky News*. He is the author of 10 books including *The End of Certainty* on the politics and economics of the 1980s. His recent books include *Triumph and Demise* on the Rudd-Gillard era and *The March of Patriots* which offers a re-interpretation of Paul Keating and John Howard in office.

David Kilcullen is Professor of International and Political Studies at UNSW Canberra, and professor of practice in the School of Politics and Global Studies at Arizona State University. He is President and CEO of the global research firm Cordillera Applications Group. He was a professional soldier, diplomat, intelligence officer and policy advisor for the Australian and US governments for twenty-five years, serving as a senior counterinsurgency advisor during the wars in Iraq and Afghanistan and as Chief Strategist in the US State Department's Counterterrorism Bureau. His books include *The Accidental Guerrilla*; *Out of the Mountains: The Coming Age of the Urban Guerrilla*; and *The Dragons and the Snakes: How the Rest Learned to Fight the West*. He holds a PhD from UNSW and is a graduate of the Australian Defence College and the Royal Military College, Duntroon.

David W. Lovell is an Emeritus Professor at UNSW. After completing his PhD in the History of Ideas at the Australian National University (ANU), he joined UNSW in 1983. During the early 1990s, he edited The Political Theory Newsletter, and was managing editor of the Australian Journal of Political Science. In 1992, he was the Australian Parliamentary Political Science Fellow, and since 1993 he has been a member of the Executive Committee of the International Society for the Study of European Ideas, and was co-editor of its journal, The European Legacy, until 2017. After heading the School of Humanities and Social Sciences at UNSW Canberra (2006-2016), he was appointed Associate Dean International (2017-2020), and then Director of The John Howard Prime Ministerial Library (2020-2022). He has published a number of books in the history of political thought, post-communism, Asia-Pacific security, theatre, international humanitarian law, and Australian politics.

David Marshall began his career as an on-air radio personality before advancing to chief executive of various radio stations and networks across Adelaide, Sydney, and Canberra. In 1994, he was appointed ACT Tourism Commissioner. In 2000, he founded Talkforce Media and Communications, collaborating with law enforcement and security agencies over the next 20 years. Currently, David serves as the Chair of the Canberra Region Tourism Leaders Forum.

In addition to his professional roles, David is a Board member of the John Howard Prime Ministerial Library, chairs the Rotary District 9705 Vulnerable Youth Project, and serves on the ACT Salvation

Army Advisory Board. David earned a PhD in 2016, with his doctoral thesis focusing on how Prime Minister John Howard managed his media and strategic communications responsibilities. In recognition of his contributions to tourism, business, charities, and health organisations, David was awarded an Order of Australia in 2011.

Stephen Martin has had a long and distinguished background in the Australian Parliament, academia and the private sector. He is currently: Chairman, Bank of China (Australia) Ltd; Chairman, Applied Positive Psychology Learning Institute; Chairman, Global ICT Training & Certification, Singapore; Chairman, Advisory Board, SmartLaw Pty Ltd, Singapore and Immediate Past Chairman, Men of League Foundation.

Professor Martin represented the NSW-based electorates of Macarthur and Cunningham in the Australian Parliament 1984–2002. In government, he served as Speaker of the House of Representatives, Parliamentary Secretary for Foreign Affairs and Trade, and Chairman of the Inquiry into the Australian Banking Industry. After retiring from Parliament, Professor Martin held several senior executive roles in academia, including President/Chief Executive Officer of the University of Wollongong in Dubai, Pro Vice Chancellor International at Victoria University, Melbourne and Deputy Vice Chancellor (Strategy and Planning) at Curtin University of Technology in Perth. Between January 2011 and April 2017 Professor Martin was Chief Executive, Committee for Economic Development of Australia (CEDA). He is currently Chairman and Independent Director of business organisations in Australia and Singapore. Professor Martin received an Order of Australia (AO) in 2022 for distinguished service to the people and Parliament of Australia, to charitable organisations, and to regional sport and education.

Penelope (Pene) Mathew joined the Auckland Law School as Dean in March 2019. Specialising in international law and politics, she holds degrees from the University of Melbourne and Columbia Law School. Pene is an expert on international refugee law, has worked as a human rights lawyer, and published extensively in this field.

She has held academic roles at the University of Melbourne, the Australian National University, Michigan Law School and Griffith University, where she also served a four-year term as Dean and Head of Griffith Law School. She served for two years as legal and policy advisor to the Australian Capital Territory's Human Rights Commission, leading the work on an audit of the territory's remand centres, among other matters. In 2008, the ACT Government awarded her an International Women's Day Award for outstanding contributions to human rights and social justice. She has also worked on shorter contracts with the Jesuit Refugee Service, and as a consultant to the Australian Human Rights Commission and for the Office of the United Nations High Commissioner for Refugees.

Fiona Wade turned to academia following a 25-year career that spanned federal politics and government relations, internal and external communication, stakeholder management and media. Retraining in education in the early 2000s, Fiona has since taught at high school, vocational college, and higher education institutions both in Australia and overseas. Fiona worked as senior advisor for the Police Federation of Australia, before completing her doctorate in 2020. Prior to Charles Sturt University, she worked with Deakin University researching workplace evaluation for the Australian Army. Fiona has published and is currently researching the effect of training transfer versus skills fade in the workplace.

James Walter has broad interests in Australian politics and history. He held the chair of political science at Monash from 2002-2016, is a former head of the School of Political and Social Inquiry (2006-09), and a past president of the Australian Political Studies Association (2007-08). He is a Fellow of the Academy of Social Sciences in Australia (and served on the academy's executive from

2006-09, and 2015-present), and a former fellow of the Royal Society of Arts and Manufactures (UK) 1992-2015. Prior to his appointment at Monash, he was pro-vice-chancellor (arts) at Griffith University (1996-2002), and professor of Australian studies (1987-2002). He was professor and head of the Menzies Centre for Australian Studies at the University of London from 1990-93.

Laura Woodbridge is currently completing a PhD at Monash University in Political Science. Her dissertation focuses on public policy making and political leadership in Westminster political systems during periods of crisis. Laura is also a Research Assistant at the Australian Catholic University. Laura's recent publications include an exploration of the political leadership of Victorian Premier Daniel Andrews during the COVID-19 pandemic (published in the *Australian Journal of Political Science*).

1

A crisis of the Australian system

Paul Kelly

No government can succeed in the contemporary world without a capability in crisis management. If a prime minister does not possess this quality, then failure is guaranteed. There is no alternative. We live in an age of mounting crisis. Consider the situation of recent years – Australia has faced a global pandemic, a recession, energy attrition and geo-strategic crisis centred around China and Russia. The world is more unpredictable and inter-dependent. Crisis is occurring more frequently and that will not change. Crisis management is more important than ever. And there is no fixed rule book to manage crisis. It is a truism that government should be prepared but the reality is that each crisis is different. This is not like the annual budget process. There is no natural generic response – crisis management demands innovation, flexibility and judgment since each crisis is unique. These three propositions govern the narrative accounts in this paper.

I suspect the Howard Government might be seen as a transition point in relation to crisis. It faced many crises. Indeed, I believe it is defined, to a large extent, by its crisis management. The Howard era may be seen as that time when the tempo of politics shifted gears and crisis management became a far more prominent task in a rapidly changing world.

I want to be clear about what I am discussing and what I am not discussing. I have long argued that Australian politics over the past 15 years has entered what I call a crisis of the system – we are not delivering the national interest policies the country needs and that this is a function of our changing culture, the decline of voter loyalty to the two-party system, technological changes, the power of the negative, the rise of single issue causes and logjam in the parliament. That is about the daily business of politics and policy.

However, that is not the subject of this chapter. My subject is about management of specific crises faced by the Howard Government.

The nature of crisis can vary – in severity, origin and subject. A crisis can be short or protracted. Our sense of crisis is defined by our age – the wartime tribulations of John Curtin cast crisis in a different frame to those faced by John Howard.

There are two common features that define a crisis. Crisis reveals the true character of a prime minister. A crisis is an event beyond the ordinary. It calls forth a deeper, more elemental response – a response that exposes the leader's heart, perhaps the leader's political soul and, under pressure, the leader's flaws. When much of the mundane business of government decision-making is forgotten, history resurrects the moments of crisis because those moments define the prime minister's character.

They are not forgotten.

Second, a crisis is invariably a test of governing ability. I have long argued that our system is best understood as a model of prime ministerial government. Its face has changed from Gough Whitlam to Scott Morrison to Anthony Albanese, but prime ministerial government is the central organising principle. In 2009 I argued that Howard built a structure of prime ministerial government that gave him more power than his Liberal predecessors, Sir Robert Menzies or Malcolm Fraser.

A crisis tests the capacity of a prime minister to mobilise the necessary elements at his disposal – in the executive or the parliament or his outreach to foreign leaders and, invariably, it tests the leader's relations with the public – the ability to explain, to appeal and to persuade. A crisis typically tests the leader's standing with the people. It is in a crisis that prime ministerial government faces its supreme challenge.

In my discussion about the Howard Government and crisis management I am opening the lens wide. I adopt a broad interpretation of crisis, not a narrow interpretation, because I want to examine the Howard Government in the sheer variety of critical situations it faced. I do not want to be constrained by academic debate about what exactly constitutes a crisis. I think the 'wide lens' approach offers more insights into the Howard years.

These crises I deal with in this chapter are gun laws, the waterfront dispute, the East Timor intervention, the MV *Tampa*, the '9/11' attack and our military commitments in Afghanistan and Iraq, and finally, the Bali bombing.

I could easily have looked beyond this list. Many other events had elements of crisis, for instance, the consequences of the High Court Wik decision, the Commonwealth's intervention to take over Indigenous affairs in the Northern Territory, the shock to the economy in early 2001 from rising interest rates, a negative growth quarter and a falling currency and the drama filled week in early September 2007 when John Howard asked Alexander Downer to sound out the Cabinet on his possible resignation as prime minister.

My technique in this chapter is to assess each of the crises I have selected and draw lessons from them.

Port Arthur massacre

The first crisis coming within weeks of Howard assuming office was the Port Arthur massacre that saw 35 people killed in the use of semiautomatic weapons. The nation was shocked; an emotional memorial service was conducted at Hobart. The prime minister responded quickly and with a firm position – he wanted to impose tough gun laws including on ownership, sale and importation of semiautomatics along with a gun buyback scheme.

This was an ambitious response. It ran into significant opposition from farm and rural sectors, from influential parts of the National Party, from parts of the Liberal Party and from some states

– and support of the states was essential. There was an enduring legacy from Howard's stance – Australia's status as a democracy that shunned gun ownership was entrenched.

Howard's response reflected the two principles of crisis that I have identified. The prime minister's determined action was based on conviction. Before becoming prime minister, Howard had publicly supported tighter gun laws. He had an established, declared position. Howard's observation of America's gun culture and its consequences had sharpened his belief in the opposing vision for Australia. Without prime ministerial conviction, this change would not have happened.

It was also an example of governing authority. Coalition relations were potentially on the line. But Howard won immense support from Nationals Leader, Tim Fischer. The attitude of Queensland and Western Australia – states that had initial concerns – were vital. But Howard was determined, knew he enjoyed public support and had been prepared to take the issue to a constitutional referendum if required. It was not.

The crisis also reflected another aspect of Howard – on this issue he rejected individual rights in favour of a superior social order, a re-occurring feature of Howard's philosophy as prime minister.

Waterfront

A different but critical event for the Howard Government was the 1998 showdown on the waterfront - triggered not by a surprise event but government policy. Howard was elected on an agenda to make the waterfront internationally competitive and that meant breaking the monopoly power of the Maritime Union of Australia (MUA). At that time the MUA had achieved a high wage, poor productivity outcome. Howard described the resulting crisis as 'the most bitterly fought domestic issue of my whole time as Prime Minister,' a situation, he said, that became violent and divisive.[1]

At an early stage, Howard and Industrial Relations Minister, Peter Reith realised that reform would likely trigger an explosive confrontation. A necessary condition was an employer willing to fight and Chris Corrigan, boss of Patrick stevedoring company was that employer. Corrigan's assumption was that a trained non-union alternative workforce was essential, and the MUA would never tolerate that alternative being established.

Howard told Corrigan the government would back his campaign with one condition – that it complied with Australian law. But Howard's dilemma was that the government was not in full control – it was hostage to Corrigan. This point is fundamental to the crisis and the difficulty the government faced.

In April 1997, Corrigan dismissed his unionised workforce, put balaclava-clad security guards with dogs onto the dock. The MUA was locked out. It was a public relations disaster for Corrigan and Reith. Most media favoured the union. Scenes of violence and chaos dominated on television. Strong picket lines were set up to intimidate the non-union workforce. In the Federal Court, the MUA won a reinstatement decision that dismayed the Howard Government but a subsequent High Court ruling while backing restatement opened the way for a settlement.

In the end, the MUA monopoly stayed but its power was broken - the union lost half its workforce and its day-to-day control on the docks. Management seized the upper hand. Many new efficiencies were introduced. Corrigan got a viable business. Howard declared 'the Australian waterfront had changed forever'. He branded the waterfront reform 'one of the great achievements of the government'.

Reith was seriously damaged. His home and family needed security protection. In a conversation with Howard at the peak of the crisis Reith, given the damaging situation facing the government, offered to resign, an offer Howard would not countenance. He praised Reith for his courage and composure under relentless attack. Howard believed that losing Reith would have sent a devastating signal of political failure and retreat on industrial relations reform. As for

Corrigan, Howard saw him as a rare business leader prepared to take a stand for reform.

The absolute key to the waterfront crisis was the determination of the prime minister to prosecute the cause of reform. This was a crisis filled with uncertainty and risks for Howard, Reith and the government. Would other Liberal prime ministers, before or since, such as Malcolm Fraser, Tony Abbott, Malcolm Turnbull or Scott Morrison have engaged in such high-risk tactics for a reform mission? I doubt that very much.

For much of the time opinion was against the government despite strong support among the Coalition constituency to challenge the MUA. The outcome was in no way ordained. Court decisions were vital - initially going against the government but then opening the door to a resolution. In the end there was still uncertainty within the government about whether it had really won the politics of this battle. This was a different sort of crisis – it was a policy driven crisis.

It highlighted the paradoxical character of the Howard Government, a character that stands in contrast with subsequent Coalition governments. Howard as prime minster was shaped by two competing compulsions. He sought to be an agent of stability aspiring to a mood where people were 'relaxed and comfortable' - yet he was prepared to provoke major upheavals to pursue his reform agenda. The notable examples of the latter were his campaign for the Goods and Services Tax (GST) and his pursuit of industrial relations reform, exemplified initially in the waterfront campaign and then in his final term with *WorkChoices*. They point to a prime minister of policy beliefs and a temperament willing to take a risk.

Timor-Leste

I have no hesitation in including in my crisis list what John Howard called the East Timor liberation story. This was a transforming event for Howard – the point at which he passed the threshold to become a national security leader. This crisis empowered Howard – as a military and diplomatic prime minister.

In September 1999 acting under authority of a United Nations (UN) Security Council resolution an international force led by Australia was dispatched to East Timor to impose order on the province after its vote for independence from Indonesia in a national plebiscite. This was Australia's most vital military commitment since the Vietnam War. It followed slaughter, population relocation and 'scorched earth' tactics against East Timorese by local pro-Indonesian military with support from the highest levels of the Indonesian army. Intelligence suggested the risk of large-scale killings. Howard told UN Secretary-General, Kofi Annan, that Australia would make a major troop commitment to the international enforcement contingent but would insist on leadership of the intervention. Annan agreed. Howard launched a diplomatic campaign to secure contributions from a range of nations.

The key was obtaining the consent of the Indonesian government. The Clinton administration, initially slow to react, delivered high level warnings to Indonesian President Habibie to help secure his acquiescence. But the Indonesian government was divided and there were real fears the Australian-led force would face military resistance. The Australian commander, Major General, Peter Cosgrove (later Chief of the Australian Defence Force and Governor-General) told me he had expected 'perhaps scores' of Australian casualties.[2] Visiting the troops in Townsville before their departure Howard was conscious that some of these young men might face an early death.

This was an unprecedented moment in Howard's prime ministership. For the first time he was putting Australian lives at risk. The opening days of the deployment were the most dangerous of Howard's time as prime minister to that point. Indonesian troops in East and West Timor vastly outnumbered the size of the intervention force. If it had been challenged the consequences would have been dire. Cosgrove did a brilliant job in being both firm yet working with the Indonesian military.

The backdrop was an agitated, often hysterical mood at home

with Labor and much of the media attacking the government for not supporting an international force into the province before the independence vote. This was never an option: President Habibie had made this clear in the most singular fashion. However, within the Labor Party and much of the media this idea became embedded as apparent proof of the government's so-called appeasement of Jakarta.

With Australian public opinion firmly behind East Timor and hostile to Jakarta the extent of hysteria was amply revealed in a *Sydney Morning Herald* editorial calling upon Howard to declare Australia's unilateral intention to intervene even without UN authority, a step that would have invited war with Indonesia. Such advocacy was divorced from any military or political reality and promoted Howard to say that 'it was an option no responsible government could have contemplated'.[3]

The operation overall was a remarkable success. For the first time Australia was a leader, not a follower, in a major UN intervention. For the first time Howard had conducted an international diplomatic campaign with a range of national leaders to secure commitments to participate in the force. For the first time he had engaged with and influenced a US president – President Clinton – in striking agreements over military and political tactics. Obviously, relations with Indonesia were damaged. Foreign Minister Downer said: 'They loved us a lot less but respected us a lot more'.[4]

The East Timor crisis brought to full maturity the operation of the National Security Committee of Cabinet (NSC). While the NSC had been a Howard Government initiative (and discussed in a later chapter) its enduring value as a decision-making forum was entrenched at this time. The legacy is vast. At the height of the East Timor drama, the NSC met twice a day. Fundamental to its structure and value was having the few senior ministers involved sitting with the critical security, policy and military advisers. This decision-making model worked effectively on East Timor and was later used at length by the Howard Government in relation to Afghanistan, Iraq and national security decisions against Islamist terrorism.

Indeed, the NSC as a model won enduring bipartisan support. During the Coalition era 2013–22 it became a defined feature of the operation of government where it proved over time to be an efficient instrument of decision-making. But the NSC had two crucial consequences.

First, the NSC enhanced the centralising influence and power of the prime minister. It became integral to the notion of prime ministerial government. It brought all elements of the military and security system into the one room where the prime minister would dominate. It gave every prime minister who operated within the NSC for any time a sense of empowerment and created within the office a permanent legacy of national security guardianship with the electoral dividends this involved. It meant that all elements of the national security system were effectively 'locked into' the final agreed decisions. It also meant that the heads of the intelligence and security agencies won regular access to the highest levels of government decision-making, on par with heads of the major policy departments – a situation that enhanced their influence within government and with successive prime ministers.

The East Timor story began with a policy change – when Howard and Downer changed two and a half decades of Australian policy by launching an initiative to President Habibie proposing a ballot thereby opening the possibility of East Timor's separation from Indonesia. The protracted legacy constituted a series of crises running over months – diplomatic, political and military. But the operation's success has concealed the extent of risk and danger.

It verifies my thesis about crisis – Howard's convictions, backed by Downer, were critical: that Australia, ultimately, must support an independent East Timor and that we must lead in delivering that transition. At each point prime ministerial governance was pivotal – Howard realised that while the decision to commit the Australian

Defence Force (ADF) was a shared Cabinet decision his ministers 'instinctively left the final decision to me'. If Howard had said 'no' his ministers would have accepted that. East Timor was a classic crisis revealing the operation of prime ministerial authority.

This event produced another legacy. It showed that success in crisis can change a prime minister. The upshot was a more seasoned, more triumphant, bolder John Howard.

MV *Tampa*

East Timor was the prelude to another, more prolonged phase in the Howard Government and crisis management – an era of far-reaching disruption from August 2001 to late 2003. This was defined by a series of crises and their consequences that, while separate events, had powerful connecting national security themes – the four standout events being the 2001 *Tampa* interception, the 9/11 Islamist attack on the United States leading to the invoking of the ANZUS Treaty and our military commitment to Afghanistan, third, the Bali bombing of October 2022 that saw 88 Australians killed, the largest number of our casualties in peacetime, and finally, the March 2003 commitment to the Iraq War with devastating consequences as the invasion turned counter-productive.

These events transformed the Howard Government – from the eve of the 2001 election campaign until well into its third term. The government, while conducting its economic and social decision-making tasks, was plunged into a series of shock, national security and military responses and political opportunities that defined John Howard's character, polarised views about his government, ignited his supporters in ideological conviction and provoked a bitter campaign of moralistic hostility against him. Many of the most vivid, long lasting and contentious memories of the Howard Government come from this period. The government's response to these events while exercises in crisis management constitute a much larger story – of a government whose identity was framed by crisis, its response to crisis and a prime minister who turned crisis into extraordinary electoral advantages.

These events were conspicuous for the emotions they unleashed and for the core principles they involved. They called forth, as never before, John Howard's convictions about national sovereignty, border security, the American alliance and national security in a way that defines his government before history.

The dilemma raised by the Norwegian freighter *Tampa* would pivot on a clash of principles – the right of a liberal democratic state to protect its borders and decide who becomes part of its community and the principle of universal human rights obligating rich nations to accept asylum seekers arriving on their doorstep. The world has devised no agreed answer to this conflict. Australia has long accepted refugees in its offshore program. But its capacity as an island continent able to protect its borders has promoted a political culture that opposes unauthorised arrivals.

In August 2001 the *Tampa* had collected more than 430 asylum seekers from a stricken vessel but its captain had been forced under pressure to change course and head to Christmas Island. The moment that ignited Howard and his Cabinet was when they realised the captain had lost control of his ship. Howard took an immediate, instinctive stand on principle – he would not tolerate asylum seekers effectively hijacking a merchant ship to enter Australia.

Tampa became an opportunity for Howard to confront the steady influx of boat arrivals to Australia over the previous three years. A range of policies had been put in place with little impact. A frustrated Howard had been losing his battle with the people smugglers. Howard felt to give landfall to *Tampa* was tantamount to an act of surrender. This was his mindset; it is the reason he resorted to military force. He chose confrontation to uphold sovereignty. After the *Tampa* entered Australian waters, the government ordered the SAS to board and take control of the ship. It was a popular move but filled with danger.

What would happen to the asylum seekers? The government had no solution. Indonesia and Norway at head of government level had refused to help. At this point having taken a stand on principle Howard had to mobilise the resources of government – legal, diplomatic and financial – to solve the deadlock he had created. There was a sense of desperation and panic within the government. Operating in uncharted territory Howard authorised a bill to validate the military action and then, secured what became known as the 'Pacific Solution' – relocating the *Tampa* asylum seekers to other Pacific nations, notably Nauru and New Zealand to ensure they would not land in Australia. Alexander Downer (foreign minister) and Peter Reith (defence minister) worked overtime to procure solutions. Reith visited Nauru to finalise that deal while New Zealand's prime minister, Helen Clark, did Howard an immense favour by accepting some asylum seekers.

On the water the ADF was deployed to prevent vessels reaching Australia. The strains within Australia's system of government at these unorthodox policies were immense. Yet the determination of the government reflected a 'whatever it takes' mentality. The key event domestically was the full Federal Court decision supporting the validity of the government's actions against *Tampa* and its asylum seekers.

The country seemed to divide into Howard admirers and haters, the former being a majority. His statement at the campaign launch that 'we decide who comes to this country and the circumstances in which they come' put the principle in a way guaranteed to have popular support. But the *Tampa* became a launch point for human rights advocates and progressive and media critics to cast Howard as morally unsuitable for office. His policy response to the *Tampa*, essentially improvisation under pressure, constituted an enduring change to Australia's asylum seekers policies and delivered on the government's goal of border protection.

This was a crisis where Howard's response resulted in the erection of a new set of legal, administrative, immigration and defence policies that would have previously been regarded as unacceptable.

Australia's stance has had regional and global ramifications. The *Tampa* was a crisis that changed Australia. It saw the implementation of a new border protection regime, adopted by the political system and supported by the public – despite a strong dissenting minority denouncing Howard on moral grounds. Once again, the key factor at work was the determination of the prime minister having decided the asylum seekers were not to land in Australia at that time. There was, however, a postscript – in the end, after processing of claims offshore, Australia did accept a small number of the asylum seekers.

In summary, the *Tampa* contains a series of lessons about crisis management. First, a leader needs a profound and clearly understood political principle on which to base such a contentious and complex response – and Howard had that in national sovereignty. Second, the government must win in the courts – defeat in the courts means the entire position unravels. Third, the *Tampa* reveals the sheer power that an Australian government can deploy when desperate in terms of summoning support from within the region. Fourth, the *Tampa* story, again, reminds of the immense risks that crisis can involve with Howard having stopped the boat before knowing what to do with the asylum seekers. Finally, it shows that if the leader comes through the political rewards can be decisive.

War on terrorism

Within days an epic global incident had occurred – the Islamist attack on New York and Washington on 11 September 2001 when Howard was in the United States' capital, Washington, DC, holding official talks with President George W. Bush. The attack transformed global politics – it turned Bush into a war president pursuing the instigators, al Qaeda, into Afghanistan, launching a 'war on terrorism' and, in 2003, invading Iraq to overthrow Saddam Hussein. The day before the attack Howard and Bush had bonded in their talks with Howard saying he and Bush 'are very close friends'.

Being in Washington the next day, experiencing the ruthlessness of the attacks, absorbing the disbelief, anger and vulnerability of Americans, Howard said he felt the tragedy 'even more keenly'. In the coming days, he made some of the most fateful decisions of his prime ministership.

Howard's reaction was instinctive. Declaring his support for 'our American friends' he said: 'We will stand by them. We will help them'. Howard saw 9/11 as an epoch changing event. He believed 'that it was going to change the way we lived'. He condemned the attack as an 'outrageous act of war'. Before leaving Washington, he said: 'I've also indicated that Australia will provide all support that might be requested of us by the United States in relation to any action that might be taken'.

The implication was unmistakable: that Australia would participate, if asked, in any future military action by the United States. Howard did not have to make such a call. He did so deliberately. This is the origin of Australia's involvement in wars in Afghanistan and Iraq. Before sunset on 9/11 Howard's mind was set.

In his first interview on Australian radio after the attack, Howard said: 'I just can't overstate the sympathy, the solidarity, the empathy I feel for the American nation and the American people at the present time'. He said the attack on civilians was 'in some respects worse than Pearl Harbor'. But his grasp of the crisis went directly to Australia. Howard saw this as an assault 'on the way of life that we hold dear in common'. He believed the strategic implications were global given the universality of al Qaeda's campaign. On returning home he told the Australian people that 9/11 was also 'an attack upon the people and values of Australia'.[5]

In short, Howard's proximity to the attack, his instinctive view of its meaning and his conception of the crisis as a threat in common to America, Australia and the civilised world became the unshakeable foundation for his future actions. For Howard, this was not an emotional over-reaction but a profound statement of belief. These were his words, not those of his advisers. They came from a leader, embolden by past crisis with a firm view of the 9/11 attack.

It was the audacity of Howard's response and the immense political benefits he mobilised that revealed a prime minister now operating with great confidence and faith in his own judgment. At this point Howard exercised a supreme leadership role. 'In making that commitment I spoke for my government and the people of Australia', he said later.[6] This was Howard, claiming as prime minister, his right to speak for the nation, harnessing a political authority that arose from the crisis itself.

En route back to Australia Howard spoke to Downer and they agreed, at Downer's suggestion, that the ANZUS Treaty be invoked. The Cabinet formalised the decision on Howard's return. After the meeting he announced that Australia was ready to assist the US 'within the limits of its capability'.

War on terror

Australia was unaware that when Bush convened his senior administration figures at Camp David to debate their response to 9/11, the first item of discussion was Iraq – with a decision not to act against Iraq at this point. The second item was to target al Qaeda and the Taliban in Afghanistan.

The crisis provided a further elaboration of Howard's view about the US alliance. He saw the alliance as a two-way street: it applied not just to threats to Australia but to threats to America. He sensed America would judge its true friends by their responses. Howard saw the alliance in global terms, not just as restricted to the 'Pacific area'. These events brought the alliance partners together in a new project – with Howard making clear he saw Islamist terrorism as a threat to Australia. Howard's commitment, however, made him hostage to Bush as a war president and Bush would prove to have serious limitations in that capacity.

Australia's contribution to the Afghanistan campaign involved special forces, aircraft and naval support and had bipartisan support at home. Its initial success meant almost nobody imagined this would become Australia's longest war. The deeper 9/11 legacy for

Australia, however, was Howard's decision to support Bush in the invasion of Iraq.

Howard was always going to Iraq with Bush. Staying aloof from the Iraq War would have defied his history, values and instincts. Yet this became the most contentious foreign policy decision of his career. The March 2003 decision to participate in the Iraq War can be traced directly back to the 9/11 attack 18 months earlier.

The real significance of 9/11 is that it was a crisis for America but not Australia. Howard, by tying Australia to the US crisis, transformed the nature of the US alliance. He used the crisis to achieve goals he had long sought. Under Bush and Howard, the US alliance was deepened in its strategic, intelligence, military inter-operability and economic dimensions. These were permanent changes. It was 9/11 that turned Howard and Bush into brothers-in-arms and their partnership became the most significant in the history of the alliance.

While the Afghanistan commitment was bipartisan, Iraq was different. The United States' military action did not have UN authorisation. The Australian Labor Party opposed both the US action and Australia's participation. It testifies to Howard's authority in his party that there was no dissent from his war decision. Future historians will find that result remarkable. In justifying his decision Howard put much emphasis on the dangers posed by Iraq's assumed possession of a Weapons of Mass Destruction (WMD) capability – he genuinely believed these claims that were subsequently shown to be false.

The NSC decision-making process was flawed since participants knew Howard was determined to commit to the war. The entire NSC debate was about how, not why. The criticism of Howard is that he participated in a US-led intervention without a full appreciation of what the war meant, without any assessment of the intervention's strategic prospects or of what it might mean for the region.

But Howard was extremely tactical in his war commitment. He

told the Americans that Australia would be involved 'at the pointy end' but then withdraw. It was a limited Australian commitment and there were no fatalities in combat. Howard understood the risks – he knew if Australia had taken significant casualties in such a politically disputed war that the price paid would be his prime ministership.

In summary, the 9/11 aftermath saw a seasoned Howard using the crisis to achieve long-run foreign policy goals while harnessing domestic political advantage as a strong leader. That advantage soon turned into a negative when the US intervention became counterproductive and the absence of any WMD capability invited a hostile retrospective judgment on the intervention. Howard, however, always defended his decision.

The previous year in 2002 Islamist extremists had killed 202 people including 88 Australians at Bali, the worst slaughter of Australians since World War Two. It was a shattering event that touched the Australian soul – young, innocent, holiday-makers, going abroad for adventure and recreation, had met a violent death. Howard travelled to Bali, comforted the grieving relatives, legitimised their anger and delivered a private message to weeping families: 'We'll get the bastards'.

Explaining his response to the author Howard said that 'reason controls anger'. He spoke as a people's prime minister. Later at the Parliament House Memorial Service held on 12 October – conspicuously a religious service led by then Bishop to the Australian Defence Force, Right Reverend Tom Frame – Howard said Australians were 'as tough as tungsten' but also 'a soft and loving people who will wrap our arms around those who have lost so much'.[7]

This was not Australia's 9/11; it was not an attack on the Australian homeland. But Howard revealed two qualities in response – an empathy for a nation in tragedy drawing upon his own emotions and language and a political judgment that turned the crisis into an opportunity to deepen ties with Indonesia.

The Bali attack was part of a de facto civil war within Islam that would have inevitable consequences for Australia. The government promoted a joint Indonesian-Australian police investigation into the bombing that became the prelude to police, intelligence and counter-terrorism co-operation between the two nations. The Australian public did not blame Indonesia for the Bali attack, but this was partly a reflection of the Howard Government's stance. In the end, the main perpetrators were either brought to trial or killed.

In strategic terms Bali crossed a threshold – terrorism moved to centre-stage as an immediate security problem for Australia, in the region and at home. The upshot was a renewed priority on resources and powers for the security agencies and the most intense passage of national security laws since the Second World War.

Lessons learned

The first and most serious failure of the Howard Government was its refusal to seek a full strategic assessment of the implications of the Iraq War and the prospects of Western intervention succeeding and achieving its declared aims. Second, I think there was too much hubris surrounding the success of the East Timor intervention. In an interview later Howard – while not using the words – endorsed the idea of Australia being a 'deputy sheriff' to the United States. That damaging branding would run for years.

Finally, on the waterfront issue – this may be more a consequence than a direct failure – but the union campaign was run by a young Greg Combet who learnt so much in the process. When the Howard Government launched its *WorkChoices* agenda years later, Combet then head of the union movement, was ready. The waterfront was the prelude to *WorkChoices*. It taught Combet how to fight and win the bigger showdown. That became a decisive industrial and political event in our history and was a tangible factor in Howard's demise as prime minister.

Endnotes

1. John Howard, *Lazarus Rising*, HarperCollinsPublishers, Sydney 2010, p. 287.
2. Paul Kelly, *The March of Patriots*, Melbourne University Press, Melbourne 2009, p. 511.
3. Ibid., p. 507.
4. Ibid., p. 482.
5. Ibid., pp. 585–6.
6. Howard, p. 385.
7. Paul Kelly, 'Bali: Beyond the Flames', *The Weekend Australian*, 11 October 2003.

2

WATERFRONT CRISIS: EFFICIENCY CRISIS OR UNION BASHING?

Shaun Carney

Some crises land on governments uninvited – an external event or series of events, such as the COVID-19 pandemic and what is referred to in the Northern Hemisphere as the Great Recession but is better known in Australia as the Global Financial Crisis. And some are all a government's own work. Exhibit A in the latter category is the waterfront dispute of 1996-1998. It was 1) a genuine crisis, the most bitterly fought domestic issue of the Howard era and 2) a domestically created one, wholly inspired and generated by the Howard Government, aided and abetted by Patrick Stevedores' Chris Corrigan and the National Farmers Federation (NFF), with an honourable mention for their antagonists, the Maritime Union of Australia (MUA) and the Australian Council of Trade Unions (ACTU), which escalated the dispute once battle had been joined. The union, by its own rights, had no choice: it was fighting for its life.

It is important to distinguish the waterfront confrontation from many of the other crises of the Howard era because it was fully homegrown, the product of the policy desires of the government's senior personnel. It was not a mistake or something that got out of hand. Breaking the union monopoly on waterfront labour was on the Howard Government's 'shopping list' when it was elected in March 1996. There would be no easy way to do it and the government knew that from the outset. Security guards in balaclavas and ferocious-looking dogs – which live on as enduring images from the dispute at its height during the autumn of 1998 – were not on the list. Nor did the list include the union-sponsored pickets – at one crucial stage 4000-strong in Melbourne, almost certainly the biggest picket line in Australian history. But the single-minded drive to introduce or ultimately impose substantial, lasting reforms on our docks definitely was on the government's priority list.

From this distance, and with the performance and attitudes of recent governments in mind, it takes a degree of intellectual readjustment to credit that a government of any political stripe could come to office possessing firmly held policy ambitions that had been gestating within its upper echelons for many years, get to work on implementing them immediately and then not bother to be deterred when the going got exceedingly rough. The unwillingness to fixate on political angles and look for potential exit strategies is the most striking element. Contrast the Howard Government's refusal to step back on its waterfront ambitions with the Rudd Labor Government's decision to defer its proposed emissions trading scheme in 2010 after its Carbon Pollution Reduction Scheme legislation was defeated in the Senate. Or the Abbott Coalition Government's modification of, or retreat on, several tough measures in its first budget. Or the Morrison Government's descent into policy stasis and ceaseless wedge politics after its unexpected 2019 election win, chiefly in order to keep itself politically alive.

The conduct of the waterfront dispute and its ramifications have been canvassed and analysed extensively,[1] and some of the dispute's practical aspects will be examined and assessed later in this chapter. However, when assessing the dispute as a deliberately created crisis, it is important to understand more fully just why the Howard Government was so committed to its course of action. The seeds of the waterfront crisis were sown in the 20 years leading up to the government's election to office. John Howard's steady parliamentary ascent began soon after he was elected as the member for Bennelong in 1974. He spent only ten months as a backbencher before being elevated to the front bench by the new Leader of the Opposition Malcolm Fraser in March 1975. After the coalition parties won in a landslide in the post-Dismissal election later that year Howard was appointed Minister for Business and Consumer Affairs. Only two years later, aged 38, he took over as treasurer, the youngest to do so in the nation's history. In April 1982, during the Fraser Government's third and final term, he was elected deputy leader of the Liberal Party.

In terms of advancement, his seven-plus years as a minister were times of great success. But Howard disagreed with Fraser on economic policy. Given that he was Fraser's chief economic policymaker, this was no small thing; as treasurer, he was frustrated. According to Howard, Fraser was a throwback, 'a creature of the Menzies-McEwen period of economic management, when plenty of benign and protective government intervention appeared to work'.[2] Howard's view was that Fraser's belief that there was no need to move on from the old model in favour of neoliberal economic settings was wrong-headed. He was not alone inside the government in holding this view and in its final years, the party room formed groups based on this Fraser-Howard economic policy divide. The 'Dries' advocated for neoliberalism, while the 'Wets' hewed closer to the existing settlement that looked benignly on financial controls, centralised wage-fixing, and tariff protection. Howard became an unofficial standard-bearer of the 'Dries' worldview.

After the Fraser Government was defeated, the divide continued, with the Melbourne-based moderate and member for Kooyong Andrew Peacock succeeding Fraser as leader and Howard continuing as deputy leader. The tussle for supremacy between the two men lasted for the remainder of the decade. Howard replaced Peacock as leader in September 1985 and lasted until May 1989, when Peacock returned to the Liberal throne, such as it was. While this ideological and personal tussle continued, what was transpiring on the other side of politics was just as troubling. Between March 1983 and March 1996, the Coalition parties lived through a political era that had hitherto been unimaginable for people on both sides of politics. They lost five elections in a row to a Labor Party that for most of its life had been an election-losing machine. In the 1950s and 60s, the ALP lost eight elections on the trot. And when Labor eventually took office under Gough Whitlam in 1972, its government lasted less than three tumultuous years. The experience in 1980s and early 1990s was altogether different.

The Prices and Incomes Accord ('the Accord'), a corporatist arrangement in which the union movement's peak council worked alongside the Hawke and Keating governments on incomes policy, taxation and welfare measures and other economic settings, prompted an earthquake in the Liberal and National parties. It was, in many respects, the non-Labor parties' worst nightmare: a successful, effective Labor government that enjoyed continued popular support and was treated seriously by the mainstream press. It was one thing to lose four times to Hawke, a once-in-a-generation political phenomenon whose charisma seduced most who encountered him, from Arbitration Commission judges to businessmen to voters and world leaders. But it was something else again to lose, at the 1993 election, to the man who ejected the great election-winner Hawke out of the prime ministership, the abrasive and in many ways unknowable Paul Keating.

All this unthinkable stuff reverberated through conservative circles. Howard's first stint as leader prompted the emergence of an ideological movement sometimes referred to in the media as the New Right, that sought to put meat on the bones of the Dries' agenda. Some of its activities focused on union-busting industrial relations policy through the HR Nicholls Society, which included in its number such leading business figures and advocates as Ray Evans from Western Mining Corporation and a young Melbourne barrister Peter Costello. The Accord sparked a radicalisation among several employer and producer groups. Prominent among them was the National Farmers Federation, led by pastoralist and businessman Ian McLachlan, which pushed hard for the Coalition parties to take up the cause of reform of the docks to lower costs and reduce bottlenecks. Within the Liberal Party, the weight of opinion shifted back and forth depending on who was leader. In opposition, the

Liberals cycled through leaders, going from Peacock to Howard, back to Howard, on to John Hewson and then Alexander Downer before Howard eventually prevailed. In the early summer months of 1994–95, with all other reasonable alternatives exhausted, he was the last man standing. He took over as the Hawke-Keating era was coming to an end, with a clapped-out government peopled by less than stellar ministers and a tacked-together agenda. Howard's path to the prime minister's chair was strengthened from the moment he returned to the leadership.

Looking for an early win

By the time the old order had been re-established with the 1996 landslide victory, the hunger for a policy win – a real, targeted win that could pierce the heart of the labour movement – was profound. But Howard had to choose with great care the issue on which he wanted to get that win. On his return as leader, he had imposed constraints upon himself and the Coalition in order to guarantee that they would emerge triumphant, with the largest possible majority, at the election. Picking up on the public's 'reform fatigue' under Keating, he presented himself as a changed man. A key example of this transformation was his acknowledgement that Labor's landmark universal health scheme *Medicare* – long opposed by the Liberals was popular and entrenched and would be retained by a Howard Government. This was a signal that unlike Hewson, who had led the Liberals to a surprise defeat at the previous election by wearing his radicalism proudly, Howard would not be a disruptor across the board.

The Howard Government established a low-key style in most areas. Its moderately reformist workplace relations legislation had to be secured through consultation and negotiation, with Workplace Relations Minister Peter Reith working delicately and patiently on a compromise with the Australian Democrats' Cheryl Kernot and Andrew Murray in order to get the changes through the Senate. Its renewed proposal for a broad-based goods and services tax, so deadly for the Coalition at the 1993 election, under Howard's leadership had to be couched in sensitive language before being put to the public again at the next election, likely to be held in 1998. Sweeteners in the form of income tax cuts would have to be attached to the policy package. And there would then have to be negotiations with the Senate cross bench on the way to legislating for the new tax system, should the government be re-elected. This was not unilateralism, it was compromise.

The waterfront dispute could be different, a policy arena where Howard's innate instincts to follow his convictions could be let loose. It would also would not involve parliamentary trade-offs. The necessary legislation that would help that along had already been passed as part of the new workplace laws, allowing for individual employment contracts. Hemmed in by Howard's pre-election promise to make Australians 'comfortable and relaxed' – code for not too much economic reform that would reach into homes or cause voters to question their preconceptions and normative views of Australian society and its history – the government needed to focus its reform impulses.

It was natural that under Howard the waterfront – which had long been a totemic issue for business – would be where he landed. Success would satisfy city corporates, small businesses and the primary industry producers who formed the National Party base. The waterfront policy was in place before the 1996 election. It noted that Melbourne's crane loading rates had not changed under the Hawke Government's 1991 waterfront reform package and were substantially below ports overseas. The Coalition policy promised to make Australian ports internationally competitive by ending compulsory unionism and by ensuring that operators would, in Howard's words, 'be given power to manage their own enterprises; the monopoly stranglehold of the MUA was to be terminated'.[3]

It was driven by the policy desires and personalities of John Howard, Peter Reith, and the Nationals' transport and regional development reformer John Sharp. Reith was a man in a hurry compared with most politicians. He could never see the point of not taking advantage of incumbency by taking action. As he wrote in his diaries published in 2015, 'anyone can say that they are an activist; the test is what you do about it'.[4] Within weeks of being sworn in as a minister, Reith was combing through polling about voters' attitudes to the pay and practices of waterfront workers and devising ways to persuade Australians that serious change was necessary. Sharp, as Transport Minister, was also a true believer going back a long way. In 1991, Bob Hawke as prime minister had personally invested heavily in trying – and mostly failing – to bring about transformative change on the docks. At one point, echoing his days as ACTU president, he oversaw a 19-hour negotiation with the MUA and waterside employers. The resulting reform package, agreed upon by the union and employers, led to a substantial reduction in the waterfront workforce and some changes in work practices, but not enough to make a real difference in productivity or profitability.

Soon after the deal was sealed, Sharp as shadow transport minister told the House of Representatives on 7 May, 1991:

> At Question Time today we heard the Prime Minister say that he had involved everybody on the waterfront in the negotiations over the past fortnight, and how happy and delighted they were with the deal. However, the Prime Minister forgot to mention the one group that actually pays for it all: the users – the farmers, manufacturers, retailers and consumers who will pay for it.

Howard, then the shadow minister for industrial relations, interjected, 'They're not important!', to which Sharp responded, 'No, they are not important. For goodness' sake, they are not the government's mates. Its mates are the wharfies, so it will do a good deal for them!'. In this, years before either man would have an opportunity to do anything about it, was the sense of conviction: changes that severely restricted or even wiped out the MUA was unfinished business. Howard in particular was dismissive, writing later that the 'problem under Fraser and Hawke had been that the reform process had been undertaken through the traditional tripartite process of government, employers and unions'.[5]

Although Reith tried holding talks with the MUA and ACTU early on, tripartism was never the government's preferred course. Instead, the search was on for a stevedoring employer who wanted change as much as the government, but who would be there to take up the fight and see it through? Howard had been sceptical because of past experience.

> I had grown tired over the years of receiving lectures from business figures about the need for the government to stand up to militant militancy on the waterfront, only to witness those same lecturers running for cover when the possibility of firm action threatened, however temporarily, their companies' livelihoods.[6]

The government hit paydirt in April 1997 when four officers from the Department of Workplace Relations met with a director of the Australian-owned stevedoring company Patrick, John Young, and a partner from the Melbourne office of the law firm, Graeme Smith. The lead departmental officer, Derren Gillespie, noted later that of the two major stevedoring companies, Patrick appeared more amenable to radical change than its chief competitor, P&O Ports. Patrick was considering two options: corporate restructuring and getting rid of its entire workforce. 'The restructuring option would entail the use of new corporate arrangements to possibly separate the labour elements of stevedoring operations from the infrastructure-hardware component,' Gillespie wrote in his notes of the meeting.[7] Patrick was uncertain about this path for legal and financial reasons. As it turned out, the company managed to blend the two options over the following twelve months. But importantly, here was the company that Howard, more than anyone else in the government, had been looking for. Gillespie prepared a briefing paper and recommended an interventionist approach.

> The interventionist approach undoubtedly entails substantial risks and would almost inevitably involve a major waterfront stoppage, in which the government will be actively involved and which will in the short term impose high economic cost ... There is no doubt that if the government decides to go down this track, it would be imperative to achieve as swift a victory as possible.[8]

Howard signed off on the interventionist strategy in a letter to John Sharp on 21 April 1997. Copies went to Peter Reith, the Treasurer Peter Costello, and the Finance Minister John Fahey. The government's path, decades in the making, was set. Chris Corrigan's Patrick fully embraced the cause. The government judged that one company would be enough to break the MUA. But Sharp would not be there for the fight; in late 1997, he resigned as a minister amid a controversy over the filling-in of travel allowance forms – he was subsequently exonerated of any wrongdoing – and from then carriage of the issue fell exclusively to Reith.

Getting past the obstacles

The government's key problem, when the battle was truly joined, was that it was not itself a direct stake-holder in the stevedoring business. No matter how radical and far-reaching its goals, it was limited in what it could do directly to determine the outcome of a confrontation between the stevedoring companies and the members of the MUA. The government could encourage. It could defend. It could advise. It could act as a banker. Once Patrick had set itself on a path of ridding itself of its unionised workforce, replacing it with new non-unionised employees, the government stumped up soft loans to finance the redundancy payments. But it could not directly run the dispute, a substantial obstacle that left it exposed.

The government was hamstrung by some of the unorthodox methods Patrick used, such as its ill-fated establishment of a training base for a replacement workforce in Dubai in late 1997. The notion that such a thing could be kept secret was folly. Corrigan initially denied knowledge of it before admitting later that this was not true. The government was inevitably drawn into this web of half-truths. As a key player and the initiator, it needed to know a lot, but how much? If it was acting in the public interest, which it believed it was, and providing hundreds of millions of dollars in public money should it not have known everything?

The Government was also taking a gamble in how the courts would view this attempt at reform. Patrick attempted to dispose of its unionised employees by surreptitiously offloading them to four separate companies that were then declared bankrupt. The ACTU fought this in the courts, as it had to, because if this had been allowed to pass, the same technique could have been used right across the workforce. Ultimately, the Federal Court of Australia and the High Court of Australia denied the government and the employers a comprehensive win. Essentially, the courts called it a draw, enabling the MUA to survive as the chief union representing waterside labour but giving the stevedoring businesses – Patrick and P&O – the opportunity to achieve greater productivity. Just how much direct economic benefit it produced compared with the psychological satisfaction it gave members and backers of the Coalition parties is not easily quantified but it is fair to say there was upside in both parts of that equation.

Following the victory of the Australian Labor Party under the leadership of Anthony Albanese in 2022, ending another period in which the Liberal and National parties held office, we can compare three Coalition governments – Fraser, Howard and Abbott/Turnbull/Morrison. Of that troika, the Howard Government is the outlier. Four terms, possessing at the beginning clear ideas about what it wanted to do rather than undo. In its first term, it implemented new budgetary processes and guidelines, new workplace laws, rearranged education funding to accelerate and underpin a fundamental shift towards private schools, set about selling the idea of a broad-based consumption tax, and, as we know, went to extraordinary lengths to create change on the waterfront, getting half of what it was after. Add to that its creation of laws in response to the Port Arthur massacre that ensured Australian society would never develop an American-style gun culture. The political dividend was that the 'conviction' tag stuck to the government, and Howard, in particular, for most of its remaining time in office. This was so despite the fact that in its third and fourth terms the government experienced problems on a range of fronts: its pursuit of further reform; budgetary discipline; settling on a firm climate change policy; and the failure to seek an electoral mandate for what came to be known as *WorkChoices* at the 2004 election.

The outlier PM

By contrast the two other Coalition governments were born chiefly out of pure oppositionism and a heightened sense of political crisis within the Labor governments they were fighting in 1975 and 2013. They were highly effective in securing office, both vanquishing two-term Labor governments. But once installed, their policy goals – the value-based systems and policy architecture they wanted to create – were far from clear. These governments both endured for three terms and were characterised by Liberal leadership challenges. In Malcolm Fraser's case, he was able to fend off an assault by Andrew Peacock. But Tony Abbott was unable to survive a challenge from Malcolm Turnbull, and Turnbull was forced to make way for Scott Morrison. While what the Howard Government wanted to do involved serious risk, it also involved conviction: a commitment to do something disruptive and meaningful on an issue that reflected the worldview of the government's leading figures – a manifestation of their reason for being in politics. When members of a government of either persuasion say they are serving 'the national interest', this is generally what they mean.

Was the waterfront dispute an efficiency crisis, or was it union bashing? Surely it was a combination of the two – a fortuitous issue in which the Government's natural ideological anti-union inclinations converged with the need to fix a practical problem when other possible ways forward had seemingly been exhausted. That said, there were obvious efficiency improvements once the dispute had passed, so the government was justified in driving for change. But for all the improvements the crisis produced, the government did not score an unalloyed win. The MUA survived; it still represents most waterside and maritime workers. Greg Combet, who in his role as ACTU assistant secretary co-ordinated the union movement's response to the dispute, later judged that the winners had been the MUA and Corrigan, who wound up with a highly profitable business.[9] And Combet was able to deploy campaigning techniques he learned during the dispute to devastating effect several years later to defeat Howard's *WorkChoices* workplace laws.

There were other shortcomings in the Government's approach. Its deployment of class warfare tactics to sway public opinion ultimately flopped. By attempting to drum up public outrage over the high wages earned by wharfies, the government found itself grasping at smoke. The campaign worked initially but once the dispute reached its zenith, public attitudes switched in favour of the watersiders on the time-honoured Australian attitude of 'half your luck!'. This same impulse worked in the Coalition's favour during the 2019 election campaign when it ran hard – and successfully – on Labor's intention to curtail franking credits and negative gearing, benefits that did not flow to most Australians.

Similarly, the Government's resort to spin, such as Peter Reith's office telling gullible journalists that the High Court judgement was a win and not a split-the-difference result, and backgrounding from other sources against the members of the Federal Court chiefly because they did not find in the government's favour took away from the legitimate gains the government had made.[10] Spin is not a way to promote good governance or maintain the public's trust. The Government also was not always reliable in telling the public what it knew and how closely it was working with Patrick and other key players. To a degree it did have the tiger by the tail once it threw its weight behind Patrick because Patrick, as the employer, had to take the running. But that did not automatically mean the Government was completely in the dark. Reith tended towards finely worded, legalistic answers to legitimate questions about the Government's prior knowledge of the Dubai exercise. On the night that Corrigan sacked his workers and locked them out in April 1998, Reith issued a statement simultaneously with Patrick's own announcement. He then held a press conference – this was close to midnight – and the legislation guaranteeing the redundancy money, which had already been approved by Cabinet, was ready to go the next day. That implied a substantial degree of information sharing.

But for Howard, none of this mattered. In his memoirs, he described waterfront reform as 'one of the great achievements of the government.' Importantly for him, it made up for the economic policy disappointments he and other Liberals had experienced in his early years as a minister between 1975 and 1983: 'It kept faith with that vast army of people who supported the government and who had felt the Fraser Government had failed the reform test.'[11] Reith, who left politics in 2004, also judged that the exercise was worthwhile, given that previously 'no government in living memory had achieved any substantial reform'.[12] The crisis exacted a heavy toll on Reith. Before it, he had been considered a possible future leader, a rival of Peter Costello. But the dispute's controversies marked his leadership card and dimmed his future prospects. He later reflected on the political consequences of his experience, writing that he had always expected to be isolated, and this was how it had turned out. 'While I had the full support of the prime minister, there were very few other public supporters among my colleagues. In fact, there was a deafening silence from nearly all my senior colleagues … Apart from Howard, and (Alexander) Downer, who was often overseas, (Senator) Amanda Vanstone was the only minister who was fighting in my corner.'[13] Nonetheless, he had no regrets. 'For the people who want to do something in politics, there's no such thing as easy reform. That's why not many can lay claim to be true reformers.'[14]

Early in 2022, as he began the election year campaign, Anthony Albanese attracted scorn from some quarters when he referred to John Howard's observation that the hard work of economic reform is never finished. The suggestion was that he was trying to model himself as some sort of political descendant of Howard. This was untrue; he was merely endorsing Howard's aphoristic contribution. Soon after, the following article was published in the business section of *The Australian* newspaper.

> The nation's ports are close to breaking point with surging stevedore charges, rising union power and poor transport links, adding to business costs and fuelling inflation. Dozens of the nation's biggest port users from miners, grain exporters, steel makers and key importers from builders to food producers have hit out at the dysfunction in ports which is adding to higher prices and undermining the nation's recovery ...[15]

Surely this underscored the wisdom of Howard – and Albanese's – truism. Most things that are old eventually become new again. Even the boldest reforms will eventually need refurbishment or replacement. It is likely that we will know the nation is heading for another national waterfront dispute if, sometime in the future, reports like that move from the business section to the political pages. The great unknown is whether Australia's leaders of tomorrow will have the wherewithal to keep going should the dispute become a crisis.

ENDNOTES

1. Tom Frame (ed.), *Back From the Brink, 1997–2001 – The Howard Government, Volume II*, New South, Sydney, 2018, Chapter 10, Shaun Carney, 'The waterfront dispute: high-risk industrial relations reform'. See also Helen Trinca and Anne Davies, *Waterfront – the Battle That Changed Australia*, Doubleday, Sydney, 2000; and Paul Kelly, *The March of the Patriots*, Melbourne University Press, Melbourne, 2009.
2. John Howard, *Lazarus Rising*, HarperCollins, Sydney, 2010, p. 135.
3. Ibid., p. 288.
4. Peter Reith, *The Reith Diaries*, Melbourne University Press, Melbourne, 2015, p. 167.
5. Howard, p. 288.
6. Ibid., p. 290.
7. Trinca and Davies, *Waterfront*, p. 36.
8. Ibid., p. 37.
9. Kelly, *The March of the Patriots*, p. 387.
10. Trinca and Davies, *Waterfront*, p. 249.
11. Howard, p. 387.
12. Reith, p. 200.
13. Ibid.
14. Ibid., p. 201.
15. Eric Johnston, 'Australian ports "close to breaking point" as costs surge', *The Australian*, 17 March 2022.

3

Refugee crisis or playing the populist card?

Penelope (Pene) Mathew

Life is mostly froth and bubble,
Two things stand like stone,
Kindness in another's trouble,
Courage in your own,

from *Ye Wearie Wayfarer*,
Adam Lindsay Gordon, Scottish-Australian poet
(1833–1870)

When invited to speak at the Howard Library conference on the topic of 'Refugee Crisis or Playing the Populist Card?', I accepted with alacrity. The invitation offered an intriguing opportunity in the presence of the former prime minister, to speak about the legacy of the Howard Government's handling of the *Tampa*. My chapter invites readers to consider whether the handling of the *Tampa* was a crisis of our own making and whether a more considered approach that utilises the normal processes of migration management is yet a possibility.

Whose crisis?

We are in the middle of several ongoing refugee crises. Some are recent, like the Ukrainian war refugee exodus, and some are protracted, as is the case for Palestinian and Afghan refugee populations. Some refugees meet the international definition of a refugee set out in the 1951 Convention relating to the Status of Refugees,[1] while others, such as war or conflict refugees, may or may not meet the Refugee Convention definition.[2]

When we watch the scenes unfolding in Ukraine – as we can in the modern era – we feel the pain of those leaving their homeland, pushed out by an unprovoked armed attack. They are in crisis. But if they arrive here without a visa and ask for our protection, does that mean we have a crisis on our hands also?[3]

The etymology of the word 'crisis' is Greek. Intriguingly, the term 'Krisis' means decision.[4] Back in August 2001 as the Norwegian freighter, MV *Tampa*, headed for Australia with 433 asylum seekers rescued from a vessel in distress, the Australian Government decided not to allow them to set foot on Australian soil. Rather, they were transferred via Australian naval ship (HMAS *Manoora*) to Nauru. Shortly afterwards, the so-called 'Pacific Solution' was developed to ensure that any person seeking asylum, travelling by boat and without a visa could be intercepted and sent to Nauru or Manus Island in Papua New Guinea. There, they were held in indefinite detention. During the Australian election that followed, then Prime Minister Howard famously declared, 'we decide who comes to this country and the circumstances in which they come'.[5]

But do we decide the circumstances in which people come; are we ignoring the circumstances in which they leave, along with the rules we have agreed on to govern this situation? It is evident that 'we' in Australia (or any other country of refuge) do not decide when Vladimir Putin invades or when other actors violate human rights or persecute people based on characteristics like race or religion that they cannot or should not have to change. Along with most of the international community, Australia has agreed to cooperate with other countries by following a set of rules in the 1951 Convention and other human rights treaties to ensure that refugees are given protection. While it is perfectly correct to say that in general, immigration is a process controlled by each sovereign State, these rules require that we do not just assume someone is not a refugee,[6] we do not penalise asylum seekers simply for arriving without a visa,[7] we recognise that refugees are human beings,[8] and we provide protection where necessary because refugees have lost the protection of their home country.[9] What, then, do Mr Howard's words 'we decide' signify?

'We decide' as a populist call to arms

Viewed in context, the phrase, 'we decide', is a populist call to the people of the country – the 'we' or 'us' – to say that we are still in control and if we decide to, we will ignore criticisms from outsiders and depart from our own long-standing practice. To begin with, the phrase 'we decide' conveniently disregards Australia's prior and voluntary acceptance of rules to govern the arrival and treatment of asylum seekers. A second relevant factor is the populist political discourse stoked by Pauline Hanson's One Nation Party at the relevant time.[10] Finally, Mr Howard's own conception of Australians' views strongly suggests a populist connotation to the phrase 'we decide'.

In light of Mr Howard's previous speeches, such as the 'Headland' speech of 1995,[11] it is apparent that 'we' are 'mainstream Australia.' Mainstream Australia,[12] according to the 'Headland' speech, was frustrated by 'government decisions increasingly driven by the noisy, self-interested clamour of powerful vested interests with scant regard for the national interest.'[13] This is a populist argument – that government is dominated, corrupted even, by powerful interests that stand against the values of 'the people'.[14]

Who, then, is included in that phrase 'we decide'? Obviously not asylum seekers and refugees. They are outsiders and 'we' will decide whether they are fit to become one of us. 'We' may not be the same as 'we the peoples' of the United Nations, under whose auspices the 1951 Convention was adopted, unless the Australian interpretation of the Convention is accepted.[15] Asylum seeker advocates are also not included – they are just part of the noise getting in the way of governing in the national interest and who ignore the purportedly unwelcome nature of asylum seekers arriving without prior authorisation.

As the *Tampa* episode unfolded, asylum seekers arriving by boat were portrayed as undesirable outsiders who were not fit to join our community, and indeed, a threat to the community: a crisis to be averted. Boat arrivals were wrongly associated with terrorism, which became a heightened concern for government following the terrorist attacks on New York and Washington on September 11, 2001. For example, when asked by radio presenter, Derryn Hinch (later a senator for Victoria), whether the boat arrivals might include 'Bin Laden appointees', Defence Minister Peter Reith replied, that 'you've got to be able to manage people coming into your country', and then went on to say 'otherwise it can be a pipeline for terrorists to come in and use your country as a staging post for terrorist activities.'[16] The idea that a person intent on committing a terrorist act in Australia would attempt to arrive on a people smuggler's boat was unlikely, to say the least. Readers will also recall the 'Children Overboard Affair', in which asylum seekers were portrayed as people who throw their children overboard, even though this had not occurred in that instance.[17]

Irregular migration was also associated with national security more broadly. For example, in his campaign speech, Prime Minister Howard said that 'national security is … about a proper response to terrorism', 'a far sighted, strong, well thought out defence policy' and 'an uncompromising view about the fundamental right of this country to protect its borders.'[18] The securitisation of borders is a trend that has swept the Western world since the end of the Cold War.[19] It has transformed immigration from something viewed as economically valuable or humanitarian or compassionate in nature and dealt with as a routine administrative matter, into a potential threat to the nation. This could be a physical threat (as with the unjustified link to terrorism) or a threat to the values and cohesion of the nation. This threat is dealt with by extraordinary measures. In the case of the *Tampa*, the Special Air Service was called in, and a militarised program of maritime interception is now accepted as the norm in Australia. The response to the *Tampa* and its aftermath is an example of the populist's 'performance of crisis'.[20]

THE AUSTRALIAN (RE)INTERPRETATION OF THE RULES

Alongside the populist narrative of threat and crisis a legal justification of Australia's actions against boat arrivals during the Howard Government was vigorously prosecuted by the Minister for Immigration, Philip Ruddock. According to the Australian interpretation of the Refugee Convention, in particular Articles 31 and 33, very few unauthorised boat arrivals needed protection in Australia as they had supposedly foregone some form of protection elsewhere and could, indeed should be treated less favourably than those arriving with a visa.

Article 31 of the Refugee Convention is almost as important as the prohibition on returning refugees to a place of danger, known by the French term as the obligation of *non-refoulement* and set out in Article 33. Article 31 prohibits the imposition of penalties on refugees who are in, or who enter a country in contravention of domestic immigration law. Those responsible for writing the Convention acknowledged that refugees would often have little choice but to breach immigration laws given their flight and the difficulty of securing valid documentation.[21]

Article 31 does contain some limiting language. To avoid penalties, an asylum seeker must, among other things, have 'come directly' and 'show good cause'. However, an amendment to the draft Convention which would have limited the protection of Article 31 to a refugee 'unable to find asylum even temporarily in a country other than one in which his life or freedom would be threatened' was ultimately discarded.[22] The Department of Immigration and Multicultural and Indigenous Affairs acknowledged this in a paper prepared for the Global Consultations held during the 50th anniversary of the Refugee Convention in 2001.[23] Nevertheless, the Department stated that:

> In view of Australia's position as an island far from most current refugee source countries, few asylum seekers – especially those arriving unauthorised since 1999 – ar-

> rive in direct flight from their country of origin. Most have engaged in secondary movement, often aided by well-organised people smuggling networks operating for financial gain.[24]

In any event, according to the Department, none of the measures Australia had adopted over the years, such as mandatory detention, temporary protection, offshore 'processing' or interception, amounted to a penalty.[25]

The Department also noted, rather optimistically, that the obligation of *non-refoulement* in Article 33 does not require entry, as opposed to non-return, and that 'through negotiating entry with other countries, it may be met anywhere in the world by those States who honour the non-refoulement obligation.'[26] While the latter statement is true, securing return of refugees to countries they had transited *en route* to Australia was never going to work. Not only were these countries under no obligation to readmit non-nationals, but they were often not party to the Convention and/or did not have national equivalents of protection. Indeed, the insecurity for refugees and asylum seekers in such countries, was documented at the time[27] and provided an obvious reason for their departure. This of course is why Australia had to offer additional aid to Nauru, which was not a party to the Refugee Convention back in 2001,[28] to secure its participation in the Pacific Solution. Similarly, Australia's extant aid program explained why Papua New Guinea was prepared to be involved.[29]

While the Australian Government may have hoped those asylum seekers sent offshore and determined to be refugees would be resettled in another country, the majority of those found to be refugees, 705, were resettled in Australia, with New Zealand taking 401, and very few other countries taking any.[30] Thus, the majority of those determined to be refugees came to Australia and in 2008 the Rudd Government brought the first iteration of the Pacific Solution to an end.[31] That end was short-lived. With the arrival of around 20,000 boats in 2012 and relentless sloganeering around 'stopping the boats' by the Tony Abbott-led opposition, the offshore detention arrangements were reinstated in August 2012 by the Gillard Labor Government, and later, Prime Minister Rudd introduced so-called regional resettlement arrangements with Papua New Guinea and Nauru.

Resettlement in these countries was never an option; nor was it an option in the third country added to the mix under the Abbott Government, Cambodia.[32] Resettlement to other countries was slow in coming. The United States deal to accept some of the refugees held on Nauru and Papua New Guinea came late (towards the end of 2006) and has seen 1006 people resettled as of 31 May 2022.[33] New Zealand's offer to take 150 refugees per annum for three years was accepted in 2022, a decade after the offer was first made.[34] As of 31 December 2021, there were 105 people still in in Papua New Guinea, and as of 31 May 2022, 112 on Nauru,[35] all of whom were apparently living in the community.[36] Australia's arrangement with Papua New Guinea came to an end in December 2021.[37]

Consequences and context

The Howard Government's response to the *Tampa* did not emerge out of nowhere. The legal parsing of penalties and *non-refoulement* which emerged during the Howard era has a neat fit with an older political narrative, to which I will return, about 'queue jumping'. From the late 1980s onwards, there has been a steady accumulation of deterrence measures including maritime interception and return; variants of detention – mandatory, offshore, indefinite; and temporary, rather than permanent, protection visas for refugees. However, the response to *Tampa* marked a turning point from which it has proved nigh impossible to retrieve a more humane policy, and the consequences for refugees and asylum seekers arriving by boat have been extraordinarily harsh.

The situation for those refugees held in detention on Nauru and Papua New Guinea, a deprivation of liberty for which Australia retained responsibility,[38] has been described in numerous reports and inquiries, as well as media stories and some excellent books.[39] One of these is Behrouz Boochani's autobiography *No Friend But the Mountains.*[40] Mr Boochani is now resident in Aotearoa New Zealand. His book is a harrowing read, revealing in vivid detail the degradation and decline of those subjected to this harsh regime.

For refugees transferred from offshore to Australia for medical assessment or treatment under the short-lived medevac laws, the 'solution' was indefinite detention in hotels, with releases occurring abruptly and often with little fanfare.[41] The appalling experience of indefinite detention must surely resonate with Australians now, given our own experiences of rather shorter periods of effective home detention and/or hotel quarantine for public health reasons during the COVID-19 pandemic. Unlike the generally lawfully imposed restrictions on liberty and freedom of movement in Australia during the pandemic, in many cases, there appears to be no good reason for the continued detention of refugees and asylum seekers. Their detention is arbitrary, and thus a violation of Article 9 of the International Covenant on Civil and Political Rights.

Many other asylum seekers and refugees have lived in constant uncertainty on bridging visas or temporary protection visas, and indeed, rolling temporary protection visas that do not allow people to sponsor their families to live with them or, more generally, to move on with their lives.[42] Our own, usually less profound experiences of separation from family and inability to plan our lives during the pandemic must have given Australians some insight into the resulting torment for refugees.

Australia's policy on unauthorised arrivals has been in limbo, too. Refusing to accept that these refugees may have nowhere else to go and need to get on with their lives, Australia has suffered a crisis of nondecision[43] for the last twenty years. Our 'crises' over the *Tampa* and the 20,000 odd boat arrivals in 2012 may usefully be contrasted with the European Union's decisive response to millions of Ukrainian war refugees in 2022.[44]

As indicated earlier, *Tampa* was a low point in a steep decline in

Australia's treatment of asylum seekers arriving without a visa. This can be dated back to the late 1980s and the mandatory detention of a group of Cambodian asylum seekers. Various narratives have been constructed as justifications for these policies, which have assisted in entrenching the perception that the measures are necessary or acceptable. One such narrative has been the idea of a queue constructed between Australia and the regions of conflict and persecution from which refugees have fled.

The origins of the term 'queue' in the asylum context are debated[45] but the response to the Indo-Chinese refugee crisis, including components of orderly departure from Vietnam and resettlement from countries of first asylum may have assisted the entrenchment of this idea.[46] Unlike the response to Vietnamese refugees in the 70s and 80s, however, there are usually very few resettlement places available in most refugee crises, and orderly departure programs or evacuations are rarely initiated.[47] Generally, less than one per cent of the world's refugees are able to access a resettlement place;[48] the pandemic meant that far fewer refugees were resettled in 2020–2021.[49] The queue is factually non-existent; legally, there is no requirement to join this factually non-existent queue. Queuing for nothing is pointless and a queue to nowhere for refugees is dangerous given the risk of *refoulement* or return to their country of origin.

More recently, particularly during the Gillard era, a purportedly humanitarian rationale of 'breaking the people smugglers' business model' and 'preventing deaths at sea' emerged.[50] The problem is that through interception and detention, we have supplemented life-threatening journeys to safety with a black hole of despair and sometimes death, as documented in Boochani's book and numerous other records. We have created the possibility of 'constructive' or 'disguised' *refoulement* where people are forced to return to dangerous countries of origin, pressured into leaving by the appalling circumstances in which they find themselves.[51] The interception program has been extremely risky, and the focus on interception, rather than pro-active search and rescue made it more likely that sinkings such as SIEV X could occur.[52] Temporary protection visas have encouraged family members to get on boats, thus adding to dangerous journeys.[53] And the Australian approach – whether supported by a populist or paternalist narrative – has migrated. One only has to look at Italy while Berlusconi or Salvini were in charge[54] and the UK's Rwanda proposal[55] to see this.

The contagious effect of Australian policy means that those countries with the means to do so push the responsibility for refugees back onto less able countries which struggle to meet the needs of refugees and their own citizens. It is untenable to argue that the asylum seekers on board the *Tampa* or the 20,000 boat arrivals in 2012 could not have been accommodated in Australia or that this posed a risk to Australian citizens. Why should this responsibility be passed to other countries?

There have also been detrimental impacts on Australian democracy and the rule of law. Playing on people's fears – whether of cultural difference or competition for jobs – provides an excuse for government not to take real action on the sorts of issues that make us fearful, be it unemployment and wage stagnation or climate change. And rational discussion about boat arrivals has become almost impossible.

Let us think about the discussion around the inquiry into the publicisation of a boat arrival on election day in 2022.[56] An inquiry was clearly merited. But the fact that secrecy about 'on water' or 'operational' matters was ever thought appropriate, and has been maintained for so long, should be extremely concerning in a liberal democracy.[57] The public deserves to know whether Australia complied with its international obligations and ensured the people on board were safe. Apparently they were flown back, rather than being subject to a tow back.[58] We were told there was a thorough screening of the passengers.[59] Where did this take place – on board, or on Christmas Island? With legal assistance and interpreters? Finally, what are the appeal avenues and is there a role for the courts here?

The framing of even one or two boat arrivals as a national emergency has meant that the courts are seen as a problem for swift executive action, rather than an important safeguard for the rights of the people seeking safety. In contrast, tennis player Novak Djokovic, who made world headlines when he attempted to enter Australia for the Australian Open claiming an exemption from the vaccination mandate, had the benefit of two court hearings prior to his eventual deportation.[60] Sadly, it appears that the special interest group of elite tennis players gets a better hearing than people seeking our protection.

Conclusion

At the beginning of my chapter, I quote some much-loved lines from a poet formerly described as the national poet.[61] In fact Gordon's brave words masked a world of pain. His family's wealth was built, in part, on slavery[62] and he violently took his own life. Yet, he once had enormous appeal as a 'rebellious, devil-may-care underdog, shy, caring, loyal, fearless, with a well-hidden sensitive side [who] fits the kind of legend that later became the Anzac legend; part of the concept of being Australian that Australians like to accept as part of themselves'.[63]

Gordon's words and the title of his poem seem particularly apt given the subject-matter of my chapter. But like Gordon himself, Australians' reactions to asylum seekers are complex. We are reacting with fear in times of trouble, blaming others for it and theirs. This seems only marginally better as a response than that proposed by Dame Edna Everage, who once advised us to 'laugh at other people's troubles, it helps to bear your own.'

I understand why it is thought to be political suicide to suggest that the policy of turning back boats should be abandoned. We all saw how the Coalition used boat arrivals to its advantage during the Rudd/Gillard Government, and the opposition will use their arrival in exactly the same way during the current parliamentary term. But I think it is important to question the populist impetus to close borders and think about what mainstream Australian values really are. Let us stop talking about the right and wrong ways to enter Australia and focus on our own processes and obligations – the matters we really do control.

There is a right way to return people who do not need protection: it involves a fair hearing with avenues of appeal so as to guard against mistakes. It is wrong to put people in a rightless black hole of detention offshore as a deterrent to others. We should remember that the grant of asylum avoids complicity in the harms that could occur if we return someone to a place of danger, and that treating them with dignity and allowing them to contribute to our country, as so many refugees have done,[64] is to our advantage. We also need to remember that the signal we send when we do not respect the right to seek asylum in our country, is that other countries should not either. If that took hold, no refugee would ever find safety. Is that a 'fair go'?

Endnotes

1. Convention relating to the Status of Refugees, opened for signature 28 July 1951, 189 UNTS 150 (entered into force 22 April 1954) as modified by the Protocol relating to the Status of Refugees, opened for signature 31 January 1967, 606 UNTS 267 (entered into force 4 October 1967) (hereinafter 'Refugee Convention'). Under Article 1A(2) of the Convention (as modified by the Protocol) a refugee is, in essence, someone who is outside their country of origin and unable to return owing to a well-founded fear of being persecuted for reasons of race, religion, nationality, membership of a particular social group or political opinion.
2. See UNHCR, 'Guidelines on International Protection No. 12: Claims for refugee status related to situations of armed conflict and violence under Article 1A(2) of the 1951 Convention and/or 1967 Protocol relating to the Status of Refugees and the regional refugee definitions', HCR/GIP/16/12, 2 December 2016; Cornelis (Kees) Wouters, 'Conflict Refugees' in Cathryn Costello, Michelle Foster and Jane McAdam (eds) *The Oxford Handbook of International Refugee* Law, OUP, Oxford, 2021, pp. 815-31.

3. Presumably no Ukrainians have travelled to Australia on a people smuggler's boat; available monthly updates regarding Operation Sovereign Borders during the relevant period speak only of Sri Lankan asylum seekers. Ukrainians have been authorised to travel to Australia (on tourist visas, for example), and visa extensions and temporary humanitarian visas have been available for Ukrainians in Australia.
4. Reinhart Kosselleck, 'Crisis', *Journal of the History of Ideas*, vol. 62, no. 2, 2006, pp. 357-400, p. 358.
5. John Howard, Election Speech, Sydney, 28 October 2001<https://electionspeeches.moadoph.gov.au/speeches/2001-john-howard>
6. If anything, the opposite is true: Rainer Hofmann and Tillmann Löhr, 'Introduction to Chapter V: Requirements for Refugee Status Determination Procedures' in Andreas Zimmermann (ed.) *The 1951 Convention relating to the Status of Refugees and its 1967 Protocol. A commentary*, OUP, Oxford, 2011, pp. 1082-128, p.1126. For discussion of international standards for the process of determining who meets the definition of a refugee, see Álvaro Botero and Jens Vedsted-Hansen, 'Asylum Procedure' in Cathryn Costello, Michelle Foster and Jane McAdam (eds) *The Oxford Handbook of International Refugee* Law, OUP, Oxford, 2021, pp. 588-606, pp. 599-605.
7. Refugee Convention, Article 31.
8. Refugees are entitled to most of the protections of the UN human rights treaties to which Australia is a party.
9. Refugee protection is often described as 'surrogate' protection: James C. Hathaway & Michelle Foster, *The Law of Refugee Protection*, 2nd edition, CUP, Cambridge, 2014, p. 51. This 'gloss' on the words of the Refugee Convention must be handled with care, however. See Guy S. Goodwin-Gill & Jane McAdam, *The Refugee in International* Law, 4th edition, OUP, Oxford, 2021, p. 8.
10. For discussion of the Howard Government's approach to One Nation, see Robert Manne, 'Reflections on the *Tampa* "crisis"', *Postcolonial Studies*, vol. 5, no.1, 2002, pp. 29-36; Lucy Wark, 'John Howard did not slay the One Nation Dragon', 6 September 2016, *Sydney Morning Herald*, <https://www.smh.com.au/opinion/john-howard-did-not-slay-the-one-nation-dragon-20160906-gr9py9.html>

11. John Howard, The Role of Government, Headland Speech, 1995 <https://australianpolitics.com/1995/06/06/john-howard-headland-speech-role-of-govt.html>
12. Marian Sawer, 'Framing Feminists: Market Populism and its Impact on Public Policy in Australia and Canada' in Yasmeen Abu-Laban (ed.) *Gendering the Nation-State: Canadian and Comparative Perspectives*, UBC Press, Vancouver, 2008, pp. 120-38, p.126.
13. Howard, Headland Speech, 1995.
14. See Sawer, 2008, pp. 120-1. See also Robert Manne, 'The Howard Years: a Political Interpretation', in Robert Manne (ed.) *The Howard Years*, Black Inc, Melbourne, 2004, pp. 3-53, p. 44.
15. See for example, Commonwealth of Australia, Department of Immigration and Multicultural and Indigenous Affairs, *Interpreting the Refugees Convention – an Australian contribution*, Australian Government, Canberra, 2002. In 2014, Australia adopted a statutory interpretation for national purposes of various aspects of the Refugee Convention definition: *Migration Act 1958* ss 5H-5M.
16. David Marr and Marian Wilkinson, *Dark Victory*, Allen & Unwin, Sydney, 2003, p. 151.
17. Commonwealth of Australia, Report of the Senate Select Committee, 'A Certain Maritime Incident', 23 October 2002, chs 3-6.
18. Howard, Election Speech, 28 October 2001.
19. Didier Bigo, 'Security and immigration: toward a critique of the governmentality of unease', *Alternatives: global, local, political*, vol. 27, no. 1, 2002, pp. 63-92.
20. Benjamin Moffitt, 'How to Perform Crisis: A Model for Understanding the Key Role of Crisis in Contemporary Populism', *Government and Opposition*, vol. 50, no. 2, 2006, pp. 189-217.
21. Draft Report of the Ad Hoc Committee on Statelessness and Related Problems. Proposed Draft Convention relating to the Status of Refugees: E/AC.32.L.38, 15 February 1950; Annex II (comments p. 57), cited in Guy S. Goodwin-Gill, 'Article 31 of the Refugee Convention: Non-penalization, Detention and Protection' in Erika Feller, Volker Türk and Frances Nicholson (eds) *Refugee Protection in International Law: UNHCR's Global Consultations on International Protection*, CUP, Cambridge, 2003, pp. 185-252, p. 190.

22. Conference of Plenipotentiaries on the Status of Refugees and Stateless Persons, Summary Records, A/CONF.2/SR.14, 22 November 1951, pp. 10-11 and 13, cited and discussed in Guy S. Goodwin-Gill, 2003, pp. 192-3. See also discussion in Cathryn Costello and Yulia Ioffe, 'Non penalization and non-criminalization' in Cathryn Costello, Michelle Foster and Jane McAdam (eds) *The Oxford Handbook of International Refugee* Law, OUP, Oxford, 2021, pp. 917-32, p. 923.
23. Commonwealth of Australia, *Interpreting the Refugees Convention*, 2002, p. 127.
24. Ibid., p. 135.
25. Ibid., p. 146. Admittedly, some interesting questions concerning the application of Article 31 are raised – for example, when interception occurs prior to entry into state territory and outside the territorial sea.
26. Ibid., p. 130.
27. Human Rights Watch, 'By Invitation Only:' Australian Asylum Policy, Vol 14, No10(C), December 2002, ch III & IV <https://www.hrw.org/reports/2002/australia/australia1202.pdf>
28. Nauru's instrument of accession was received on 26/6/2011 and the Convention entered into force for Nauru on 26/9/2011. Regarding the additional aid to Nauru, see Commonwealth of Australia, 'A Certain Maritime Incident', 2002, [11.68].
29. See Greg Fry, 'The "Pacific Solution"?' in William Maley et al, *Refugees and the Myth of the Borderless World*, ANU, Canberra, 2002, pp. 23-31, pp. 26-27; Savitri Taylor, 'The Pacific Solution or a Pacific Nightmare? The Difference between Burden Shifting and Burden Sharing', *Asian-Pacific Law & Policy Journal*, vol. 6, no. 1, 2005, pp. 1-43, pp. 28-30.
30. Ariane Rummery, 'Australia's "Pacific Solution" draws to a close', UNHCR, 11 February 2008 <https://www.unhcr.org/news/latest/2008/2/47b04d074/australias-pacific-solution-draws-close.html>
31. Rummery, 2008.
32. Andrew & Renata Kaldor Centre for International Refugee Law, Fact sheet, 'Australia—Cambodia Agreement for Refugees in Nau-

ru', 1 October 2019 <https://www.kaldorcentre.unsw.edu.au/publication/cambodia-and-refugee-protection>

33. Australian Government, Regional Processing and Resettlement <https://www.homeaffairs.gov.au/about-us/what-we-do/border-protection/regional-processing-and-resettlement>.
34. Michael Neilson, 'New Zealand and Australia reach deal over refugee resettlement offer', New Zealand Herald, 24 March 2022 <https://www.nzherald.co.nz/nz/new-zealand-and-australia-reach-deal-over-refugee-resettlement-offer/K3GTXNYUXX2JNN2EN2TI2NSC2Y/>.
35. Refugee Council of Australia, Offshore Processing Statistics, 13 June 2022 <https://www.refugeecouncil.org.au/operation-sovereign-borders-offshore-detention-statistics/>
36. 'Transitory persons' (i.e., refugees and asylum seekers transferred from Australia) live in the community on Nauru, according to the regular Operation Sovereign Borders updates: Australian Border Force, 'Operation Sovereign Borders Monthly Update: June 2022', 29 July 2022 <https://www.abf.gov.au/newsroom-subsite/Pages/Operation-Sovereign-Borders-monthly-update-June-2022.aspx>.
37. The arrangement came to an end on 31 December 2021: Australian Government, Regional Processing and Resettlement <https://www.homeaffairs.gov.au/about-us/what-we-do/border-protection/regional-processing-and-resettlement>.
38. There are several ways in which Australia may be held responsible. When an individual remains within the power or effective control of a country, the human rights obligations accepted by that country still apply. Further, where one country aids and abets another in the violation of human rights (for example, by paying for the construction of a detention centre), both countries may be held responsible.
39. Madeline Gleeson's book is a comprehensive account: Madeline Gleeson, *Offshore: Behind the Wire on Manus and Nauru*, NewSouth Publishing, Sydney, 2016.
40. Behrouz Boochani, *No Friend but the Mountains*, Picador, Sydney, 2020. For other memoirs, see Abbas Nazari, *After the Tampa: From Afghanistan to New* Zealand, Allen & Unwin, Auckland, 2021; Jaivet Ealom, *Escape from Manus: The untold true story*, Penguin Random House Australia, 2021.

41. Cait Kelly, 'A Form of Cruelty: 51 Asylum Seekers brought to Australia under medevac laws still languish in detention', *The Guardian*, 20 March 2022 <https://www.theguardian.com/australia-news/2022/mar/21/a-form-of-cruelty-51-asylum-seekers-brought-to-australia-under-medevac-laws-still-languish-in-detention>
42. See Mary Anne Kenny, Nicholas Procter and Carol Grech, Policy Brief 13, 'Temporary Protection Visas in Australia: A reform Proposal', Kaldor Centre, June 2022. Temporary protection for persons determined to be refugees should be distinguished from the temporary protection afforded in a mass influx (such as Ukrainians in the EU) which is a short-term measure designed in part to ease the strain on individual refugee status determination procedures.
43. The Meriam Webster dictionary defines a nondecision as 'an inadequate decision: a statement or determination that is presented as a decision but that avoids or leaves unresolved the issue being considered.'
44. The EU has applied a document known as the Temporary Protection Directive. Under the Temporary Protection Directive, a temporary form of protection may be granted to displaced people during a mass influx. Displaced persons are those 'unable to return in safe and durable conditions because of the situation prevailing in [their] country', in particular, those who are fleeing armed conflict, endemic violence and systematic or generalised violations of human rights. Council Directive 2001/55/EC of 20 July 2001 on Minimum Standards for Giving Temporary Protection in the Event of a Mass Influx of Displaced Persons and Bearing the Consequences Thereof [2001] OJ L212/12, Article 2(c).
45. The term was used in the late 1970s and Klaus Neumann attributes it to Gough Whitlam: Klaus Neumann, *Across the Seas: Australia's Response to Refugees – A History*, Black Inc, Melbourne, 2015, p. 276.
46. Gareth Evans, for example, once stated that 'the reality that we must all acknowledge is that there are many Vietnamese who will simply not be willing to wait in the Orderly Departure queue, and who will go on chasing the dream of a life elsewhere so long as the prospect of ultimate resettlement has not been absolutely excluded.' Gareth Evans, International Conference on Indo-Chinese Refugees, State-

ment by the Australian Delegation, Delivered by Senator the Honourable Gareth Evans QC, Minister for Foreign Affairs and Trade, Geneva, 13 June 1989, UNHCR Fonds 11 Series 3, 391.89, UNHCR Archives.

47. For some examples of 'protected entry procedures' enabling people to apply for protection from their home countries or transit countries, see Claire Higgins, Policy Brief 8, 'Safe Journeys and Sound Policy: Expanding Protected entry for refugees', Kaldor Centre, November 2019.
48. UNHCR, Resettlement, <https://www.unhcr.org/resettlement.html>.
49. UNHCR, 'Global Trends: Forced Displacement in 2021', 16 June 2022, p. 38.
50. Sharon Pickering and Leanne Weber, 'New Deterrence Scripts in Australia's Rejuvenated Offshore Detention Regime for Asylum Seekers', *Law & Social Inquiry*, vol. 39, no. 4, 2014, pp. 1006-26, p. 1009.
51. For discussion see Penelope Mathew, 'Constructive Refoulement' in Satvinder Singh Juss (ed.) *Research Handbook on International Refugee Law*, Edward Elgar, Cheltenham, 2019, pp. 207-223; Penelope Mathew, '*Non-refoulement*' in Cathryn Costello, Michelle Foster and Jane McAdam (eds) *The Oxford Handbook of International Refugee* Law, OUP, Oxford, 2021, pp. 899-916, pp. 913-5.
52. Marr and Wilkinson, 2003, pp. 228-9.
53. See for example, the story of Sundous Ibrahim and her three little girls who were unable to join Sundous' husband, Ahmaed Al-Zalimi, because of his temporary protection visa, and travelled on the ill-fated SIEV X (Suspected Illegal Entry Vessel 'X'), resulting in the deaths of all three children: Marr and Wilkinson, 2003, ch 17.
54. See for example, Jacquelin Magnay, Italy Immigration: New Interior Minister Matteo Salvini promises to 'stop the death boats', *The Australian*, 4 June 2018.
55. The language of queue jumping and breaking the business model of the people smugglers was used by Prime Minister Johnson: Alistair Smout & Clement Uwiringiyimana 'Britain Plans to send migrants to Rwanda under tougher asylum policy', Reuters, 15 April 2022 <https://www.reuters.com/world/uk/uks-johnson-seeks-put-fine-behind-him-with-immigration-plan-2022-04-13/>.

56. Letter to Clare O'Neil, Minister of Home Affairs, from Michael Pezzullo, Secretary of the Department of Home Affairs, 1 June 2022; appendix 'SIEV 915 and the Commander Joint Agency Task Force Operation Sovereign Borders Public Statement', https://minister.homeaffairs.gov.au/ClareONeil/Documents/siev-915-JATFOSB-statement.pdf. (Hereinafter Pezzullo report.)
57. The protocols around information are purportedly designed to protect against undesirable consequences such as informing the strategies of people smugglers. See Pezzullo report, 2022, pp. 2-4.
58. Karen Middleton, 'Claims Coalition colluded in election day boat arrival', *The Saturday Paper*, 28 May-3 June 2022.
59. Stephanie Borys, 'Labor sends election-day boat arrivals back to Sri Lanka, slamming mass text "disgrace"', *ABC News*, 24 May 2022 < https://www.abc.net.au/news/2022–05-24/labor-turns-back-election-day-asylum-seeker-boat-arrival/101095322>.
60. Sherryn Groch, 'Djokovic is gone. How did the case unfold and what does it mean for Australia's border rules?' *The Age*, 17 January 2022.
61. Frank Davidson, 'Adam Lindsay Gordon (1833-1870) – a Great Scottish-Australian Poet?', *Journal of the Sydney Society for Scottish History*, vol. 12, 2010, pp. 27-46.
62. Georgina Arnott, 'Australia's deep connection with enslavement', *The Age*, 16 June 2020.
63. Davidson, 'Adam Lindsay Gordon', 2010, p. 46.
64. Graeme Hugo, *Economic, Social and Civic Contributions of First and Second Generation Humanitarian Entrants: Final Report to the Department of Immigration and Citizenship*, Department of Immigration and Citizenship, June 2011.

4

Terrorism crisis: cosying up to the Americans?

David Kilcullen

Introduction

This chapter explores how terrorism – specifically, the outbreak of the Global War on Terrorism on September 11th, 2001, and Australia's subsequent response to transnational jihadism – emerged as an unexpected crisis at the beginning of the 21st century, and how Prime Minister John Howard's response to that crisis shaped, and was shaped by, the broader experience of crisis management within the Howard Government. It argues that, contrary to a narrative popular at the time, Australia was not instinctively 'cosying-up to the Americans' or acting as Washington's 'deputy sheriff'.[1] Rather, the Howard Government's crisis response to the 9/11 attacks produced a calibrated commitment to global counterterrorism under US leadership, while simultaneously allowing Australia to exercise regional leadership independent of US priorities, and creating space for a distinctively Australian domestic approach to terrorism.

The chapter is organised into three sections. The first examines the circumstances surrounding the outbreak of the Global War on Terrorism (GWOT) and how they shaped the Howard Government's strategic framing of the conflict. The second examines three levels of Australia's engagement with the terrorism threat after 9/11: global commitment (in Afghanistan and Iraq), regional cooperation (with Indonesia and other like-minded countries in Australia's neighbourhood) and domestic deterrence and response. The final section offers observations and conclusions about terrorism as it relates to the broader theme of crisis management in the Howard Government.

Outbreak of the War on Terrorism

Prime Minister John Howard was famously, in Washington, DC, on 9/11. He was visiting the United States to commemorate the 50th anniversary of the signing of the 1951 ANZUS treaty, to hold his first meeting with US president George W. Bush who had taken office several months before, and to discuss negotiations for the Australia-US Free Trade Agreement (eventually signed in May 2004). Howard had held talks on 10 September, including a four-hour meeting with President Bush, and participated in an ANZUS ceremony at the Washington Navy Yard in Washington, DC, before retiring to his hotel. He later described that day, in an interview with Richard Fidler of ABC Radio, as 'the last day of the old order.'[2]

The following morning, 11th September, as he was at the hotel preparing to speak with reporters about the collapse of Ansett airlines, first one jet airliner and then another struck the twin towers of the World Trade Center in New York City. The prime minister immediately held a press conference to express solidarity with the United States; he was partway through when a third aircraft struck the nearby Pentagon, close enough for Mr. Howard to see smoke rising from the building.[3] A fourth airliner, downed by passengers courageously fighting back against the hijackers, crashed in a field near Shanksville, Pennsylvania. It was immediately obvious the United States was at war and would respond accordingly.

Howard and his delegation were quickly 'bundled off to a bunker underneath the Australian embassy' a few blocks from the White House.[4] In the bunker, Howard conferred with intelligence, military and diplomatic personnel on Australia's response.[5] On arrival back in Australia three days later he invoked the Australia, New Zealand, United States Security Treaty (ANZUS) treaty for the first time in its history, framing 9/11 as an act of war, and one that, with '80 or 90 Australians unaccounted for', should be seen as an attack on Australia also.[6] He argued that 'at no stage should any Australian regard this as something that is just confined to the United States. It is an attack upon the way of life we hold dear in common with the Americans' and announced that Australia was 'willing to participate [in military operations] to the limit of our capability. The Americans haven't at this stage made any requests for particular support but we will consider any request that is made'.[7] A few weeks later, as the invasion of Afghanistan began, the government (with bipartisan support) initiated Operation Slipper, embedded Australian planners in US headquarters, and deployed Special Operations Forces (SOF) and support elements to Afghanistan.[8]

The Government's strategic framing comprised, in effect, five key elements: 9/11 was (1) an act of war, (2) an attack on both the United States and Australia, (3) a situation covered by the ANZUS treaty, in which Australia would (4) support the United States 'to the limit of our capability' and (5) 'consider any request' for military support. This five-part framing came to define Australia's war aims throughout the GWOT, both for the Howard Government and for subsequent Australian governments of both main political parties. It framed Australia's participation in alliance terms – supporting the United States under ANZUS – rather than setting campaign-specific objectives for the wars in Afghanistan or, subsequently, Iraq.

Howard later said that 9/11 'was not an occasion for Australia to be a 70 or 80 per cent ally, it was an occasion to be a 100 per cent ally'.[9] But the maximalism of Australia's declaratory policy (which did, indeed, give rise to a perception of 'cosying up to the Americans') was combined with subtle practical restraint. Far from stating an unlimited commitment, Howard set the tone for subsequent limited Australian participation by telegraphing that Canberra would cap its commitment at a level it considered to be within available capability and consider US requests on a case-by-case basis rather than committing to open-ended support. In practice, Australia tended to prioritise crises closer to home (in the Solomon Islands after 2003 or East Timor in 2006) while tailoring its expeditionary commitments to specific, limited-purpose forces drawn from whatever spare capacity remained once higher-priority regional tasks had been resourced. Arguably, this combination of rhetorical maximalism with practical restraint enabled Australia to gain significant strategic advantage – consolidating its position as a US ally – for relatively low cost.

Clausewitz famously wrote that

> the first, the supreme, the most far-reaching act of judgment that the statesman and commander have to make is rightly to establish ... the kind of war on which they are embarking; neither mistaking it for, nor trying to turn it into, something that is alien to its nature.[10]

Likewise, British and Australian military doctrine identifies 'selection and maintenance of the aim' as the first, most important principle of war.[11] Unsurprisingly, because of the circumstances just described Australian political and military decision-makers' conceptualisation of 9/11 (the 'kind of war on which they [were] embarking') was in alliance terms. Australia's war aim – selected in the immediate aftermath of 9/11 and maintained through successive changes of government – was to demonstrate Australia's reliability and competence as an ally, thereby cementing the ANZUS relationship, which both major parties (and the bulk of the Australian people) saw as the cornerstone of our national security. That framing had positive and negative consequences.

Australia's global participation

The alliance-support framing drove the upper, global layer of Australia's participation in the war on terror. An Australian Special Operations Task Group (SOTG) deployed in November 2001 for the invasion of Afghanistan, remaining until the end of 2002, but then disengaging from post-invasion occupation tasks. This aligned with decisions made immediately after the invasion, with Cabinet on 10 December 2001 expressing concern over the possible length of a protracted conflict in Afghanistan, and noting that 'the government was not inclined to commit significant [defence] assets or personnel to any medium-term or long-term stabilisation or peace keeping force'.[12] Another SOTG (in August 2005) then a reconstruction task force (in August 2006) were recommitted under the International Security Assistance Force (ISAF), but deployed into an Australian Area of Responsibility (AOR) in Uruzgan province, with separate, specific tasks rather than a blanket commitment to U.S.-led combat operations.[13]

The war in Iraq saw a similar pattern – an initial SOTG deployment for the invasion in March 2003, disengagement from occupation tasks once combat concluded, then recommitment, in early 2005, of a stabilisation task group within a distinct Australian AOR with separate tasks and rules of engagement.[14] Participation in the invasion phase of each conflict (in both cases, as part of a very small group of allies willing to deploy directly into combat alongside US forces) gained Australia significant alliance credibility; stepping back from post-invasion stabilisation – and subsequently committing only to limited tasks – let Australia minimise the long-term costs of what became protracted, inconclusive conflicts.

Conceptualising the commitment to each of these major conflicts in alliance terms meant that Australian forces were not trying to win either war; indeed, this approach ceded ultimate responsibility for victory to the coalition's lead nation, the United States. If Australian forces continued to provide valuable contributions to the coalition, preserving our alliance credibility, they were achieving the national war aim—whether the war ended in victory or not. In effect, if a nation's war aim is to participate, and be seen to participate, as a credible ally, this aim is achieved from the outset of any deployment. Assuming an acceptable level of military competence (and Australians were generally seen as competent by our allies) the only thing that could undermine that aim would be to withdraw too early, giving the appearance of leaving allies in the lurch.[15]

Given that Australia's level of effort was decoupled from the war's ultimate outcome, Canberra was free to calibrate Australia's commitment and casualties accordingly. This did not always go down well with the United States or other allies, particularly the United Kingdom (UK), who (especially in Iraq) sometimes saw Australia as reaping the benefits of coalition participation without putting in the same effort, or suffering the same costs.[16] Casualty figures tend to support this criticism: in Afghanistan, the US lost 2355 killed (including 9 CIA officers) and British forces 456; Australia lost 41 killed, of whom 34 were combat casualties. In Iraq, US forces lost 4,459 killed and the UK lost 179 killed. Two Australian servicemen died in Iraq, neither of them in combat – one was killed by an accidental gunshot, and one died in an aircraft crash.[17] While any death is a tragedy, to the extent that casualty rates reflect combat commitment, Australia's effort was calibrated at a different level than that of the United States or the United Kingdom.

The approach also placed a significant burden on Australia's Special Operations Command (SOCOMD), which was tapped to provide a succession of overseas SOTGs while simultaneously retaining its key military counterterrorism task within Australia, the responsibility for the two high-readiness Tactical Assault Groups (TAGs) in Perth and Sydney. The heavy reliance on SOCOMD also telegraphed a certain lack of government confidence in the rest of the Australian Defence Force, with negative effects both for the readiness of an over-tasked SOCOMD and the morale of the wider defence force.

These operational disadvantages were offset by the crucial strategic advantage of an approach that allowed Australia to retain strategic freedom of action, tailoring troop commitments to available capacity and sequencing them in response to specific US requests. This meant that Australia, despite deployments in Iraq and Afghanistan, retained sufficient assets to respond in a timely manner to regional developments including the Regional Assistance Mission in the Solomon Islands from 2003, the humanitarian response to the Indian Ocean tsunami of December 2004, and the East Timor security crisis of 2006, as well as several smaller commitments, including advisory and peace support missions in Bougainville and Papua New Guinea, and ongoing United Nations peacekeeping efforts. The imposition of careful limits on Australia's global expeditionary commitments in the GWOT also allowed Australia to respond to the regional challenge of terrorism in the Asia-Pacific.

Australia's regional response to terrorism

In October 2002, Indonesia's regional ally Jemaah Islamiyah bombed two nightclubs in Bali, injuring 209 people and killing 202, including 88 Australians.[18] The bombing brought the immediacy of the regional terrorism threat home to the Australian people and Government alike: most of the victims were Australian citizens, and more Australians were killed and injured, as a proportion of population, in the Bali bombing than Americans on 9/11.

Australia's response was to launch a cooperative counterterrorism effort in partnership with the Indonesian government. The Howard Government made clear that it saw the bombing as part of an ongoing threat to both Indonesia and Australia, and therefore one that required a collaborative effort in response. Again, the prime minister set the tone, in remarks delivered in Bali one week after the attack, suggesting that as Australians we

> try and comprehend what has happened, let us gather ourselves together, let us wrap our arms not only around our fellow Australians but our arms around the people of Indonesia, of Bali.[19]

Indonesia was undergoing a transition to democracy at the time, after almost four decades of military dictatorship; Howard's collaborative framing of the regional terrorism challenge allowed Canberra to accelerate the process of reconciliation with Jakarta after the contentious Australian-led intervention in East Timor. This had occurred in 1999 under a different Indonesian government but remained a source of tension in the relationship: the Bali bombing, and the cooperative effort that followed, contributed to the East

Timor intervention 'fading from public consciousness' in both Australia and Indonesia.[20]

The framing of terrorism as a common threat to Australia and the region (rather than a threat to Australia from the region) enabled collaborative efforts including the establishment of the Jakarta Centre for Law Enforcement Cooperation as a permanent platform for regional counterterrorism cooperation.[21] It prompted deep and enduring collaboration between the Australian Federal Police (AFP) and Indonesia's national police service, along with cooperation between the Australian Intelligence Community and Indonesian intelligence services.[22] And it gave impetus to an Australian-Indonesian joint regional effort, the Bali Counterterrorism Process, that drew together partners across the Asia-Pacific to collaborate on and fund counterterrorism efforts.[23]

Thus, unlike the global level of the war on terrorism – where Australia's goal was to demonstrate loyalty and effectiveness as an alliance partner, irrespective of the outcome of each individual campaign – at the regional level Australia asserted substantive leadership alongside like-minded countries, with definite campaign goals in mind. The United States and other global allies were welcome to participate (and did so) but Australia took the lead in working with regional partners, rather than waiting for US leadership. This approach became the cornerstone for the Howard Government's counterterrorism white paper of 2004, *Protecting Australia Against Terrorism*, and for counterterrorism strategies issued by subsequent governments in 2010 and 2017.[24]

The approach paid dividends in October 2005, in response to a second bombing in which Jemaah Islamiyah again targeted sites frequented by Australian and international tourists in Bali. The death toll from the second Bali bombing – 23 people, including the three suicide bombers – was an order of magnitude smaller than the first bombing, while Australian and Indonesian intelligence and law enforcement cooperation, established and deepened in the three years after the first bombing, enabled rapid response by both countries and a quick roll-up of the terrorist network responsible for the attack.[25] The regional partnership only came into its own, however, well after the end of the Howard Government, when it enabled regional partners to ramp up their cooperation in response to Jemaah Islamiyah's resurgence and the emergence of Islamic State in Southeast Asia after 2016.[26] This, in effect, adds a layer of complexity to the public narrative on the Howard Government's response to terrorism: rather than a blind commitment to the United States, that response saw carefully-calibrated global engagement paired with a regional response alongside like-minded partners.

The domestic level of Australia's response

Simultaneously with these global and regional approaches, the third layer of Australia's response involved domestic law enforcement, intelligence, border security and internal security. This commenced immediately after 9/11: by 2 October 2001, Cabinet was already considering a submission on 'options for defence enhancement for domestic security.'[27] A few weeks later, the Government commissioned a review into Australia's counterterrorism capabilities by Robert Cornall, secretary of the Attorney-General's Department. The Cornall Review (the first of several since 9/11) drove enhancements, operational and legislative, to Australia's counterterrorism efforts. The government subsequently introduced legislation creating new terrorism-related offences, enabling proscription of terrorist organisations, enhancing the powers of customs officers and airport security officials, and improving coordination and information-sharing for critical infrastructure resilience.[28] The Australian Commonwealth, state and territory governments agreed an intergovernmental framework for nationwide coordination of counterterrorism arrangements.[29]

After the Bali bombing, the government's domestic response focused on better early warning and intelligence for terrorism threats, along with closer coordination among agencies responding to them.

The government established a National Counter-Terrorism Committee to coordinate interagency efforts, created a National Threat Assessment Centre within the Australian Security Intelligence Organisation (ASIO) to manage terrorism threat warnings, and appointed a Counter-Terrorism Ambassador within the Department of Foreign Affairs and Trade to coordinate overseas collaboration. Joint Counter Terrorism Teams (JCTTs) were established including the AFP, state and territory police forces, ASIO and other agencies.[30] ASIO and police forces were granted enhanced detention and questioning powers, along with powers to preventively detain individuals to prevent an imminent terrorist attack.[31] The government also began the process – not fully completed until 2017 – of unifying a series of disparate customs, immigration, border security, law enforcement and intelligence agencies into what subsequently became the Department of Home Affairs. Taken together, these measures gave Australia one of the most robust domestic counterterrorism regimes anywhere in the democratic world, provoking civil liberties concerns even as its effectiveness in disrupting terrorist attacks became apparent.[32]

Against the heightened threat driven by 9/11, the Bali bombing and the wars in Afghanistan and Iraq, which saw multiple terrorism plots within Australia, these capabilities enabled a series of effective operations. Most notably, Operation Pendennis – a joint ASIO/AFP investigation in cooperation with the Victoria and New South Wales state police – became Australia's longest-running terrorism investigation, disrupting two terrorist cells and culminating in a series of arrests between November 2005 and March 2006 that resulted in terrorism charges against thirteen individuals in Melbourne and nine in Sydney.[33] Several other operations disrupted individual or smaller-scale threats: in 2003, Zaky Mallah became the first individual charged under the new legislation while in 2006, Faheem Lodhi was convicted of terrorist offences relating to planning a terrorist attack.[34]

Militarily, the Howard Government built on lessons already

learned during the Interfet deployment in East Timor to improve or accelerate existing efforts to enhance defence capabilities against terrorism. These included the establishment of Tactical Assault Group (East) as a counterpart to the existing Perth-based TAG to cover counterterrorism response on Australia's east coast, and the raising of an Australian Regular Army commando capability in the form of the 2nd Commando Regiment, responsible for TAG (East) and for SOTG deployments. In addition, a domestic high-risk search and Chemical, Biological, Radiological and Nuclear Explosive (CBRNE) capability – originally created for the 2001 Sydney Olympic Games – was expanded into the Special Operations Engineer Regiment.

As noted above, the enhanced anti-terrorism powers established by the Howard Government after 9/11, though receiving bipartisan support in Parliament and thorough legal review through amendments to the Crimes Act (1914) and the passage of the federal anti-terrorism bill of 2005, were contentious within the Australian community. There were legitimate concerns over civil liberties, coercive questioning and preventive detention. Notably, however, subsequent governments have not substantially altered the direction established by the Howard Government after 9/11, and over time the approach seems to have attained a degree of bipartisan support and public acceptance. In effect, despite acrimonious political debate at times, the direction set by the Howard Government on domestic anti-terrorism and homeland security has endured.

Observations

The terrorist attacks of September 11th, 2001 marked Australia's most important national security and foreign policy crisis in a generation. As noted in other papers, even before 9/11 the Howard Government had an experienced national security team, with key decision-makers and government personnel already in office through multiple crises before 9/11. The deep personal commitment shown by John Howard, and the prime minister's visceral understanding of the terrorism threat, through the accident of being present in Washington, DC, as the attacks on 9/11 unfolded, set the tone for Australia's subsequent response, and also allowed for a rapid reaction to the crisis with key Cabinet decisions occurring within days of the attacks.

Inevitably, for the same reason, Australia's strategic response to 9/11, and our participation in the subsequent GWOT, was framed as one of ANZUS commitment and of demonstrating that Australia was a reliable and competent ally. The alliance relationship was central to Australia's wartime strategic calculus – Australia's role in the GWOT was not as a regional deputy sheriff, but as a global partner. But, as we have seen, this was a carefully calibrated level of effort in which Canberra ensured it retained freedom of action for other issues and regional priorities, while limiting its costs from the wars in Afghanistan and Iraq, to the occasional envy of other coalition partners such as the United Kingdom.

The centrality of the alliance commitment gave Australia a clear war aim, selected early and maintained through multiple successive governments of both parties, creating consistency and enabling sustained efforts over two decades, with important benefits for regional counterterrorism efforts and domestic security policy. However, as we have seen, it ceded responsibility for the ultimate outcome of the wars to the United States, tying Australia to US strategy in Afghanistan, Iraq and subsequently in the campaign to counter the Islamic State.

The risk here – which we might call the risk of major-ally incompetence – is real. Since none of the junior allies controlled the overall strategy, when a series of administrations in the United States proved unable to stabilise Iraq or Afghanistan, or to successfully terminate either conflict in a politically sustainable timeframe, the allies were trapped. They could neither generate sufficient leverage to alter the course of events, nor exit the effort without being seen as disloyal or ineffective, thus undermining their alliance-centric war aims. But this was true of all coalition partners and allies – Australia managed the issue better than most, largely because of the Howard Government's framing of the issue in such a way as to retain Australia's regional and domestic freedom of action while limiting cost and keeping commitments at a manageable level.

The Howard Government's approach to the global, regional and domestic layers of the terrorism problem, though established within days of the 9/11 attacks and thus arguably a product of crisis planning, set the direction for subsequent governments of both parties. As such – and, as we have seen, with both advantages and disadvantages – it created an enduring policy legacy for the Howard Government. While Australia may have appeared to be cosying up to the Americans, this was a superficial impression only. The reality was multi-layered and much more nuanced than that. At all levels including the global layer of expeditionary commitments to the war on terrorism, the hallmark of Australia's response was careful calibration of support, in such a way that we retained regional and local freedom of action. Arguably that fact, along with support from mainstream Australian public opinion, explains why the direction set by John Howard on the morning of 9/11 has endured.

Endnotes

1. See for example 'Howard dubbed 'deputy sheriff'' in *The Sydney Morning Herald,* 3 December 2002, at https://www.smh.com.au/national/howard-dubbed-deputy-sheriff-20021203-gdfwl4.html
2. Australian Broadcasting Corporation (2011), *ABC Conversations with Richard Fidler: John Howard Interview Transcript,* online at https://www.abc.net.au/reslib/201109/r826557_7555516.pdf , p. 1.
3. Sky News Australia, *Former Australian Prime Minister remembers 9/11 attacks in the US,* 9 September 2021, at https://www.skynews.com.au/opinion/andrew-bolt/former-australian-prime-minister-remembers-911-attacks-in-the-us/video/ae27f05753be46899f1202dada5293d4
4. Ibid.
5. Ibid.
6. See 'Transcript of portions of a joint press conference held at Parliament House, Canberra, by John Howard and Alexander

Downer', 14th September 2001, at https://australianpolitics.com/2001/09/14/government-invokes-anzus-treaty.html

7. Ibid.
8. See Australian War Memorial, *Operation Slipper*, at https://www.awm.gov.au/collection/E84816
9. Charlie Moore, 'John Howard reveals he feared SYDNEY would be attacked next after 9/11 – as he defends decision to send Australians to war in Afghanistan alongside the US', *The Daily Mail*, 5 September 2021, at https://www.dailymail.co.uk/news/article-9960875/John-Howard-reveals-feared-SYDNEY-attacked-9-11-defends-Afghanistan-war.html
10. Carl Von Clausewitz (Michael Howard and Peter Paret, eds.) (1989, first published 1832) *On War*, Princeton, NJ: Princeton University Press, p. 88.
11. Ministry of Defence, Joint Doctrine Publication 0–01, *UK Defence Doctrine*, Shrivenham: Development, Concepts and Doctrine Centre, 2014, p. 30.
12. Jonathan Kearsley, 'Cabinet papers from 2001 reveal Howard Government was concerned by length of Afghanistan war', Nine News, 1 January 2022, at https://www.9news.com.au/national/cabinet-papers-2001-howard-government-afghanistan-war-september-11-attacks-ansett-deal/8a4bdfed-8c1d-4e90-b919-0391fea111ac. For the original Cabinet decisions on Afghanistan see National Archives of Australia, Cabinet Decision JH01/0337/NS - Reference copy of Afghanistan - Australian Defence Force deployment - Without Submission, NAA: A14370, JH2001/337, 10 December 2001; and Cabinet Decision JH01/0347/CAB – UK Request for Australian Contribution to Multinational Stabilisation Force in Afghanistan – Without Submission, NAA: A14370, JH2001/347, 17 December 2001.
13. For a detailed chronology see Parliament of Australia, Parliamentary Library, *Australia's military involvement in Afghanistan since 2001: a chronology*, 16 July 2010, at https://www.aph.gov.au/About_Parliament/Parliamentary_Departments/Parliamentary_Library/pubs/BN/1011/MilitaryInvolvementAfghanistan
14. For a detailed chronology see John Blaxland, Marcus Fielding and Thea Gellerfy, *Niche Wars: Australia in Afghanistan and Iraq, 2001–2014*, Canberra: ANU Press, 2020, pp. 357-64.

15. For an Australian perspective on coalition perceptions of Australian performance see Dan McDaniel, 'Australia's intervention in Afghanistan, 2001-2 in Blaxland et al, *Niche Wars*, pp. 67-70. For a US Army perspective see Stephen A. Carney (2011) *Allied Participation in Operation Iraqi Freedom*, Washington, DC: US Army Center of Military History, pp. 39-41.
16. Author's discussion with British officers of MNF-I in Baghdad, May 2007 and at ISAF headquarters, Kabul, December 2009.
17. See 'Coalition casualties in Afghanistan' at https://en.wikipedia.org/wiki/Coalition_casualties_in_Afghanistan and 'Casualties of the Iraq War: Coalition Military Casualties' at https://en.wikipedia.org/wiki/Casualties_of_the_Iraq_War#Coalition_military_casualties
18. SBS News, Bali Bombings: Full List of Victims Names, at https://www.sbs.com.au/news/article/bali-bombings-full-list-of-victims-names/5gqu3ovvr
19. National Museum of Australia, Defining Moments: Bali Bombings, at https://www.nma.gov.au/defining-moments/resources/bali-bombings
20. John Blaxland (ed) (2015) *East Timor Intervention: A Retrospective on INTERFET*, Melbourne: Melbourne University Press, p. 364.
21. For an overview see Michelle Teo, *Jakarta Bombing 2004: Why Target Australia?*, IDSS Commentaries.
22. 22 September 2004, at https://www.rsis.edu.sg/wp-content/uploads/2014/07/CO04045.pdf and John Coyne, "The future of the Jakarta Centre for Law Enforcement Cooperation" in *ASPI Strategist*, 21st February 2017, at https://www.aspistrategist.org.au/future-jakarta-centre-law-enforcement-cooperation/
23. See Jacinta Carroll, Australia and Indonesia: Indispensable Partners in Counterterrorism, Australian Strategic Policy Institute, 17th February 2017, at https://www.aspi.org.au/opinion/australia-and-indonesia-indispensable-partners-counterterrorism
24. See Ministry of Foreign Affairs, Japan, Bali Counter-Terrorism Process: Report of the Australian and Indonesian Co-Chairs, August 2006, at https://www.mofa.go.jp/policy/terrorism/report0608.html
25. See Commonwealth of Australia (2004), Protecting Australia

Against Terrorism, Canberra: Department of Prime Minister and Cabinet, at http://repository.jeffmalone.org/files/CT/paat_2004.pdf

26. See 'Indonesia's measured response to terror' in East Asia Forum, 29 February 2016, at https://www.eastasiaforum.org/2016/02/29/indonesias-measured-response-to-terror/. For an assessment of successful counterterrorism capacity building in the wake of the first bombing see Celina Realuyo and Scott Stapleton, 'Response to Bali: An International Success Story' in Economic Perspectives, September 2004, pp. 14-17 at https://ciaotest.cc.columbia.edu/olj/ep/ep_sep04/ep_sep04e.pdf
27. See Bilveer Singh and Kumar Ramakrishna, 'Islamic State's Wilayah Philippines: Implications for Southeast Asia' in *RSIS Commentaries*, 187, 21 July 2016, at https://www.rsis.edu.sg/wp-content/uploads/2016/07/CO16187.pdf. See also Kanupriya Kapoor and Fathin Ungku, 'Southeast Asian nations step up cooperation as Islamic State threat mounts', Reuters, 4 June 2017, at https://www.reuters.com/article/us-asia-security-islamicstate-idUSKBN18V0JI
28. Chris Wallace (2022) The 2001 Cabinet Papers in Context, Canberra: National Archives of Australia, online at https://www.naa.gov.au/sites/default/files/2021-12/The%202001%20Cabinet%20papers%20in%20context.pdf. See National Archives of Australia, Cabinet Submission JH01/0304 - Reference copy of Options for Defence enhancement for domestic security - Decision JH01/0304/NS, NAA: A14370, JH2001/304, 2 October 2001.
29. Department of Prime Minister and Cabinet (2015) Review of Australia's Counter-Terrorism Machinery, Canberra, ACT: Commonwealth of Australia, pp. 2-6.
30. See Council of Australian Governments (2013) Council of Australian Governments Review of Counter-Terrorism Legislation, Canberra: Commonwealth of Australia, pp. 1-3.
31. Ibid.
32. See Nick Evershed and Michael Safi, 'All of Australia's national security changes since 9/11 in a timeline' in *The Guardian*, 19 October 2015, at https://www.theguardian.com/australia-news/ng-interactive/2015/oct/19/all-of-australias-national-security-changes-since-911-in-a-timeline

33. For an assessment, see Ashutosh Misra (2018) 'Australia's Counter-Terrorism Policies Since September 11, 2001: Harmonising National Security, Independent Oversight and Individual Liberties,' *Strategic Analysis*, vol. 42, no. 2, pp. 103-18.
34. See Bart Schuurman, Shandon Harris-Hogan, Andrew Zammit and Peter Lentini (2014) 'Operation Pendennis: a case study of an Australian terrorist plot' in *Perspectives on Terrorism*, vol. 8, no. 4, pp. 91-9.
35. Prime Minister and Cabinet, Review of Australia's Counter-Terrorism Machinery, pp. 5-6.

5

Crisis in remote Indigenous Australia

Mal Brough

It was just before two o'clock on the afternoon of Monday, 18 June 2007. My colleagues were making their way into the House of Representatives chamber for Question Time. I arrived early and had taken my seat on the front bench. Shortly after, the prime minister arrived. His usual practice was to head straight for his chair at the dispatch box, however, on this occasion he stopped in front of me and uttered a few words. He said something like 'we need to ban the booze'. There was no other detail. No context. I was startled, to say the least. I tried to clarify with him what he had just said, but he pivoted in his chair to take his first question from the opposition.

I sent a message to my office requesting they urgently speak with the prime minister's office. The message came back: in response to a question from radio announcer, John Laws relating to the recently released 'Little Children are Sacred' report from the Northern Territory (NT) Government into child abuse, the prime minister said he would consider 'banning alcohol in these communities'. I was gobsmacked. This was no small gesture. The findings of child sexual abuse throughout remote NT communities were shocking and he clearly wanted to act. Naturally, I was in full agreement.

Addressing the devastating issue of child abuse in remote communities had been a priority from my earliest days in the Indigenous Affairs portfolio. I needed to share my thoughts with the prime minister at the earliest opportunity. At the conclusion of Question Time, we walked together back to his office. It was a short conversation. I felt we needed to do more than just 'ban the booze'. I proposed an action agenda to be considered by Cabinet. He agreed. Thirty minutes later he addressed his colleagues at our regular Cabinet meeting. Howard spoke of his shock at the findings of the report and had asked me to develop a plan. My colleagues were in full agreement.

The far reaching and unprecedented response announced on 21 June 2007 ensured the media was forced to focus on the true extent of abuse and neglect being perpetrated on children in isolated communities across the Northern Territory. Senior members of the Canberra press gallery shared with me later they had no idea why the prime minister had called a major press conference at that time. Aboriginal child abuse was clearly not on their radar. Not even the release of a report with the first recommendation stating clearly, 'The Aboriginal child sexual abuse in the Northern Territory be designated as an issue of urgent national significance by both the Australian and Northern Territory governments' had elicited interest among mainstream media. What was more needed to gain the attention of the Canberra press gallery?

Without the urgent response from the Howard Government the disturbing findings of this report – and the plight of these children – may not have entered the consciousness of the general population. Notably, the Northern Territory Government received the final report in January 2007, almost six months before making it public and failed to provide a copy to the Commonwealth Government. A clear breakdown in Commonwealth-state relations.

Time to step up

I was appointed to this portfolio in January 2006, following Liberal Senator Amanda Vanstone (2003-2006), Philip Ruddock (2001-2003) and Liberal Senator Dr John Herron (1996-2001) respectively. The Aboriginal and Torres Strait Island Island Commission (ATSIC), which had been formed in 1990 by the Hawke Government was responsible for the development and delivery of most federally funded programs for Aboriginal and Torres Strait

Islander peoples. However, Labor Minister Carmen Lawrence had concluded that ATSIC had been under-resourcing health programs and had restored the funding responsibility to the Health Department in 1995. Labour market programs were maintained by Department of Employment and Workplace Relations. The legislation governing ATSIC limited the scope and capacity for the Minister to develop or implement programs and initiatives within the portfolio. This would remain the case until ATSIC was abolished in 2005.

In a clear demonstration of the Howard Government's policy priorities, Senator Herron, a trained surgeon, introduced the Army Aboriginal Community Assistance program – which continues to this day. This practical program delivers targeted and measurable results in health, housing, and infrastructure to remote communities.

In 1997 the 'Bringing Them Home' report relating to the separation of Aboriginal and Torres Strait Islander children from their families was tabled in the House of Representatives. The Howard Government again responded with practical assistance, initiating family reunion and counselling services.

In March, the $27 million 'Indigenous National Literacy and Numeracy Strategy' was launched. At the launch the prime minister declared the strategy was 'very much an exercise in practical reconciliation' – a hallmark of the Howard Government's approach. The Coalition's approach to Indigenous affairs and reconciliation at this time is best summed up by the words expressed by the prime minister when speaking to a motion on Aboriginal Reconciliation in the House of Representatives in May 1997:

> In the remarks that I made to the Reconciliation Convention yesterday, I deliberately said, and I repeat it in the House today, that we believe that the essence of reconciliation lies not in symbolic gestures – although some of them are important; this motion in a sense is a symbolic gesture. It is important on these issues that the parliament,

> as far as possible, speak with one voice – not in overblown rhetoric but in a practical determination to address the areas of disadvantage that indigenous people suffer.

Further, on 26 August 1999, after the election of Democrat Senator Aden Ridgeway (New South Wales) – the second person of Aboriginal descent to be elected to the Senate after Liberal's Neville Bonner (Queensland) – the prime minister co-sponsored with Senator Ridgeway a motion of reconciliation stating

> [d]eep and sincere regret that indigenous Australians suffered injustices under the practices of past generations, and for the hurt and trauma that many indigenous people continue to feel as a consequence of those practices.

The motion was passed without the support of the Australian Labor Party.

In 2000, Howard announced 'Reconciliation Square' would be constructed in the national capital along with the granting of $5.6 million to establish Reconciliation Australia. This not-for-profit foundation (established in January 2001) works to continue the 'people's movement' for reconciliation. My colleagues, Philip Ruddock and Amanda Vanstone worked to advance this theme of practical reconciliation.

With the abolition of ATSIC in 2005, government departments and their officials were again responsible for delivery of programs, services, and policies to the Aboriginal and Torres Strait communities throughout Australia. Accompanying these changes was the commencement of Council of Australian Governments (CoAG) trials of a whole-of-government approach. Initiatives such as 'No school, no pool' were introduced along with Shared Responsibility Agreements and Regional Partnership agreements. This period saw policies directed at freeing up land tenure possibilities on communal land, encouraging private home ownership and providing employment and training opportunities in lieu of Community Development Employment Projects along with the passage of the *Native Title Amendment Act 1997* in response to the High Court's Wik decision. Practical action being the driver of change.

It is clear from this abbreviated history of the period that while the Howard Government's priority was to achieve tangible 'practical' outcomes it had envisaged benefiting Indigenous families and communities it was not at the expense of making appropriate and measured symbolic gestures. It is also clear that many within the 'established' Aboriginal leadership and media would never be satisfied with the actions of the Howard Government in relation to reconciliation as their views and prejudice were too deep seated. Any attempt to 'win' them over would be a waste of time.

By January 2006 the situation was very different to that experienced by my predecessors: ATSIC was no more, native title was off the agenda, the government was in a very strong financial position, and I had responsibility for a department with a significant budget. Howard's instructions outlined in my charter letter (a letter provided to incoming ministers) were clear: address passive welfare in Indigenous communities, provide ongoing leadership and guidance (as Chairman of the Ministerial Taskforce on Indigenous Affairs), develop shared responsibility agreements, and promote Indigenous home ownership on communal land. These priorities, directed at regional and remote communities, were to be the sole focus of my attention and determination.

Town camps

My first trip to remote communities was to Galiwin'ku, Groote Island and Nhulunbuy, all on the west coast of the Gulf of Carpentaria. We flew into Darwin and met with Claire Martin, then Northern Territory Chief Minister. Martin had been an advocate for 99-year leases and private home ownership on communal land. Beyond introducing myself, the meeting was planned to be a discussion on progressing these initiatives on Galiwin'ku. The Chief Minister appeared shocked and denied having any prior knowledge of my intentions. She backed away with haste from any commitment to leases and countered that her number one priority was addressing social disfunction and the poor physical state of 'town camps' in Alice Springs. Sensing a shift in the sands, I immediately agreed to visit and would seek to work cooperatively with her to find practical solutions. I learnt a valuable lesson in politics that day.

The town camps are small suburbs of Alice Springs operated and managed by an Indigenous organisation, Tangentyere Council, an organisation independent of the Alice Springs local government. Tangentyere Council receives funding for a multitude of functions including youth programs, municipal services, housing and security. Like many Indigenous communities, town camps were hampered by land tenure issues. It was this very issue we sought to address and in doing so aim to lift the infrastructure to the same standards applied to the remainder of Alice Springs.

I visited the town camps by day *and* night for obvious reasons. A visit by day was standard fair whereby a Minister would be shown around a quiet clean environment by polite locals. Returning to the same place at night as part of 'Night Patrol', was another story. Alcohol, abuse, and fighting was the norm. The goal of 'Night Patrol' was to keep the peace, ferry intoxicated persons to the hospital or 'dry out' clinics, and support police. I was confident no other federal minister had ever seen this side of these communities. No child should be exposed to this environment *and* no child could be expected to flourish from this mayhem. I was determined to make a difference for these children.

I returned to the town camps on numerous occasions searching for an agreeable way forward and each time my efforts were thwarted by those who controlled Tangentyere Council. Over the next 12 months, I travelled extensively visiting remote communities from Cape York in Queensland to the Anangu Pitjantjatjara Yankunytjatjara (APY) Lands in South Australia, Kalumbura in the far north of Western Australia, and Wadeye in the Northern Territory. It is worth recounting an experience in Wadeye encompassing the disconnect between what was occurring on the ground *and* what the media thought newsworthy.

Wadeye

Wadeye is a home to a floating population of around two thousand people drawn from several language groups. The township is cut off by monsoonal rains for many months each year and only accessible by barge and plane. My visit was planned to be the typical four-to-six-hour ministerial sideshow. These are well rehearsed events that generally include visiting an arts centre, viewing a work program and chatting with leaders of the community – basically, being shown what the community leaders want you to see, not what you need to see or hear. On this occasion, local events made this impossible.

Before I arrived there had been a riot resulting in some 25 houses being destroyed, with one person receiving a spear wound to the leg. The one shop, the health clinic and local school were closed due to community safety concerns. The NT Police Force 'riot squad' was enroute from Darwin arriving the next day. There is much more to this story however the point I make is that if it were not for a journalist from the now defunct *The Bulletin* magazine covering this story, no person outside of this community or representatives of the Northern Territory Government would have known this had happened. Imagine if a similar event occurred in Melbourne. There would no doubt be wall to wall coverage, a major enquiry into how and why it happened, and remedial action put in place. Sadly, not in Wadeye.

It was also during this visit a plea from a grandmother came asking to reduce the supply of cash in the township. Her story was simple: when she was called on to take responsibility to feed and care for her grandchildren when the parents either could not or would not it would mean her needing to access cash from an automatic teller machine to withdraw cash to buy food for her grandchildren. Too often she would be forced to give that money over to older relatives for 'Gunga' (drugs). She made it clear that preventing this from happening was her biggest priority. Sadly, her story was not unique: it was typical of most townships.

On 21 June 2007, I announced the Howard Government would

> [r]educe discretionary disposable income by quarantining 50 per cent of all Australian Government income support and family assistance payments, and CDEP wages, for an initial period of twelve months, for people who have been, or become, in receipt of payment for two years or longer for residents in prescribed [Northern Territory] communities, with those outside of these communities decided on a case by case basis by Centrelink.

The introduction of the 'BasicsCard' to ensure monies were spent on the welfare of children (food, clothing and health) commenced three months later.

Misinformation

Social justice, treaties, constitutional recognition, modes of representation and land rights have dominated Indigenous affairs debates in recent times. They are all significant issues deserving of consideration. However, the issues and policies that have resulted in poor health, lower educational outcomes, high unemployment, high incarceration rates, violence, substance abuse, child abuse and neglect are largely ignored. This is perplexing. These are difficult issues, they are confronting, and they should be discussed. Indigenous children have a right to a better future. It appears that only when the focus and attention is on these issues for prolonged periods of time that governments act. This is a failure of leadership.

Housing shortages, deaths in custody and alcohol abuse are in the media spotlight from time-to-time, but not for long. Generally, the facts presented are incorrect. When misinformation seeps into the nation's conscience and accepted as fact, this creates an environment to find answers and solutions to the wrong questions. The Royal Commission into Aboriginal Deaths in Custody (reported in 1991) found '[I]ndigenous people were no more likely than non-Indigenous people to die in custody but were considerably more likely to be arrested and imprisoned'.

To many, this statement would come as a surprise given the continual media portrayal to the contrary. Not only is it true but this fact was known to the Commission within weeks of commencing. Rather than request a change of reference to embrace the universal blight of deaths in custody, as would have been appropriate, the Commission continued for years leaving most Australians under the misapprehension that Indigenous Australian's die at the hands of the police far more than the general prison population. This is important because it shapes the debate and public opinion, potentially resulting in policy responses that are inconsistent with the facts. At best this is unsatisfactory and at worst dangerous or destructive. The same can be said for the 'Aboriginal housing crises'.

Housing

A consistent theme throughout the townships is there being too few houses. This results in overcrowding leading to health and domestic violence consequences. The logical conclusion to this reporting is that insufficient housing has been provided by government and that if only more money was spent, we would prevent overcrowding and associated consequences. I am going to dig into this proposition as a way of explaining my approach to the portfolio within the framework of the government's priority: achieving practical outcomes and challenging the status quo.

The images presented on evening news bulletins when reporting overcrowding almost always show footage of remote communities. What they do not show is the hundreds of houses that have been either destroyed or abandoned. Ask yourself how many abandoned or destroyed houses are in your neighbourhood? None or very few, no doubt. Why would there be so many homes in this state where the need is the greatest? There are many causes and if we are to improve the situation we must first understand *how* and *why* this happens.

Referring to my earlier visit to Wadeye (when two dozen houses were destroyed in a day), it was told to me the houses were destroyed as part of a long running dispute between two warring tribal groups. The cause of the fighting is said to be complex, and I do not have space here to explain it, however, the outcome was clear: some one hundred people became homeless overnight. The only solution being for most people to 'bunk' with relatives some distance from their community. The social housing in this community would be considered a health hazard in any other part of the country with graffiti and rubbish scattered throughout. The living conditions would shock most people. I found the situation unacceptable.

Wudapili is a small community fifty kilometres along the Port Keats Road. Described by the NT Government as a 'Family Outstation' it has a population of 16; with 11 government-funded dwellings. When visiting one time, at least three uninhabitable houses required a complete rebuild: with the remaining houses in poor condition at best. Given the community is home to one 'mob' and there being no clan disputes, I was left asking why were these houses destroyed, as well?

Like so many other outstations or homeland communities, Wudapili is occupied only during the dry season. Access to food and services during the wet season (between November and April) is problematic. Much of the year houses remain empty with residents seeking shelter in neighbouring areas such as Darwin, Wadeye or Daly River – resulting in the conundrum of overcrowded houses in one location and empty houses in another.

One kilometre away from the main community is a single house occupied by an elderly couple, traditional owners of the land. Their house was in pristine condition with a well-kept garden and a kitchen floor so clean you could eat off. After the filth and destruction in Wudapili and Wadeye, I was pleasantly taken aback. I chatted happily with the house-proud couple and asked why they chose to live in an isolated location. Their response was enlightening. They disapproved of the behaviour by some in the communities and felt safer and more in control where they lived. The contrast could not be starker. Most Australians have the choice where to live but for this Indigenous couple their choice of survival was made possible only through government funding.

Wudupili is one of many outstations across remote Australia where housing and infrastructure have been built and yet either cannot be or are not occupied for much of the year. In some cases, communities have been abandoned all together. The question then is how we can expect better health, education, and employment outcomes if we keep supporting (and building) communities where opportunities and services simply do not exist. Perhaps one answer lies with the voice of an Aboriginal elder.

Calling on respected elder and former Australian of the Year, Galarrwuy Yunupingu AM, he invited me to sit with him on his porch. I was happy to oblige. Looking out across the water stream adjacent to his house, a fulsome conversation ensued. Having touched on the complexity of social and economic wellbeing, Yunupingu leaned in,

> You don't get it. Homelands are not traditional living places. They are where families run to get away from the grog and violence. You (the government) then build houses for them. The grog and violence catch up and they move on, and the cycle starts all over again.

He was right. Governments do not learn from their mistakes.

Recently, over two-hundred million dollars ($223 million) was allocated for remote housing in the 2022–23 Commonwealth Budget, with activists calling for a further investment of five billion dollars. These calls are ignorant as this would continue the social and cultural decay evident for all to see. Yunipingu's words remain forever etched in my memory.

Land tenure

This leads to the next restriction on the housing market, land tenure. In the Northern Territory, all community land, including towns such as Wadeye, are held in an Aboriginal land trust as inalienable freehold (meaning it cannot be sold). A decision taken in 1976 ensured no Aboriginal person could aspire to own their own home in their community placing limitations on potential housing stock. This was a policy I took on with gusto. Through establishing 99-year leases, the Commonwealth allowed the same secure tenure for people residing in the Northern Territory as provided to homeowners living in the nation's capital, Canberra.

The Tiwi Island 'Nguiu' community were the first to embrace this policy initiative. I spoke to a Tiwi community member asking how things are now. He responded:

> … I would have to say that the best project that has worked from day one and is only getting better by the year ... is your Township leasing. Tiwi's have built homes and businesses and jobs have been created.

I was delighted for him and his people.

There was, of course, resistance from Labor Party politicians and self-interest groups, but the strong leadership of the Tiwi elders prevailed. Reflecting on those heated negotiations, my friend recalled it this way: 'ahh, the memories of those early days when all the haters said we will all burn in hell, haha!'. Leadership in action.

As minister, I also had responsibility for an annual funding round for Indigenous Housing. This program funded between 500 and 1000 new or renovated dwellings each year via grants to Indigenous Community Housing Organisations (ICHO). In 2006 there were 496 'ICHO's' managing 21,758 permanent dwellings. The problems with this program are too many to cover in detail, however, it is true the model did not meet community standards for governance, fiscal management, or sustainability. The program did not deliver the best and most equitable outcome for the people it was designed to support. I had to act.

In tackling these issues inevitable pushback came from those who had benefitted from the 'flowing cash'. Investigations uncovered houses being sold to benefit individuals and local governments forced to sell homes to meet unpaid rates. To rub salt in the wound, we discovered the Commonwealth Government had no legal recourse to address this fraudulent activity. The result being money earmarked for housing was forever lost. A shameful act perpetrated by those who should have known better.

Lessons learned

There are many generic lessons that flow from my time as Minister for Indigenous Affairs. Some of them include vested interests fighting hard to retain their position of influence and power regardless of cost to community; accepting more of the same will deliver improved outcomes is folly; and leadership at both the political and community level are essential in effecting change. I undertook the challenges presented to me in this portfolio much the same way I did throughout my career in the Australian Army: get a good understanding of the facts on the ground, and charge forward with a practical plan of action. I make no apology for treading on toes or upsetting some in the Aboriginal industry. My sole focus was on improving the lives of young Indigenous children. Only time will tell if I made a difference.

Endnotes

See Mal Brough (Minister for Families, Community Services and Indigenous Affairs), National emergency response to protect Aboriginal Children in the NT, media release, 21 June 2007, http://parlinfo.aph.gov.au/parlInfo/search/display/display.w3p;query=Id%3A%22media%2Fpressrel%2F8ZFN6%22

6

Political leadership

Richard Alston

There is no shortage of books on leadership. Google says there are at least 15,000 books on the subject and thousands more articles appear every year. But most of these are about business and I would argue that political leadership is a protean art that defies simple definition. It is also an extremely difficult art to master.

Prominent economic historian, Niall Ferguson, says that every secretary of state and national security adviser must make choices between bad and worse options. The same can be said of political leaders. Ferguson also says, presciently, that anger has replaced dialogue to carry out disputes, especially in the social media age.

In my time as Liberal Party President (state and federal) and a senator from Victoria, I have had dealings with 11 prime ministers and over 40 state premiers, not to mention quite a few political leaders offshore. Hopefully I learned a few lessons along the way.

All good leaders are different, whether it be Mahatma Gandhi, Nelson Mandela (whom I met at the inauguration of his successor in Pretoria in 1999) or Martin Luther King Jr. Their achievements depended on their unique socio-cultural contexts.

A new book on leadership written by the legendary 99-year-old Henry Kissinger strongly emphasises the importance of great men and women in bringing about major changes. He sees the role of leaders as being to guide and inspire and he identifies five critical qualities: tellers of hard truths, visionary, bold, capable of spending time on their own and not fearing to be divisive. There are very few leaders, past or present, who have exhibited even most of these characteristics.

One who probably did meet all these exacting standards was one of Kissinger's six subjects, Lew Kuan Yew, first prime minister of Singapore between 1959 and 1990. He started public life as a socialist firebrand but later converted to free enterprise and turned his small island state of Singapore into a global success story. Perhaps his greatest attributes were transparent incorruptibility and a fierce determination to pursue his economic dream.

One of Kissinger's most interesting requirements is spending time reflecting on your own. In our time, Kevin Rudd (prime minister 2007-2010; 2013) and Malcolm Turnbull (prime minister 2015-2018) clearly lacked this ability, whereas John Howard (prime minister 1996-2007) and Robert Menzies (prime minister 1939-1941; 1949-1966), especially in their 'wilderness years', clearly did.

It is sometimes said that leaders are born, not made. But it is certainly not just a case of genetics, as many leaders have emerged from modest, even poverty-stricken, families. To name just two: Bill Clinton was born after his father died and his mother was an alcoholic who married three times – hardly a promising start. Abraham Lincoln was born into poverty in a log cabin. He lifted himself up by his bootstraps, educated himself and became a lawyer. The American Civil War (1861-1865) made him.

It is much more likely that leadership skills are a product of one's environment. In other words, growing up listening, learning, thinking, planning and drawing on vital lived experiences. That is why parliamentarians who were in politics a long time before becoming prime minister are usually much more successful – compare Paul Keating and John Howard with Julia Gillard (prime minister 2010-2013) and Kevin Rudd, certainly Malcolm Turnbull and perhaps even Scott Morrison (prime minister 2018-2022). Bob Hawke (prime minister 1983-1991) was a special case – he had been playing politics at high levels all his adult life.

The key to successful stewardship is understanding economics. Both Howard and Keating (prime minister 1991–1996) learnt a lot as treasurers and simply being immersed in political issues for more than two decades. In contrast, Rudd may have had some theoretical understandings, Gillard very little. Gough Whitlam (prime minister 1972-1975) and Tony Abbott (prime minister 2013-2015) both eschewed economics, and it showed.

In his latest political biography, Anthony Seldon, the doyen of British political biographers says of former United Kingdom (UK) Prime Minister Theresa May (2016-2019): 'She came to office knowing little about economics, which prevented her from understanding better the complexities involved. She understood little about government, including the powers and limitations of her office, how to make Cabinet government and the civil service work for her, and how to advocate and persuade. These skills were not optional extras for the task in hand'.[1] This is a devastating indictment of a prime minister completely out of her depth but, at least to a lesser extent, the same could be said of some other recent prime ministers in Australia.

Rudd, Turnbull, John Hewson (leader of the Liberal Party, 1990-1994) and John Gorton (prime minister 1968-1971) all prided themselves on being party outsiders, but this proved to be a weakness not a strength. Howard had been a vice president in the New South Wales Liberals and understood the critical importance of keeping the party on side and understanding its concerns – first, look after the base!

Doris Kearns Goodwin, the renowned American political historian, says the vital qualities of leadership are intelligence, energy, empathy, verbal and written gifts and skills in dealing with people. I would add a fierce ambition, which Andrew Peacock (former Leader of the Opposition (1983-1985; 1989-1990) lacked, but Howard had in spades, plus perseverance and a strong work ethic.

Howard also has a memory like an elephant, so he never needed speech notes. Perhaps some of the most powerful and enduring words ever uttered in public life were spoken by him in the heat of battle during the 2001 election campaign launch held in Sydney:

'We will decide who comes to this country and the circumstances in which they come'. I was there – you could hear a pin drop, as his words sank in.

Leadership is not just about achieving outcomes. It is taking people with you, as John Howard did, by giving everyone a 'fair go' in Cabinet, with the result being very few leaks to the media. He was constantly in touch with backbench members. While I was busy preparing for Question Time in my office eating a sandwich, he was often found in the dining room with colleagues.

Great leaders are judged by their character, and they inspire others through integrity, displayed in their actions and words. As Tony Abbott said recently of the Howard years: 'Good leadership is about character, convictions and courage'.

It is also not just about 'the vision thing', as George H. W. Bush somewhat derisively dismissed it. Visionaries do not have a great track record – no doubt Hitler regarded himself a visionary, so too, perhaps, Julius Caesar and Napoleon. It ended badly for all of them.

When John Howard was asked about his aspirations in the lead up to the 1996 Federal election, he said that he wanted Australians to be 'comfortable and relaxed'.[2] This comment evoked howls of derision as it was seen as lacking in vision. Yet it struck a chord with middle Australia, who had grown tired of being preached to and wanted simply to be understood and appreciated.

Longevity is not necessarily proof of quality leadership. Angela Merkel served as German Chancellor for 16 years and was frequently referred to as the 'de facto leader of the European Union', but I think the reality was that there was no one else – think French presidents Nicolas Sarkozy (2007-2012) and Francois Hollande (2012-2017), and prime minister of Italy, Silvio Berlusconi (1994 to 1995, 2001 to 2006 and 2008 to 2011). She was much more concerned with German pre-eminence than European success. Keeping the euro low was a real boon for German exports, but a killer for small countries such as Greece.

Good political leaders are hard to find. After all it is a very difficult job and you are under the pump every day, so temperament is critical. Howard had a certain calmness – I never heard him swear or lose his temper. His long experience had solidified into political wisdom – he had seen it all and instinctively knew the right response. He had a good sense of humour and never let his ego take over – he was always extremely patient and courteous towards others.

Howard was upfront about his intentions, not like Keating who promised not to privatise the Commonwealth Bank and Qantas and, notoriously, not to repeal 'L-A-W' tax cuts. But when he reversed his previously staunch opposition to a goods and services tax, Howard took it to an election with a major compensation package – a high-risk strategy but the ultimate in electoral transparency.

Busy prime ministers often find it convenient to delegate a range of responsibilities including attendance at various events, but this can have its downside. When he established the Prime Minister's Science Engineering and Innovation Committee (of which I was a member) Howard made a point of not only attending but chairing every meeting. He had clearly learned the lesson from reports that Keating had attended meetings of his predecessor body in desultory fashion – arrived late, left early – clearly only nominally engaged.

Howard recognised the importance of these regular meetings of the great and the good of the scientific community, from whom we all learned a great deal. His enthusiastic participation not only inspired confidence among attendees but delivered a very important political bonus.

At the start of the 2001 election year the science natives were getting restless. But when we released a comprehensive, multi-facetted, five-year $3 billion innovation action plan ('Backing Australia's Ability') they quickly realised its seminal importance and strongly supported it. There is no doubt that Howard's attendance, energy, and leadership convinced some, if not, all, involved of the government's commitment to science and innovation.

Howard strongly believed in continuous communication and was therefore effectively in constant election mode. He took every opportunity to drive home his messages by speaking directly to people, particularly via talk back radio, which went to the audience without intermediation by journalists or editors, unlike with the written media, who were always keen to put their 'spin' on issues.

Howard had impressive management skills, and did not just 'enjoy the problem', as many are wont to do. He was careful to select high quality office staff with people of the calibre of Arthur Sinodinos, a Treasury economist and Graeme Morris a highly skilled political operative. He also appointed excellent chairmen of the Cabinet Policy Unit in Michael L'Estrange (former Rhodes Scholar and executive director of the Menzies Research Centre) and Paul McClintock (acting as the prime minister's most senior personal adviser on strategic directions in policy formulation), both of whom went on to forge successful careers in the private sector.

He was also very respectful of the public service, whose capacity to leak when unhappy was a constant factor. Accordingly, when he rejected advice, he was careful to ensure he explained his reasons to those who mattered.

If there was a single key to Howard's prolonged success it was his mastery of politics. He knew that it determined electoral outcomes even more than good policies. He was acutely aware that you must compete constantly and hard in the life and death game of politics. This might seem axiomatic, but leaders and senior Cabinet ministers often persuade themselves that good policies alone will deliver good political rewards. They do not.

This was clearly not the case in the recent 2022 election, where Labor was the ultimate policy small target and spent most of its time denigrating Scott Morrison and turning him into a hate figure. Morrison was sound at economics but strangely reluctant to tackle Labor opponents such as Mike McGowan (Premier of Western Australia), Daniel Andrews (Premier of Victoria) and Anthony

Albanese (Leader of the Opposition), not to mention the Australian Broadcasting Corporation (ABC). Leaving his best policy of 'super for housing' until the last week of the campaign, when more than 40 per cent of eligible voters had cast their ballot, left many political operators and media commentators baffled.

At the end of his monumental political career Robert Menzies said that building a strong coalition with the Country Party (now the Nationals) was not only crucial but one of his proudest achievements. Howard was quick to agree. He made sure that he was in constant contact with their leaders, Tim Fischer (deputy prime minister 1996-1999), John Anderson (1999-2005) and Mark Vaile (2005-2007), all of whom were not only admirable human beings but very effective leaders.

It took me a while to work out that many of them had almost identical views to right of centre Liberals and this was often because there were no Liberal Party branches in their electorates, so they simply went with the local strength. This made our political task a lot easier, but Howard never took any chances.

Malcolm Fraser was prime minister of Australia (1975-1983) for the duration of my three-year term as Victorian Liberal state president, so I had many dealings with him. I suspect history will say that he did not take full advantage of his opportunities, particularly when he had the numbers in the Senate. Shortly after my election I crossed swords on ABC television with Sir Robert Sparks, then-powerful National Party state president in Queensland. This clearly alarmed Fraser who promptly invited me to dinner at the prime minister's official residence, 'The Lodge', but he squandered his opportunity. He lectured me endlessly about the importance of the National Party, without ever asking me what my thoughts were on the subject. As a result, Fraser missed the chance to work with me (and the Victorian Division) on the issue.

In those years I felt it was important that the Liberal Party contested every seat so that its loyal supporters could be accommodated at the ballot box. However, this ran squarely into Fraser's keen desire to protect his close friend Peter Nixon in Gippsland from competition. He won the argument, but only after some heavy browbeating. He even went so far as to suggest privately that he and Doug Anthony (then leader of the National Party) could form another party, implying that the Liberal Party was only a flag of convenience, which did not impress me very much. It was not long before I came to realise what a profoundly important figure Nixon was, and I have since admired him greatly.

Fraser was from the land and clearly regarded the powerful National party triumvirate of Anthony, Ian Sinclair and Peter Nixon as soulmates. Whereas Menzies and later Howard were able to strike the right inter-party balance, Fraser seemed almost anti-Liberal at times and could not conceal his disdain for key Liberal policies such as privatisation.

At this point it is worthwhile reflecting on several players who did not quite make it to the top. Andrew Peacock came closest, having been Leader of the Opposition on two occasions. He was not lacking in charisma but did not quite have the killer instinct needed in politics. In contrast, Howard was obsessed with politics, while Peacock merely enjoyed it, along with other extra-curricular activities.

Alexander Downer (Leader of the Opposition, 1994-1995) was capable but probably came to the job of opposition leader too early. He never really recovered from being filmed putting on fishnet stockings and several other gaffes (his 'Things that Batter' remark in 1994), ruthlessly exploited by a master politician in Paul Keating. The Labor prime minister had already seen off Downer's predecessor, John Hewson, who was regarded as a Party outsider and a political parvenue. His economic policy instincts in those days were generally sound but he was not really interested in cultivating key interest groups or tailoring his cloth to suit the political demands. Accordingly, Hewson pressed ahead with Fightback! – his economic brainchild – with little consideration for the fact that the Goods and Services Tax (GST) was a complex subject needing to be carefully and patiently explained to the masses, as Howard and Costello were later able to do successfully when arguing for taxation reform.

Peter Costello (Treasurer, 1996-2007) had a very good mind and would have achieved great success if he had stayed at the Bar. However, having shared an apartment in Canberra with him for some seven years, my impression was that he enjoyed the cut and thrust on the floor of the Parliament and getting his head around complex economic issues, but he had little interest in the art of politics which was a very different challenge. At no point did he ever raise with me his interest or willingness in challenging for the leadership of the Liberal Party.

Another outsider worth mentioning is John Elliott. In his prime, Elliott was one of Australia's leading businessmen, with a very good brain and a fierce dedication to the Liberal cause. Apart from serving as Federal President of the Liberal Party he almost singlehandedly formed the 'Victorian 500 Club' (500 members at $500 each), as a major fundraising entity. He was interested in getting into politics and, as he had stood aside for me to become Victorian State President, I was happy to help. But his business interests proved too enticing and ultimately led to his downfall.

World leaders

Since the Second World War there have been few outstanding political leaders. Certainly, none in Europe in the last 25 years. Very few in the United States of America, since Ronald Reagan (president 1981-1989) and Bill Clinton (president 1993-2001), whom I met several times, and who also addressed Federal Cabinet. I last saw him in Los Angeles a few years ago at the Eli Broad Museum opening – the old magic was still there!

When Harold Macmillan, United Kingdom prime minister (1957-1963) was asked what the greatest challenge for a statesman was, he replied: 'Events, dear boy, events' – a telling insight, as many big happenings come out of a clear blue sky – only recently, the Global Financial Crisis, Ukraine and Covid-19. Domestically, take the Port Arthur massacre, which happened barely eight weeks after John Howard became prime minister. Gun control was the ultimate political test for a Liberal leader as it potentially pitched the Liberals at odds with their Coalition colleagues, the Nationals. Yet Howard's resolute determination and cool head under pressure carried the day. He stayed the course and carried the nation.

Margaret Thatcher, prime minister for over eleven and a half years (1979-1990) was in a class of her own – thereafter only Tony Blair (prime minister 1997-2007) really stood out and then for his political skills, having brought a left leaning Labor party in from the cold, rather than any major policy achievements. The same could be said of David Cameron (prime minister 2010-2016), who followed Gordon Brown's disappointing two years in office.

I met Margaret Thatcher several times, but she was then rather in her dotage. She was of course a policy wonk, backed by steadfast beliefs in the righteousness of the cause. She loved to project strength – 'TINA' (There is no Alternative), and 'The Lady is not for turning' said it all. She forever revelled in the glory of being nicknamed 'the iron lady' – intended to be a putdown but to her it was the supreme compliment. It must be said that the times suited her. England was in the middle of the winter of discontent and was being constantly derided as 'the sick man of Europe'. Unlike Rudd, who was obsessed with capturing the four-hour news cycle, Howard focused on making the big things count. He may have learned this from Margaret Thatcher.

Historians will recall with admiration how she took on the coal miners in the North and the print unions in London, both major contributors to the UK's declining economic performance. Together with the deregulation of the UK financial markets she greatly reduced the power of the trade unions to hold governments to ransom and made Britain competitive once again.

I remember a select lunch in London in 2005 with John Howard where he said he was a social conservative. She reacted strongly: 'I'm not, I'm a real conservative!'. She clearly thought that he was describing himself as a party animal! She remained a conviction driven politician to the end.

Perhaps the supreme compliment to her success in getting the country back on track was that both Blair and Brown sought to co-opt her legacy – even inviting her back to Downing Street! They dared not overturn any of her policy reforms. I recently watched a two-part documentary on Reagan and Thatcher – there is no doubt who was the dominant partner.

Boris Johnson likes playing the buffoon and his unruly mop top is clearly cultivated. He is highly intelligent, but with a light touch. He is also quite disorganised and easily distracted with few fixed political beliefs. He is certainly not alone. Of the 13 Conservative prime ministers in the 20th century (and the three to date in the 21st) only Thatcher could be regarded as right wing.

Cameron, Blair and Brown I came across with some frequency. Blair had star power – he was almost always upbeat with a light touch and could ad lib spectacularly well. Cameron had great political skills – I saw him win the leadership contest with David Davis by speaking for an hour without notes and he was always on top of his brief in the House of Commons, but I doubt that history will rate him highly. Gordon Brown was the epitome of dour – very awkward to talk to and always looking at his watch or over his shoulder. During his ten years as Chancellor of the Exchequer his main preoccupation seemed to be to blast Tony Blair out of office. But he was a weak prime minister, always playing political games.

The 2007 Australian Federal Election coincided with a Commonwealth Heads of Government Meeting (CHOGM) in Kampala, Uganda so John Howard, fighting for his life, or at least his seat, could not attend. I had the honour of leading the Australian delegation.

It was my great good fortune to spend the evening with Stephen

Harper, who was clearly one of the outstanding leaders of the 20th century, serving as Canadian prime minister for nearly ten years. Down to earth and easy to talk to, he had a great understanding of practical politics.

During the CHOGM debates Gordon Brown kept pestering me about the Australian election result and I worked out that he thought that as soon as Rudd had been declared the winner, I would have to change my line on climate change, which of course I did not. I was in good company with Helen Clark, prime minister of New Zealand (1999–2008), as we both argued that our countries should follow international norms in our climate objectives and not virtue signal by getting too far ahead of the pack.

Helen Clark was a very warm, friendly and capable leader and a good friend of Australia. In the lead up to her first election she was seen as very left wing with an approval rating of about four per cent, but quickly learned to govern as a centrist and, accordingly, stayed in power for some 10 years.

There is a lesson here, particularly for Labor leaders, as Anthony Albanese – and perhaps Bill Shorten – seem to have lately discovered. The key to success is to govern from the centre-right, catering principally for middle Australia, as Anthony Albanese looks like he is trying to do.

Leadership succession

This is a topic which is frequently discussed in corporate literature but is completely different from political succession strategies. The average business chief executive has a life span of approximately five years – rarely planning their own succession. Senior executives emerge over time as potential candidates, but ultimately chair and chief executive officer promotion, ejection and retirement are matters for the board. Lobbying in the media and canvassing internal support are often counterproductive. David Morgan, for example, killed his chances of becoming Chairman at BHP by letting it be known in the media that he was readily available.

In politics, succession is handled very differently. Very few prime ministers contemplate succession, and none plan for it, except perhaps Robert Menzies, who finally gave the game away in his seventies, leaving Harold Holt, his long serving and loyal treasurer, as his obvious replacement. Menzies remains today the only prime minister to have voluntarily stepped aside at a time of his choosing.

In politics there is no board of governors, such as the Federal Executive of the Liberal Party, to oversee the issue. In fact, it was very reluctant to ever canvass the leadership matters, let alone publicly contemplate regime change, which would have been regarded as political treason. I can speak from personal experience in saying that the Federal President of the Party does not have a role to play. Malcolm Turnbull would have been very unwise to seek my advice.

Succession is entirely the responsibility of the Parliamentary party, and they are not keen on gratuitous outside advice, let alone anointments and coronations. Extra-curricular machinations obviously need to occur as leadership contenders must count numbers to decide whether to stand for, and particularly succeed in achieving, the highest office.

Political regime change can be a very messy business. It is well documented how Malcolm Turnbull spent much of his time before becoming leader on two occasions (2008 and 2015) in publicly and privately undermining the incumbents by a non-stop media campaign which, because of his perceived left-wing leanings, was sympathetically received by many journalists, who were more than happy to assist in dethroning hate figures such as Tony Abbott.

However, Turnbull's constant guerrilla warfare campaigns against colleagues proved fatal. As Aaron Patrick says in his new book, *Ego*: 'Ultimately Turnbull lacked the most important quality needed for leadership: the ability to win his colleagues' trust'.[3] He also adds that 'Turnbull seemed to lack the emotional strength to effectively lead his party when he felt he had lost control of events'.[4] Being a good front runner is never enough.

A much quieter and more successful transition occurred when the Labor Party finally realised, on the cusp of the 1983 election, that it was headed for defeat under Bill Hayden. Privately, senior colleagues persuaded Hayden to stand aside in favour of former union leader and shadow minister, Bob Hawke. A similar situation occurred in 1995 when Alexander Downer deferred to John Howard. Coincidentally, both manque leaders went on to serve under their replacements as foreign ministers (with Hayden also later serving as a governor-general).

This would never happen in the private sector – a deposed chief executive would never become a board member. Sometimes the obvious replacement becomes impatient and seeks to force the issue by resigning from Cabinet, as both Paul Keating and Andrew Peacock did. As we all now appreciate, Keating was entitled to feel aggrieved, given that Hawke had welshed on his solemn promise before witnesses to resign.

The succession issue for the Federal Liberal Party arose quite acutely in the dying days of the Howard Government. There was some expectation that John Howard might have been persuaded to stand aside in favour of Peter Costello. I was out of the country during this time, but I did maintain contact with some of my former senior colleagues and my impressions are that:

1. John Howard, like some other political leaders, probably had some reservations about the political skills of his prospective successor – perhaps like Churchill, then in his eighties, who thought that Anthony Eden 'wasn't quite ready'.
2. Several members of the Cabinet felt that Costello was not likely to be successful in the game of politics, as he never seemed interested in political strategy discussions.
3. There was a considerable legacy of loyalty and respect towards John Howard, somewhat similar to those who supported Hawke to the very end in his doomed efforts to rebuff Paul Keating in December 1991.

Costello had a very good brain and was a tower of strength on the floor of the parliament and in arguing his case in the media. However, in Cabinet I found Peter Reith to be much more interested in the politics and substance of issues than Costello, who preferred to simply deal with Treasury matters. He was certainly available for the top job if drafted but not inclined to make much of an effort to assist his own cause. His decision to not contest the leadership and subsequently resign from politics strongly suggests he did not enjoy the politics of politics.

John Howard, in marked contrast, enjoyed every minute of politics – always keen to circulate at functions and shake every hand. I used to say that he would have done the job for nothing. He was always ready to acknowledge that he only got where he did through the Liberal Party. He had his finger on the pulse of every political manoeuvre. It was a pleasure to seek his guidance on the issue of the day. He was very quick on the uptake – he understood every aspect of my portfolio, but after attending to core business he was always happy to have a wide-ranging political chat.

There is a lot of luck in politics and my great good fortune was to have been there during the Howard ascendancy – no one else could have done it better.

Endnotes

1. Anthony Seldon, *May at 10: The Verdict*, Biteback Publishing: Great Britain, 2020.
2. See ABC Television, *Four Corners* interview with John Howard, then Leader of the Opposition, in 1996: https://www.abc.net.au/4corners/an-average-australian-bloke-1996/2841808
3. Aaron Patrick, *Ego: Malcolm Turnbull and the Liberal Party's Civil War*, HarperCollins, 2022, p. 4.
4. Ibid., p. 81.

7

Banking crisis: an issue in the making?

Stephen Martin

Introduction

The Australian financial system is interictally tied to the fortunes and misfortunes of the global economy, as well as being a player in and helping shape the domestic economy. In many respects crises that impact the Australian banking system might emerge from international circumstances that some argue are perhaps beyond the control of the government of the day.

That said, while Australia is very much at the mercy of world economic forces, decisions made by the Howard Government between 1996 and 2006 dealt with several significant underlying issues that led to emerging crises with banking implications. In the light of subsequent events these contributed to governments inheriting significant problems. Banking behaviour identified over the past three years or so clearly indicate that the seeds of a banking crisis are always present in an economy such as Australia.

There is no better vision than 20–20 hindsight. It is therefore appropriate that in examining the Howard years to working backwards from the damning revelations of the Hayne Royal Commission.[1] Current issues confronting Australian banks bring to light failures of government policy in the financial sector while on Howard's watch. Did these lead to or contribute to the negative consequences for Australia of the Global Financial Crisis (GFC) and did the wholehearted embrace of deregulation explicitly result in the raft and breadth of misconduct of Australia's financial sector exposed by Hayne?

In my view a strong economy, deregulatory zeal, a whatever it takes attitude of the banks, L-plate supervision and a government that was happy to let it rip laid the foundation for future crises in the Australian banking sector.

The Australian economy and banking

The 1990s were marked by serious financial dislocation and substantial banking sector losses at the start of the decade, from which a gradual recovery occurred throughout the decade. In contrast, the 2000s were relatively tranquil until the severe dislocation of the Global Financial Crisis (GFC), although the start of the 2000s was marked by two disruptive events- the global 'tech stock' boom and bust which had limited implications for Australia and the collapse of the major insurance company HIH in 2001.[2]

However, that period sowed the seeds of excessive lending, leverage, under-pricing of risk, and inadequate governance and regulation. Monetary and other regulatory authorities exercised a degree of restraint. Excessive profitability and remuneration issues emerged which were not seriously tackled until the Hayne Royal Commission.

An important influence on financial sector evolution was the pattern of net lending and borrowing by the various sectors in the economy. This was reflected in the shift of the household sector from net borrowers to net lenders and the increase in borrowing by the corporate sector. Compulsory superannuation and tax incentives for voluntary contributions to superannuation were also a major influence.

Despite the deregulatory zeal from government banking in Australia was and is still dominated by four major banks. Smaller banks and other financial institutions provide limited banking-type services. Many large foreign banks have a presence, but few offer retail banking although they provided a spur to competition.[3] The 1990's witnessed the beginning of increasing privatisation in

Australia, a trend that was accelerated in to 2000's. Commencing with the Commonwealth Bank the trend included many State Banks.[4]

But with deregulation came a new spirit of entrepreneurship that saw many of Australia's banks adopt a whatever it takes business approach. The consequences of this arguably unfettered and ravenous behaviour saw regulators eventually refine corporate governance standards in an effort to rein in the cowboys. To quote Gordon Gekko in the movie *Wall Street*, 'Greed, for lack of a better word, is good'.

This raises the obvious question, should the Howard Government have seen this coming with its negative consequences for Australian consumers and done more? Should the regulators certainly have been more vigorous in their pursuit of obvious bad behaviour?

In response to the internationalisation of the Australian economy, deregulation, the changing nature of banking and the need to ensure a strong and competitive financial system, governments pursued various strategies underpinned by detailed and extensive public inquiries.[5]

The Campbell Committee Report's conclusions were largely validated by the Vic Martin Review Report of 1983 following the election of the Hawke Labor Government. The new treasurer, Paul Keating, had requested the review to freshen up Campbell. It provided the impetus for the government to embrace deregulation with gusto. Floating the dollar, allowing the entry of more foreign banks and privatising the Commonwealth Bank were some of the more significant achievements.[6]

Financial deregulation, and its impact on banking, was reviewed by the House of Representatives Standing Committee on Finance and Public Administration (the Stephen Martin Committee) in 1991. Its report concluded that Australian banks were highly profitable by international standards. Deregulation had led to narrower interest margins overall but it appeared business was gaining more benefit than were consumers. Cross-subsidies were being unwound as 'user pays' became more prevalent.

The Committee concluded concerning the impact of deregulation on competition that:

> … the four major banks have retained their market share and, accordingly, their dominant position in the industry; at the regional level, vigorous competition for market share is provided by locally based State banks, regionally operating banks and non-bank financial intermediaries; and foreign banks have had limited impact …

While the Committee was broadly supportive of the impetus to competition from deregulation, it acknowledged that banks had made some mistakes in handling the transition to a deregulated market. Access to the payments system was identified as a remaining barrier to competition. The long-standing reputations and extensive branch networks of the four major banks were seen as a barrier to entry for potential competitors in the retail banking market.

These inquiries and government responses have also sought to avert any possible crises or negative consequences for the Australian economy. A fundamental question is, did it work?

Following the Howard Government's election in 1996, the Wallis Inquiry[7] sought further regulatory reform. Wallis proposed a new prudential regulator-Australian Prudential Regulation Authority (APRA) and a new market-conduct and consumer-protection regulator for financial services-Australian Securities and Investment Commission (ASIC). RBA was left responsible for monetary policy and the payments system. A Council of Financial Regulators was proposed to act as a co–ordinating forum, to discuss developments in the financial system and to co–ordinate responses to any areas of concern.[8]

Wallis was embraced by Howard, and the regulators were created as independent statutory authorities without direct oversight by a government department. Yet all was not what it seemed.

Hayne Royal Commission

Fast forward to The Royal Commission into Misconduct in the Banking, Superannuation and Financial Services Industry (Hayne Royal Commission). Established on 14 December 2017 it followed revelations of a culture of greed within several Australian financial institutions and the lack of regulatory intervention by the relevant government authorities.

Financial planning scandals, interest rate rigging and failure of financial institutions to properly develop accountability, trust, responsibility and culture were exposed. People – even dead people – were found to have been charged for services they did not receive, signatures forged, banks finding many ways to put their profits ahead of the fair treatment of their customers.[9] Later revelations indicated that financial institutions were involved in money laundering for drug syndicates, turned a blind eye to terrorism financing, and ignored statutory reporting responsibilities and impropriety in foreign exchange trading.

The final report in 2019 concluded that greed and a focus on sales and profit led to the bad behaviour, and non-compliance with the law, but that the implications for banks, regulators and the Australian economy ran deep.

In responding to the issue of 'why', the Commissioner determined that:

> … the answer seem(ed) to be greed – the pursuit of short term profit at the expense of basic standards of honesty … From the executive suite to the front line, staff were measured and rewarded by reference to profit and sales … When misconduct was revealed, it either went unpunished or the consequences did not meet the seriousness of what had been done. The conduct regulator, ASIC, rarely went to court to seek public denunciation of and punishment for misconduct. The prudential regulator, APRA, never went to court. Much more often

> than not, when misconduct was revealed, little happened beyond apology from the entity, a drawn-out remediation program and protracted negotiation with ASIC of a media release, an infringement notice, or an enforceable undertaking that acknowledged no more than that ASIC had reasonable 'concerns' about the entity's conduct. Infringement notices imposed penalties that were immaterial for the large banks. Enforceable undertakings might require a 'community benefit payment', but the amount was far less than the penalty that ASIC could properly have asked a court to impose.

Hayne stated that there could be no doubt that the primary responsibility lay with the entities concerned and those who managed and controlled those entities: their boards and senior management.[10] The Commissioner made it clear the failings extended to organisational culture, governance and remuneration. The final report also emphasised many of the key principles of good governance, particularly the importance of board challenge of management and having the right flow of information to the board for directors to discharge their duties. The regulators were especially negligent in fulfilling their mandate.

Crises?

So were there 'crises' in banking during the Howard Government that lead to such damning revelations by Hayne? Three specific areas where the seeds of potential and subsequent real crises were sown can be identified during the Howard years.

Structural issues

In 1990, the Hawke Government adopted a 'four pillars policy' in relation to banking in Australia and announced that it would reject any mergers between the big four banks as a positive way to ensure four major financial institutions could provide the necessary level of competition and services to Australia.

The policy was strengthened in that the Commonwealth Bank was fully privatised between 1991 and 1996.[11] Wallis recommended that the model be dismantled but this was rejected by the Howard Government reflecting the broad political unpopularity of further bank mergers.

Has the public interest really been served by the four pillars policy that has seen four majors thrive, developing a profit at all costs culture and often been accused of collusion on things like interest rates? Findings from the Hayne Royal Commission would suggest not. For example, the Commonwealth Bank admitted that it had charged dead people for financial advice services, engaged in 'unconscionable conduct' and manipulated the bank bill swap rate five times between February and June 2012. In 2018 it settled an interest rate rigging case brought by ASIC for $25 million.[12]

The issue of Reserve Bank of Australia independence was a significant factor during the Howard years. Howard specifically recognised the independence of the Bank by statute in August 1996. The Bank's focus was to be on price stability while taking account of economic activity and endorsed the 2–3 per cent target range for inflation. To promote transparency and accountability, the Bank would release six-monthly statements and the Governor would report to parliament once a year.[13]

The Bank's decisions on monetary policy were directly responsible for the post-1991 growth cycle that benefited the Keating and Howard Governments.[14]

The Howard years also saw the 1997 Asian Financial crisis and 2001 US tech recession play out, with implications for economic policy and corporate governance. While Howard argued both had virtually no impact on Australia, a deeper review suggests otherwise.

The 'Asian financial crisis' started in currency markets in South-East Asia but spread to other markets undermining confidence in continued high growth in the region - the so-called East Asian Miracle.

The ensuing economic downturn raised questions about the foundations of that growth, the soundness of the region's financial sectors, and the role of government in directing investment and lending. Several inter-related challenges subsequently emerged- implementing the financial sector reforms needed to attract foreign capital back into the region; establishing governance practices which will improve transparency and accountability; and developing growth strategies which are both sustainable and inclusive.[15]

At its heart, the Asian crisis was a banking crisis brought on by banks and their customers taking on too much foreign currency risk. No doubt macroeconomic policies were not always perfect, but the real problems were in the financial structure more than the macroeconomic settings. Other problems were the capacity of financial institutions and corporations to manage risk, and of the supervisors to enforce better management. The markets required to manage such risks were small or non-existent. More generally, capital markets were underdeveloped, especially local-currency denominated ones. Hence, not only were the risks concentrated in the banking system, but when the banks could no longer extend credit there was no other channel to make up the difference.[16]

It was a crisis of Asian governance- the region's financial, economic, legal and political systems were too weak to manage the demands of globalisation.[17] The crisis arrived in Howard's re-election year and was the major single influence on the formulation of Australian macroeconomic policy in 1997/98. The ensuing declines in Asian exchange rates, domestic demand and imports were relatively quickly transmitted to the Australian economy- financial markets, particularly the foreign exchange and equities markets, falling exports, a widening current account deficit and a slowing in domestic demand.[18]

The Reserve Bank of Australia however played a critical role in terms of monetary policy and had an influence in monitoring and forecasting economic developments. With central issues in the

Asian crisis being the volatility of international capital flows, the fragility of financial sectors and the role of exchange rates, this meant that much of the discussion concerned core central banking issues.[19] Howard ensured that the RBA knew the government's preferred position to not increase interest rates.[20] Was Bank independence, championed by Howard, compromised? It could be argued that it was.

A somewhat mild economic downturn occurred in 2001, particularly in the USA, but its effect on Australia was limited. Its cause can be traced to the collapse of the dotcom bubble, the 9/11 attacks, and a series of accounting scandals at major US corporations.

In the second half of 2001, the Reserve Bank of Australia continued to move monetary policy to a more expansionary stance to support growth in domestic demand, as the international economic environment weakened. The RBA lowered official interest rates on three occasions in the second half of 2001, by a total of 75 basis points, to 4.25 per cent. Two of these moves came after the events of September 11 as central banks world-wide lowered rates aggressively in the face of financial market instability and risks to the economic outlook.

In the first half of 2002, the RBA removed the additional stimulus as global economic recovery appeared to take hold and with the Australian economy continuing to make solid gains. The cash rate was 4.75 per cent in June 2002. Interestingly, a major contributor to economic growth was the rebound in dwelling investment. In 2001–02, the housing sector contributed 0.9 percentage points to GDP growth of 3.8 per cent.[21] A portent of future problems in the sector that the Howard should have responded to?

The 2001 collapse of HIH Insurance and community concern regarding growing bank profits pointed to a trend in corporate Australia that the government and its regulators should have seen coming. There were clearly implications for the wider financial services sector.[22]

Although a Royal Commission[23] found that APRA did not cause or contribute to the collapse of HIH, several shortcomings in its supervisory practices were identified. It noted that APRA eschewed 'light touch' supervision in the wake of the collapse and recommended that APRA develop 'a more sceptical, questioning and, where necessary, aggressive approach to its prudential supervision of general insurers'. While it has been argued this led to a more assertive supervisory culture in APRA, subsequent criticisms particularly during the Hayne Royal Commission show this to be a fallacy.

A serious political problem that arose for the Howard Government concerned the closure of bank branches, justified by competition and technology changes for those Australians who lived in rural, regional and remote parts of the country. These were significant constituencies for the Liberal and National Parties- an electoral crisis in the making.

In response, a parliamentary inquiry was established in 2002, reporting in January 2004 on these matters.[24] The banks responded initially by placing a moratorium on further bank closures, but this only forestalled the inevitable. Clearly the banks saw technology solving many of the problems identified as they sought to improve their bottom lines. The government meanwhile sat back, wedded to their version of deregulation, competition and getting out of the way of business. It could be argued the closure of bank branches led to many communities virtually ceasing to exist.

Interest rates and housing affordability

At the commencement of the tenure of the Howard Government, banks provided something like 78 per cent of mortgage loans, had substantial branch networks and saw the enhancement of technological change for the Australian financial sector.[25] This raised the issue of access to home ownership, particularly for first homeowners.

With ubiquitous prosperity, cheap money, and tax breaks for homeowners and investors, discussion turned to the likely emergence of a housing bubble. Australian home prices had risen about 250 per cent from 1989 to the early 2000s. All capital cities saw strong increases in property prices since 1998. These increases coincided with record low wage growth, low interest rates and record household debt equal to 130 per cent of GDP.

The influence of interest rates and banking policy on property prices should not be understated. Financial deregulation led to greater availability of credit and a variety of financial products and options. RBA maintained a low cash interest rate policy which reduced the cost of financing property purchase. In addition, the easy availability of interest-only loans made possible for property investors to borrow to purchase a property and compounding the benefits of negative gearing.[26]

While APRA tightened regulations around mortgage loans that initially led to a drop in new home loans the Howard Government should have seen this was only a temporary reprieve. The political argument that maintaining low interest rates equated to who was the better economic manager contributed to the crisis in home ownership and rising prices. However, a number of other factors that were directly controlled by the government contributed to this.

The strength of the economy between 1998 and 2008 saw real net national disposable incomes increase by 2.8 per cent a year on average from about $32,000 to about $42,000. This was accompanied by a consequent rise in the number of two-income households, relaxation of lending standards, active promotion of real estate as an investment, population growth creating demand that was not matched by supply, planning and land release issues and a tax system that was skewed in favour of property investors.

Additionally, in 1999, property sale proceeds were subject to a reduction in Capital Gains Tax from 100 to 50 per cent and in July 2000 the government introduced the First Home-Owners Grant of $7,000 for established homes, and $14,000 for newly built homes.

In response to concerns about housing affordability, Howard initiated a Productivity Commission inquiry into home ownership in Australia.[27] Its 2004 final report observed that general taxation arrangements (capital gains tax, negative gearing, capital works deductions and depreciation provisions), lending regulations, lower interest rates and planning issues lent impetus to the surge in investment in rental housing and consequent house price increases.

In what must rank as one of the most incredible responses to a major report, the government concluded that there was no conclusive evidence that the tax system has had a significant impact on house prices.

This issue remains just as alive today as it has through the past two decades. Should the government have done more? If so the current housing crisis – high prices, affordability – might have been curtailed. As noted by Hayne, banks' avarice for profits, the ready-made market for a mix of housing products and their sales incentives for staff saw little change from the mid-2000s to today. Government policy failure has exacerbated the crisis in housing affordability.

Corporate governance and crisis preparedness

One major issue identified by Hayne was already perceptible in the financial services sector in the Howard years was a portent of what else was to follow- the failure of banks to develop and impose appropriate corporate governance policies and practices, and to put people before profits. The failure of the regulators in this respect is also worth a strong mention

Consider as one example the National Australia Bank (NAB) foreign currency scandal in 2004 which had significant ramifications for the bank, customers and Australia's financial regulator.[28] It could also be argued that it had significant implications for the Howard Government. If deregulation, championed by the prime minister for years was supposed to lead Australians to the promised land of financial security, how did it go so wrong now. And did it have wider implications that potentially increased the risk of a major financial sector crisis?

In January 2004, APRA was informed of irregular activity on NAB's currency options desk. NAB immediately hired PWC to undertake an investigation that showed amongst other things final loss from the foreign exchange (FX) options unauthorised trading was $360 million; the losses significantly increased between September 2003 and January 2004; the four traders involved exploited loopholes and weaknesses in systems and processes to hide trading losses and protect bonuses; and the trading losses had been reported to management by several junior employees.[29]

The immediate effect of the trading scandal triggered several changes at NAB including the departures of Chief Executive Frank Cicutto on 2 February and then chairman Charles Allen on 16 February.[30]

APRA also launched an inquiry and released its report on 24 March 2004.[31] Essentially it concluded:

- Line Management turned a blind eye to known risk management concerns because 'Profit is king'. As long as the business unit turned a profit, other shortcomings could be overlooked.
- Operations verification procedures contained significant gaps, raising questions about the adequacy of its resourcing and skills, and whether its mandate had been weakened by pressure to reduce costs and its growing subservience to the front office.
- Market Risk failed to engage the trading desk effectively to resolve them and failed to attract the attention of higher management or otherwise escalate its concerns.
- Executive Risk Committees were particularly ineffective, missing or dismissing risk information pertinent to the problems that emerged and failing to escalate warnings.
- The Board was not sufficiently proactive on risk issues, despite often asserting that risk needed the Board's attention. Until the establishment of a separate risk committee, it ap-

peared content to leave the elevation of risk issues to its Audit Committee.

APRA concluded that cultural issues were at the heart of these failings. There was a conscious effort to embed a more commercial culture in risk management areas within NAB. Terms such as 'business partnership' and 'embedded risk management' were used frequently.

Remedial actions fell into two specific areas- fixing cultural, governance and risk management issues and fixing risk management and operational controls for traded markets area across NAB. These affected both staff and most importantly the Board. The Board was required to develop policies that promoted and supported 'whistleblowing' and to review incentive arrangements to ensure that these promoted behaviours that had appropriate regard to risk.

With respect to governance the Board, its Committees and Executive Risk Committees were required to clarify the appropriate escalation channels available to enable the Board and its committees to deliberate on serious risk issues. The Board must establish more transparent risk reporting systems and place greater reliance on independent checks and balances on executive management to enable it to discharge its duties appropriately. It was required to review, and formally approve, all market risk limits in Global Markets, set risk escalation policies, streamlining reporting lines, improve data integrity and improve accountancy reconciliation processes.

Given my previous comments on the creation of APRA and its vital importance as Australia's financial regulator it is surprising that scandals such as this occurred. In fact, there was some criticism levelled at John Laker, APRA Chair, at the time. Laker told a parliamentary committee that APRA had raised concerns with NAB regarding its risk management in early 2003 and told them to fix them. In August 2003 APRA directly raised these concerns with senior management. Why was no action apparently taken? And even more importantly, who was watching the watcher?

For the Howard Government, if deregulation, championed by the prime minister for years was supposed to lead Australians to the promised land of financial security, how did it go so wrong now. And did it have wider implications that potentially increased the risk of a major financial sector crisis?

The question must therefore be asked how much information was conveyed to the government and did they foresee a potential larger crisis emerging? Or was the protective sunscreen that is 'independent of government' used to ensure any blame was truly apportioned to the bank?

APRA has continued its (belated) pursuit of banking supervision, particularly in ensuring Australia's financial system is prepared for any potential crisis or emergency. APRA recently described how it balances the need for appropriate risk-taking by financial institutions while minimising the potential for disorderly failures that might harm bank depositors.[32] Several important pointers are given:

- Australia needs a financial system that harnesses the creative power of risk-taking, and the innovation and efficiencies derived from risk taking. On the other hand, it cannot have a system that is brittle and overly prone to failure – particularly catastrophic failure. Failure always involves pain and cost, but that cost must be acceptable.
- APRA seeks to ensure that any failures that do occur will be orderly failures. An orderly failure is one where a regulated entity hasn't reached its intended destination, but where the entitlements of protected beneficiaries and the stability of the financial system remain intact.
- Leaders need to have thought seriously about financial stress scenarios, come up with a credible plan, and then tested their institution's ability to execute this plan. If you are going to step up to the controls of one of our institutions, it is your responsibility to assure yourself that you can land it safely in the unlikely event of an emergency.

- The essence of financial contingency planning is our expectation that institutions must be ready to manage their own destiny in all reasonable circumstances. Boards of APRA-regulated institutions must be aware that it simply isn't acceptable to rely on ordinary insolvency or APRA stepping in to solve the problem.

Conclusion

While Australia might have been spared the worst in terms of international financial crises during the Howard years there is little doubt that the Australian banking sector was allowed to develop practices and procedures that were not in the spirit of deregulation and certainly not in the best interests of consumers. It can be demonstrated that significant genuine crises that emerged in banking had their genesis in policies pursued by the Howard Government.

Failure by Howard in terms of housing policy and corporate governance regulation and the wholesale embrace of free-market business philosophy coupled with significant inaction by regulators were to blame. Deregulation yes, but total hands-off no. Hayne was right – culture was and should be at the centre of banking practices. And government and its regulators have critical roles to play.

Interestingly, more recent events with both NAB and the Commonwealth Bank in foreign currency dealing and other issues would indicate that the lessons of the past have not been learned. Boards still have a lot to answer for. But APRA's renewed emphasis on culture, risk and good governance following their public humiliation by Hayne is keeping all authorised deposit-taking institutions (ADI) on their toes.

APRA has continued its (belated) pursuit of banking supervision, particularly in ensuring Australia's financial system is prepared for any potential crisis or emergency. APRA recently described how it balances the need for appropriate risk-taking by financial institutions while minimising the potential for disorderly failures that might harm bank depositors.

Endnotes

1. Kenneth Hayne, *Royal Commission into Misconduct in the Banking, Superannuation and Financial Services Industry*, Canberra, 2019.
2. Kevin Davis, *The Australian Financial System in the 2000s: Dodging the Bullet*, Reserve Bank of Australia Conference, 2011; Reserve Bank of Australia, The Australian Economy in the 2000, Proceedings of a Conference, Sydney, 15-16 August 2011; Australian Treasury, *2001-02 in review: strong growth in the midst of an international slowdown*, Economic Roundup, 11 October 2002.
3. Adam Boyton, *Liberalisation of Foreign Investment in the Australian Financial Sector*, 26th Conference of Economists, Australian Treasury, Canberra, 2009; Parliament of Australia, Department of the Parliamentary Research Service, *Foreign Bank Policy in Australia*, Current Issues Brief No. 8, 1995-6.
4. Graeme Hand, *Naked Among Cannibals: What really happens inside Australian banks*, Allen and Unwin, Sydney, 2000; Stephen Martin, *Labor and Financial Deregulation – The Hawke/Keating Governments, Banking and New Labor*, PhD Thesis, University of Wollongong, Wollongong, 1999.
5. Keith Campbell (Chairman), Committee of Inquiry into the Australian Financial System, *Australian Financial System: Final Report*, Australian Government Publishing Service, Canberra,1981; Vic Martin, *Australian Financial System*, Review Group on the Australian Financial System, AGPS, Canberra, 1984; Stephen Martin MP (Chairman), House of Representatives Standing Committee on Finance and Public Administration, *A Pocket Full of Change: Banking and Deregulation*, Australian Government Publishing Service, Canberra, 1991.
6. Stephen Martin, 1999; Paul Kelly, *The End of Certainty*, Allen and Unwin, Sydney, 1992.
7. Stan Wallis (Chairman), *Financial System Inquiry Final Report*, AGPS, Canberra, 1997. Available at https://treasury.gov.au/publication/p1996-fsi-dp

8. Parliament of Australia, Department of Parliamentary Services, Parliamentary Library Research Brief No.16, *Australia's Corporate Regulators- the ACCC, ASIC and APRA*, Canberra, 2005.

9. Ross Gittens, '*How the Morrison Government lost interest in banking reform*', *The Age*, 27 April 2022.

10. Australian Institute of Company Directors, '*After Hayne*', Company Director, March 2019.

11. Martin, 1999.

12. Hayne, 2019.

13. Glenn Stevens, *Aspects of Australian Economic Performance in 2000*, Address to the Australian Industry Group, Sydney, 22 February 2000.

14. Paul Kelly, *The March of Patriots- the Struggle for Modern Australia,* Melbourne University Press, Melbourne 2009.

15. Reserve Bank of Australia, *The Asian Crisis and the Reserve Bank*, Annual Report, Canberra, 1998.

16. Glenn Stevens, *The Asian Crisis: A retrospective*, Address to The Anika Foundation Luncheon Supported by Australian Business Economists and Macquarie Bank, Sydney – 18 July 2007; Parliament of Australia, Joint Standing Committee on Foreign Affairs, Defence and Trade, *Asian Currency Crisis and its Effect on Australia,* Canberra, 19 March 1998.

17. Kelly, 2009.

18. Ian Macfarlane, *Some Thoughts on Australia's Position in Light of Recent Events in Asia,* Talk to the Australian Stock Exchange, Australian Institute of Company Directors and The Securities Institute of Australia, Bull and Bear Luncheon, Brisbane, 26 March 1998; David Richardson, *Asian Financial Crisis*, Parliamentary Library Current Issues Brief 23, 29 June 1998; Barry Sterland, 'The Asian Financial Crisis 20 years on: Lessons learned and remaining challenges', *Australian Financial Review*, 2 July 2017; Ron Duncan and Yongzheng Yang (2000) *The Impact of the Asian Crisis on Australia's primary Exports: why it has not been so bad*, Asia Pacific School of Economics and Management, Australian National University Working Paper 2000-1, Canberra.

19. Reserve Bank of Australia, *ibid*, 1998.

20. Kelly, 2009.

21. Australian Treasury, 2002.

22. Parliament of Australia, Parliamentary Library E-Brief, *HIH Insurance Group Collapse*, Canberra 29 November 2001; Australian Treasury, *The HIH Claims Support Scheme*, Economic Roundup Issue 1, 2005.

23. Neville Owen, Report on the Royal Commission into HIH Insurance, AGPS, Canberra, 16 April 2003.

24. Parliament of Australia, Joint Committee on Corporations and Financial Services Report, *Money Matters in the Bush: Inquiry into the Level of Banking and Financial Services in Rural, Regional and Remote Areas of Australia*, Canberra, January 2004.

25. Saul Eslake, *An introduction to the Australian Economy*, Chief Economist, ANZ, 4th Edition January 2007.

26. Reserve Bank of Australia, *Productivity Commission Inquiry into First Home Ownership*, Canberra, 2007.

27. Productivity Commission, *Inquiry Report into First Home Ownership*, AGPS, Canberra, 2004.

28. Australian and New Zealand School of Government (2004) *The Australian Prudential Regulation Authority, HIH and the NAB*, 2004, https://www.anzsog.edu.au › documents › file; CPA Australia, *Corporate governance case studies*, July 2020; Dianne Thomson, *Corporate Governance Failure And Its Impact On National Australia Bank's Performance*, Journal of Business Case Studies 2(1), January 2006; Sydney Morning Herald, *APRA raised NAB concerns before scandal*, 19 February 2004; Sydney Morning Herald, *Profit-is-king NAB put back onto P-plates*, 25 March 2004.

29. *Australian Financial Review*, 'NAB haunted by foreign exchange woes more than a decade', 4 December 2018.

30. *Sydney Morning Herald*, 'Heads roll at NAB over foreign exchange scandal', 12 March 2004.

31. Australian Prudential Regulation Authority, *Report Into Irregular Currency Options Trading At The National Australia Bank*, Sydney, 23 March 2004.

32. Renee Roberts, 'Failing to plan is a Plan to fail', Speech to Risk Management Institute of Australasia Annual Conference, 31 March 2012.

8

Coronavirus (COVID-19): LESSONS LEARNED?

Peter Collignon

During 2020 and 2021, Australia was successful at limiting the spread of repeated reintroductions of the severe acute respo-ratory syndrome (SARS). This was achieved by an early closure of international borders – limiting the spread from high prevalence countries/regions (e.g., China, Italy, and the United States of America) – and by quarantining returning international travellers (until late 2021). This was a sensible approach while awaiting high levels of adult vaccination against COVID protecting against death and serious disease. By global comparison, Australia has done much better than most other countries – and are likely to remain among those countries with the lowest number of cumulative deaths related to COVID – but what are the important lessons learned during this global pandemic?

On a population basis until 28 August 2022, Australia's cumulative death rates from COVID was 530 per million people. This figure is much lower than the 3097 (USA), 1763 (Germany) and 1892 (Sweden) deaths per million people. It is similar to what was experienced in New Zealand, Japan, Singapore, Taiwan and South Korea. Importantly, excess deaths rates (i.e., deaths from all causes and not just COVID) have also been much lower in Australia than nearly all other countries over the first two and a half years of the pandemic (up to August 2022).

Despite these relatively good outcomes, COVID continues to instil a sense of fear and panic – although it is not hard to see why. Up until mid to late 2021 Australia was relatively well protected from COVID's worst effects. Through a concerted effort the spread of COVID was kept under control – through long periods of 'zero

COVID' and limited periods of severe restrictions – with Victoria an exception.

From mid-August to November 2021, the spread of COVID – with the advent of the much more transmissible delta variant – became almost unstoppable. This was despite early lockdowns in many Australian jurisdictions. With our inability to control the spread of 'Delta' and after achieving over 95 per cent vaccination in adults, in late 2021 (when Australia reopened its international borders and loosened restrictions) widespread infections started. From December 2021 to August 2022, the initial 'Delta' variant wave was followed by three overlapping waves caused by different 'Omicron' variants. We unfortunately had over 10,000 COVID-19 associated deaths in the first eight months of 2022. But why are the political and public perceptions – and levels of restrictions – dramatically different to the mindset of mid-2021? I suspect many reasons.

First, we are now a very highly vaccinated population, markedly lowering our risk of death and serious disease when infected. Second, most Australians have likely been infected over the last nine months and have now hybrid immunity. Our individual risk for hospitalisation and death is now ten to twenty-fold lower than in 2020, if we become infected. In 2020 about two per cent of those who were infected, died. Whether our current immunity is from three or four doses of the vaccine, natural infection or by a mix (hybrid immunity), this protection against serious disease likely persists for twelve months or more. On the downside, vaccines are much less effective at stopping mild infections. Onward transmission to others remains common.

Unanswered questions remain

Many unanswered questions about COVID-19 remain. We need to address these so we can better learn how to potentially decrease similar threats in the future. It is also relevant for knowing how best to limit deaths and serious disease in those people most at risk, but without excessive restrictions and consequent harm. These harms include not only social, psychological, economic, and educational but also associated health effects (e.g., delays in cancer diagnosis, surgery, and treatment for diabetes) that may be shown by an increase in 'excess deaths', even if COVID deaths are low.

Did SARS-CoV-2 virus escape from the Wuhan lab?

The short answer is we still do not know. A 'lab leak' remains a possibility that cannot be excluded, but equally there is no strong evidence available that this is what occurred either. The SARS-Cov-2 virus or its immediate predecessor appears to have come from a coronavirus initially present in bats (in China or Southeast Asia). The unresolved question is how it then infected people and spread so readily. One view is that the virus went from bats to an intermediary animal (so far not found) with the virus spreading to humans. Initial spread occurred either in the wild or via the seafood market at Wuhan, where live animals were sold.

An alternate theory is that it escaped from the research laboratory at Wuhan, which stored viruses and propagated many hundreds of different coronavirus samples from bats and other animals, after their discoveries in wild animals. The latter lab leak theory has caused political and scientific controversy, including when the Morrison Government in 2020 called for an independent World Health Organization (WHO) sponsored review.

We do need to be concerned about lab leaks. These have occurred not infrequently in the past with various viruses including smallpox, influenza virus and SARs-1. In the Wuhan lab (and other labs) there appears to have been 'gain of function' experiments done on various viruses to make them more transmissible and/or more virulent. These experiments are justified by research labs in that it helps scientists to better understand viruses and develop better drugs and/or better vaccines to combat novel infections. Despite these promises this has not happened for any novel virus (or even old ones) and patently did not happen with the coronavirus that causes COVID, even though similar viruses were held for some years at the Wuhan lab, and elsewhere.

More worrying is that for a novel virus found in animals to cause infections in people and spread, it must first be able to multiply in people and their cells. With coronaviruses in the Wuhan lab, many viruses were cultured (and therefore virus numbers multiplied exponentially) in cell lines that included both human cell lines and monkey cell lines. This seems to be a very efficient way to adapt a new virus found in animals, to then be able to multiply in people if the virus ever escaped from the lab.

We need much better controls on these types of laboratories and on cell lines used to culture any new animal derived viruses. Much of this work has been done without any obvious benefits. Certainly not the benefits that many argue justifies the types of research and processes done in many of these labs – such as it will help prevent the next pandemic or prepare us better for a new pandemic. No one can claim it helped with COVID-19 or for other infections that have spread in the last two decades before, such as Swine Flu (H1N1 influenza), SARS, Bird Flu or Ebola.

Who is most infected by COVID?

In the first two years of the pandemic, the age group with the highest infection rates have consistently been young adults aged between 20 to 29 years, followed by those people in the 30 to 39-year-old age group, due likely to their mobility and interaction with larger numbers of people. Children incorrectly continue to be the concern or belief by many, as the major source of ongoing infections in communities. In most data, however, whether based on case numbers or antibody tests, children have generally lower rates of infection than adults aged 20 to 60 years. Children below the age of ten also have lower infection rates than teenagers. This is quite different to most other respiratory infections (e.g., influenza, RSV), where young children have often had infections at five times or more higher rates than adults. The main reason for children having less infection is likely due to them having less receptors in their nose and airways before multiplying and causing infection (ACE2 receptors), compared to adults.[1]

Mortality rates

Age dependent mortality rates is another important aspect of COVID-19. The highest infection fatality rate is seen in those people aged 80 years of age or older, where in 2020, more than one in ten infected people – but not immunised – died. This compares to a much lower infection fatality rate seen in 30-year-olds, where pre-vaccination in 2020, their infection fatality rate was about one per 10,000 infections. In children the fatality rate was even lower. Likely about one per 100,000 infections and even lower still in children who do not have any underlying major health issue when infected.[2, 3]

We still do not know enough on how COVID spreads

The SARS-CoV-2 virus is present in respiratory secretions and in faeces. It can also be found on surfaces after these have had respiratory secretions deposited on them. In theory, the virus can spread via direct contact with respiratory secretions, faecal material or from innate surfaces (via hands and then inoculation of eyes, nose, or mouth). We know that close and prolonged contact indoors is the most important factor involved in the transmission of COVID e.g., within a household or workplace. Higher risk activities are being in air-conditioned or heated rooms with low humidity.[4] While the SARS-CoV-2 virus is present in faeces, the respiratory route seems to be the overwhelming way COVID-19 is transmitted. Past and current epidemiological evidence suggests that most transmission of COVID-19 in the community is through air, but this transmission is likely mainly by larger particles (droplets) rather than by aerosols. The latter are much smaller than droplets and can stay suspended in air for many hours and travel much further.

In 2020, over 700 returning (but infected) Australian residents were cared for by New South Wales Health in apartment hotels, over a two-week period, in Sydney. Staff wore surgical masks to protect their airways and face shields for eye protection. No staff members became infected. Surgical masks are said by those concerned about aerosols as giving poor protection against aerosols, compared to N95 respirator masks. N95 masks might give extra protection, but it is hard to see it would be very much, given the low rates of cross infections in our quarantine hotels in Australia that used surgical masks and eye protection properly (especially in NSW where the largest numbers of infected people were looked after). No one (staff or guests), wearing a surgical mask and eye protection when exposed to someone with an infection, became infected while staying in or working in quarantine hotels in Australia (other than some when exposed in Victoria to an inappropriately used nebuliser).

Staying away from others and work while symptomatic is an important prevention strategy. While those who are asymptomatic or pre-symptomatic, can spread the virus, most spread occurs likely from people who have symptoms. Isolation and social distancing are vital even though this was not done by many people, including healthcare workers in the past.[5]

Suppressing or eliminating COVID-19

When initial interventions to limit the spread of COVID-19 were implemented in Australia (and worldwide), it was intended to 'flatten the curve'. This meant that instead of allowing numbers of new cases to continue to rise per day (as was occurring and often rising exponentially), restrictions and interventions would cause the number of new cases per day to level off. The level and severity of restrictions put in place would be tailored with numbers of new cases occurring per day such that the health system could cope better.[6] In Australia, during our first wave in March/April 2020, we did much better than just 'flattening the curve'. The epidemic curve of daily cases decreased rapidly after about March 26 – and we had very low numbers of new cases per day by mid to late April. This resulted in an effective suppression of cases like South Korea during their first wave, and in New Zealand. After this successful suppression, some areas (e.g., New Zealand in March 2020 and then Victoria) started aiming for an 'elimination strategy'. This was done with more prolonged lockdowns compared to other states in Australia. The supposition being that if lockdowns continued so no new cases were seen for two or more incubation periods (i.e., 28 days) then it was likely the virus was eliminated from those areas.[7]

In both Victoria and New Zealand, however, there were subsequent outbreaks of COVID-19 after the initial 'elimination'. Notably, the genomics on new outbreaks that occurred in Australia and New Zealand since late 2020, show all new outbreaks were caused by newly introduced strains. This suggests that everywhere in Australia and New Zealand – including Sydney – with large cases numbers during multiple outbreaks, the virus was eliminated before new strains were reintroduced, and by some states using much less severe levels of restrictions than others. Notably, Japan, South Korea and Taiwan achieved either zero COVID and/or low levels of spread until early 2022, without resorting to widespread lockdowns. Even when achieved, elimination has been and will be very difficult to maintain in large populations over time. By August 2022, China was the only country continuing with this approach. Hong Kong was still aiming for 'dynamic covid-zero', but case numbers in August 2022 were still rising.

The symptoms in people who are aged in their 20s and 30s, are mostly very mild and/or asymptomatic and likely more so if vaccinated. Yet they can still pass on the virus to others. Even if we are not seeing cases, it can still be likely that in some areas there might be ongoing low-level transmission occurring, even if no cases are found for many weeks or even months.

Yet when SARS-CoV-2 virus is eliminated from certain populations, if 'isolation and social distancing' measures are not retained, the virus is reintroduced, spreading rapidly, especially in Winter.

Elimination will be difficult to maintain, given how widespread COVID remains globally. New case numbers can quickly escalate, as evidenced not only by what occurred in Melbourne (in the Winter of 2020), but also in Korea and in Auckland. South Korea, with its control of COVID-19, was like Australia after its first wave, but when South Korea reopened crowded facilities, particularly bars and nightclubs, a rapid increase in new cases ensued, worsening over Winter of 2020/21.[8]

COVID is not going away. It will be present for decades to come. Its spread was delayed but with the more transmissible strains (Delta and Omicron) we cannot stop it from spreading. Nor can we expect to get to COVID-zero. NSW, Victoria, and New Zealand tried but failed – as did Taiwan and Hong Kong. In August 2022, Hong Kong (like the rest of China) was still striving for 'COVID zero', but despite prolonged restrictions, this seems an unlikely achievable or sustainable goal.

Vaccines

Vaccinations have been very effective in saving lives. Data from Australia, the United States, the United Kingdom, Qatar, and Israel show that once someone is fully vaccinated that person receives high levels of protection against death, intensive care unit (ICU) admission or serious disease (hospitalisation) compared to those who remain unvaccinated. Vaccination also decreases mild disease and viral transmission, but much less so. Especially once the Omicron variants become dominant.

Vaccines in use or being used were developed and deployed

much faster than previous vaccines and were all novel. Early and large-scale studies showed all to be effective at markedly decreasing death rates and relatively safe. All vaccines, by different means, presented the spike protein component of the virus to our bodies. We then produced protective antibodies and cellular responses by our lymphocytes.

The Pfizer and Astra Zeneca (AZ) vaccines were available in Australia from about March 2021, but vaccine supplies were not available in large quantities until October 2021 due to global demand and vaccine supply issues. The Astra Zeneca/Oxford vaccine used encoded deoxyribonucleic acid (DNA) as a template to produce a spike protein delivered by injection of a non-replicating modified adenovirus vector. The Pfizer and Moderna vaccines were messenger RNA based vaccines (stored at very low temperatures). The spike protein was then made from this mRNA template in the body near the site of injection. The Novavax vaccine only became available much later in 2022. This vaccine relied on the spike protein being injected resembling a more traditional vaccine approach.

In Melbourne in the Winter of 2020 when no vaccines were available, the case fatality rate (CFR), was about four deaths per 100 people infected, although age dependent. In those vaccinated, the overall population CFR is well below one per 1000 identified cases, making the population CFRs similar to those linked to seasonal influenza.

Australia was fortunate to have had a large proportion of the adult population vaccinated before COVID spread widely – with over 90 per cent of adults vaccinated by the end of 2021. We also were able to have available to offer to those over the age of 70 years (and at highest risk of death from COVID) vaccination by mid-2021 – before widespread infection with COVID occurred. A rare side effect was noted for the AZ vaccine resulting in the death of about one per million vaccines recipients. This was caused by an unusual clotting or thrombotic event and was found to be more common in younger women. Consequently, older people deferred their vaccination opting for Pfizer vaccines.

In mid-2021, Australia had little or no COVID circulating with an expectation that 'zero COVID' could be achieved. Unfortunately, the Delta variant took hold in August 2021 resulting in many hundreds of deaths among the elderly. The mRNA vaccines also had rare but serious side effects, mainly inflammation of the heart (myocarditis), occurring more often in younger males.

There seems to have been an expectation in the community that vaccines would have no serious side effects. If you were over the age of 70, your risk of dying if infected with COVID was about one in 50, and if over 80 years of age, there was a one in ten chance of death. Even though the risk of death from the AZ vaccine was about one per million, several older Australians were not persuaded. Inconsistent advice from health experts on age eligibility – as well as an over-emphasising of adverse effects – led to the uptake of an effective vaccine being much less than it should have been. A consequence: the loss of too many lives when the inevitable spread of COVID occurred.

Outside air and ventilation

Outdoors, the risks of transmission of COVID-19 (and many other respiratory infections) are low. Several environmental factors are known to reduce the viability of viruses and other infectious pathogens in the air including variations in temperature, relative humidity, solar ultraviolet radiation, and dilution effects. One agent that reduces the viability of both viruses and bacteria outdoors, germicidal open-air factors (OAF), has not been properly recognised for decades: despite robust evidence that these factors can influence both the survival of airborne pathogens and the course of infections.

The germicidal effects of outdoor air were widely exploited during the late 19th and early 20th centuries.[9] First, in the treatment of tuberculosis patients who underwent 'open-air therapy' in sanatoria; and second, by military surgeons during the Great War. Military surgeons used the same open-air regimen in specially designed hospital wards to disinfect and heal severe wounds among injured soldiers. This method was also used on influenza patients during the 1918–19 pandemic. Later, in the 1950s, open-air disinfection and treatment of burns were proposed in the event of nuclear warfare. During the 1960s, OAF briefly returned to prominence when biodefence scientists conducted experiments proving that open air has a potent germicidal effect. When this work ended in the 1970s, interest in the OAF again fell away, remaining largely ignored.

The COVID-19 pandemic has revived interest in understanding the transmission dynamics and survival of viruses in the air. The pandemic has also stimulated research in the science and practice of improved ventilation to control respiratory infections. Such work is incomplete without an appreciation of the inactivation of viruses and other pathogens by OAF, prompting urgent further investigation. This work is important as we need to review building design regarding infection control and patient recovery. We need to act without delay. There is sufficient evidence showing public health generally improves if more emphasis is placed on increased exposure to outdoor air.

We do not know how best the germicidal and health effects of outdoor air can be preserved indoors. Given the threat to global public health from COVID-19, antimicrobial-resistant bacteria, pandemic influenza, and novel pathogens, there is merit in investigating whether and how this can be done. If so, 'rediscovering' open-air wards and the open-air regimen might benefit patients and staff in hospitals. The OAF will likely also help in reducing the transmission of many infections in schools, homes, offices, and larger buildings.

A program of testing is essential to determine the effects of

OAF on the viability of established and emerging pathogens. Research must be carried out to confirm that OAF can be preserved indoors and under what conditions. We need to recognise there is sufficient evidence already showing that public health generally improves if we place more emphasis on increased exposure to outdoor air.

Lockdowns and school closures

Despite the much lower fatality rate in children and lower infectivity risk to others (compared to the age group of parents and teachers) there were prolonged school closures, not only in Australia, but globally. This action resulted in an intergeneration trade-off leaving children worse off than older adults.

Recent analysis published by the US National Bureau of Economic Research, reveals while lockdowns did likely overall decrease deaths from COVID in most countries, lives saved were mainly those people aged over 70. This age effect was marked more in countries with high per capita gross domestic product (GDP); where even in richer countries, lockdowns did not 'save' many children's lives.[10] In contrast, in countries with low GDP's, lockdowns increased the number of children who died. While some children's lives were saved after avoiding COVID infections, overall deaths increased because of the associated severe socio-economic effects and poorer access to healthcare for non-COVID related reasons.[11]

The United Nations International Children's Emergency Fund (UNICEF) has also recently shown the detrimental effects COVID restrictions (and associated school closures) had on children. These effects were much worse in low socio-economic countries, where two years or more of schooling has been lost and unlikely to ever be recovered.[12]

In Australia, socio-economic disadvantage has effects both on health and other outcomes related to COVID. Australian Bureau of

Statistics (ABS) data shows those in lower socio-economic groups, have up to five times higher mortality rates than those who are more affluent. Many media and other reports also show that many children did not participate in much or sometimes any 'in home' schooling during lockdowns and school closures in Australia. Because of a lack of access to a computer and the Internet, and overcrowding in housing, lower socio-economic groups were disproportionately disadvantaged.

Mask mandates

Wearing masks in the community likely decreases the chances of people getting infected with COVID by about fifteen per cent. Surprisingly there are only two studies that have looked at this using good control or comparator groups. This relative lack of good research is one reason there is such controversy.[13]

Good data supporting wearing of mask use in the community remains scanty and while there are many mask studies published, they are generally of poor quality. There are data showing potential benefits but there are also many observational studies that show adjoining regions with mask mandates compared to those that that have no mandates, results in little or no differences in the numbers of cases detected on a population basis.

One argument is that cloth and surgical masks are ineffective and that we need the widespread community use of better-quality masks. When this was tried in Bavaria, Germany, however, the widespread use of N95 respiratory masks, did not seem to have an associated lower infection rate with COVID, compared to other regions not using these types of respirators/masks.

Masks are not usually worn in situations where the highest levels of transmissions occur in homes and public areas. Wearing a mask decreases the risk of contracting COVID by a small to moderate amount and should be promoted for that reason, especially the vulnerable in our community. Mask mandates and associated fines for non-compliance, do not make much difference to case numbers nor likely impact numbers in hospitals or dying from COVID.

The Howard era: pandemics and planning

During the Howard Government era, there were several infectious disease threats. In March 2003, the WHO issued a global alert recommending active worldwide surveillance for severe acute respiratory syndrome (SARS). The virus originated in China and large secondary outbreaks occurred in Vietnam, Canada, and Hong Kong. Australia adopted a border control policy and there were 138 people investigated for SARS: 111 suspect and 27 probable. No spread occurred within Australia with only five probable cases reported to the WHO.[14]

Another infection was Avian flu (H5N1 influenza). Because of its ongoing spread in birds in Asia (and sometimes elsewhere), spread to or between people was rare, but when people became infected, a case fatality rate of over 25 per cent was realised.

In June 2005, Health Minister, Tony Abbott released the Australian Management Plan for Pandemic Influenza.[15] This plan provided information for an Australian response to an influenza pandemic in the event of an outbreak. The Plan included information on major strategies to be used to respond to a pandemic, an overview of roles of various committees and agencies involved in pandemic planning, key groups involved in pandemic response, information on diagnostic testing, surveillance, disease control measures, communications strategies, and, importantly an overview of response actions.[16]

Notably, when the COVID-19 pandemic was declared in 2020, Sweden, South Korea and Japan were among the few countries to follow their respective pandemic plans. Nearly all other countries, including China, Australia and New Zealand used lockdowns and prolonged school closures as public health measures, despite those measures not prescribed in pandemic plans.

What will the near future hold?

The 'Spanish flu' of 1918–19 (Influenza A) was much worse than COVID-19 with its associated fatality rates (a case fatality rate of-about two per cent but killing tens of millions of people, disproportionately affecting those people aged 20 to 40 years). COVID-19 predominantly causes deaths in the elderly. Even before vaccines, the COVID case fatality rates in people aged 30, was about one per 10,000 cases. With the Spanish flu, the case fatality rate was one to two per cent in that younger age group, but this high mortality was only in the first two years after it circulated widely in 1918.

Spanish flu did not go away after 1920. It persisted for another 50 years or more, with new 'variants' appearing frequently. It's very high mortality rate fell to much lower levels after two years, and it became a winter seasonal illness throughout most of the world – as COVID-19 is likely to repeat. Yes, we have had lots of cases in Australia, and our cumulative number of cases per million people, now equals the United States, but delaying the introduction and spread of COVID-19 in Australia, and because of our high levels of vaccination and now lower virulence in the circulating strains, our cumulative case fatality rate is about seven times lower than in the United States. Australia's cumulative total rate is likely to stay much lower.

We, do, however, need to better target and protect our most vulnerable. We need to better ensure they are fully immunised with boosters; plus ensure access to early testing and quicker access to antiviral drugs, if infected. These steps will lead, in part, to a decrease in the risk of serious disease and a lowering of deaths resulting from COVID. Prevention is still important. Masks decrease the risk of transmitting infection to others, especially when indoors and in crowded situations. But mask mandates and fines however do not seem to have much effect on the overall community transmission. We need to change our focus from case numbers to more accurate indicators, namely deaths, hospitalisation, and intensive care unit

(ICU) numbers, as better indicators. If we want an early warning system, we need early daily reporting of sewage levels of COVID, as this information provides the best indication of the true numbers of cases (and the likely subsequent hospital demands about one to two weeks later).

Australia is now past the worst of COVID-19. We need to be optimistic about the future. Vaccines have been, and are effective, at protecting against death and serious disease. We now have antiviral drugs that decrease the risk of death and serious disease for our most vulnerable citizens. While new strains will continue to appear and be more transmissible, they are also likely to be less virulent. The Spanish flu's high mortality rates dropped dramatically after two years. We should expect a similar outcome for COVID.

Endnotes

1. Peter Collignon, 'COVID-19 and future pandemics: is isolation and social distancing the new norm?', *Internal Medicine Journal*, vol. 51, no. 5, 2021, pp. 647-53, doi: https://doi.org/10.1111/imj.15287
2. Andrew Levin et al, 'Assessing the Age Specificity of Infection Fatality Rates for COVID-19: Systematic Review, Meta-Analysis, and Public Policy Implications', *medRxiv* preprint, 6 October 2020, doi: https://doi.org/10.1101/2020.07.23.20160895
3. Peter Collignon and John Beggs, 'COVID-19 fatality risk: Why is Australia lower than South Korea?', *medRxiv* 2020, doi: https://doi.org/10.1101/2020.05.14.20101378
4. Collignon, 'COVID-19 and future pandemics: is isolation and social distancing the new norm?', pp. 647-53.
5. E. Tartari et al. 'Not sick enough to worry? "Influenza-like" symptoms and work-related behavior among healthcare workers and other professionals: Results of a global survey', PLoS One, 2020, vol. 15, no. 5: e0232168, published 13 May 2020. doi:10.1371/journal.pone.0232168
6. S. Roberts, 'Flattening the Coronavirus Curve', *New York Times*, 27 March 2020, https://www.nytimes.com/article/flatten-curve-coronavirus.html

7. M. G. Baker et al 'Successful Elimination of Covid-19 Transmission in New Zealand', *The New England Journal of Medicine*, 2020, vol. 383:e56, doi: 10.1056/NEJMc2025203.

8. Choe Sang-Hun, 'As South Korea Eases Limits, Virus Cluster Prompts Seoul to Close Bars', published online 9 May 2020, https://www.nytimes.com/2020/05/09/world/asia/coronavirus-south-korea-second-wave.html

9. Richard Hobday and Peter Collignon, 'An Old Defence Against New Infections: The Open-Air Factor and COVID-19', 20 June 2022, *Cureus*, DOI: 10.7759/cureus.26133

10. J. Herby et al, 'A Literature Review and Meta-Analysis of the Effects of Lockdowns on COVID-19 Mortality,' Studies in Applied Economics 200, The Johns Hopkins Institute for Applied Economics, Global Health, and the Study of Business Enterprise, https://sites.krieger.jhu.edu/iae/files/2022/01/A-Literature-Review-and-Meta-Analysis-of-the-Effects-of-Lockdowns-on-COVID-19-Mortality.pdf

11. L. Ma et al, The Intergenerational Mortality Trade-off of COVID-19 Lockdown Policies, (published online ahead of print, 24 April 2022), International Economic Review, 2022, https://onlinelibrary.wiley.com/doi/full/10.1111/iere.12574

12. UNICEF. 'UNICEF, EU CONCERNED ABOUT IMPACT OF SCHOOL CLOSURES ON CHILDREN: 897 MILLION SCHOOLCHILDREN WORLDWIDE WERE AFFECTED BY DISRUPTIONS TO THEIR EDUCATION DUE TO COVID-19 RELATED LOCKDOWNS.', 1 February 2021. Press Release, https://www.unicef.org/eu/press-releases/unicef-eu-concerned-about-impact-school-closures-children

13. J Conly et al, 'Use of medical face masks versus particulate respirators as a component of personal protective equipment for health care workers in the context of the COVID-19 pandemic', *Antimicrobial Resistance & Infection Control*, vol. 9, no. 1, pp. 1-7, DOI: 10.1186/s13756-020-00779-6

14. G. Samaan et al, 'Border screening for SARS in Australia: what has been learnt?', *Medical Journal of Australia*, vol. 180, no. 5, pp. 220-3.

15. Australian National Audit Office, *Australia's Preparedness for a Human Influenza Pandemic*, Audit Report No.6, 2007–08, https://www.anao.gov.au/sites/default/files/ANAO_Report_2007-2008_06.pdf

16. Parliament of Australia, prepared by N. Brew and K. Burton, 'Australia's capacity to respond to an infectious disease outbreak', Research Paper no. 3, 2004–05, 16 November 2004, https://www.aph.gov.au/About_Parliament/Parliamentary_Departments/Parliamentary_Library/pubs/rp/rp0405/05rp03

9

The National Security Committee of Cabinet: Did it provide a consistent response?

Peter Jennings

John Howard recounts in his autobiography, *Lazarus Rising*, his intention after the 1996 election 'to restore a fully functioning and orderly system of cabinet government, with all of the major decisions of the government being made by cabinet or its properly functioning committees.' Howard continued, 'As promised, I established a National Security Committee of cabinet, which was to have the task of dealing with all Foreign Affairs and Defence issues. … It was to prove one of the most successful administrative decisions I took.'[1]

Howard's positive assessment of the NSC is striking in the context of an autobiography containing some self-critical reflections about his time in office. The Howard Government's NSC strengthened the prime minister's position over Defence policy and international crisis management and has largely set the benchmark for how subsequent governments have approached these issues. At its best the NSC gave the Howard Government a flexible mechanism to handle international crises and to steer defence policy decisions, at times against the advice of officials. At its worst the NSC could be subject to group think. In some respects, the Committee took on the personality of Howard as its Chair: it was an orderly, prose driven clearing house for decisions, not given to extravagance or policy adventurism.

Over the life of the Howard Government, I interacted with the NSC in a number of different roles. As Chief of Staff to Defence Minister Ian MacLachlan from March 1996 to October 1998 I was involved in the early stages of the NSC's operations through the 'Sandline Crisis' with Papua New Guinea and some ADF deployments. As a Defence official I was closely involved in supporting the NSC's work on the East Timor stabilisation operations and later, on the Iraq and Afghanistan conflicts. In 2002-03 I was a member of Howard's Cabinet Policy Unit developing a strategic policy framework for the full Cabinet and observing the operation of the NSC in the lead up to the Iraq war.

A further connection to the NSC I should acknowledge is that I suggested it should be created when writing *A Strong Australia: Rebuilding Australia's Defence*, the policy statement John Hewson (former Leader of the Federal Parliamentary Liberal Party) took to the March 1993 election. In the *Fightback!* tradition *A Strong Australia* was a 170-page tome. It proposed the creation of a tiny National Security Office aligned to the Department of Prime Minister and Cabinet to 'ensure that briefings for Ministers and Cabinet adequately address Australian security concerns in the broad and not simply from a narrow departmental perspective.' Further, it promised that the Coalition will revamp the Cabinet Security Committee (CSC) and complained that the Hawke and Keating governments had allowed the committee to fall into disuse. The CSC had not formally met, for example, to authorise the deployment of Australian forces to the Gulf War.[2]

A Strong Australia was released in a hurry in late 1992 to get ahead of a newspaper story about to reveal its contents. The Shadow Defence Minister, Alexander Downer, lamented he did not get his name in the book such was the haste to get copies ready for the media. However, the Cabinet committee idea stuck and was repeated in the Coalition's 1996 election policy statement, *Australia's Defence*, which said: 'The Security Sub-Committee of Cabinet, which has met over recent years on an irregular and ad hoc basis, will be replaced by a National Security Committee (of Cabinet). The NSC was to be 'the focal point of decision-making on national security.'[3]

Working with Defence Minister Ian MacLachlan our early impression was that an NSC was needed to put more order into a slightly dysfunctional decision-making system. Defence, for example, had not produced an incoming government brief for MacLachlan and had clearly not spent much time looking at the Coalition's policy statements. One early order of business was to take a series of equipment acquisition proposals to the full Cabinet, supported by a folder of paperwork not much more advanced than a manufacturer's glossy brochure. At times it was possible to imagine that the Defence Department was content to run itself. Unlike in later years it seemed that responsiveness to ministers was patchy. Phone calls to senior officials and Australian Defence Force (ADF) leaders were not always quickly returned. On bad days it felt that ministers were regarded as optional extras not always essential to departmental processes.

The NSC – as Howard structured it – gave more focus and directed the attention of senior ministers and officials to policy work. Howard as prime minister chaired the meetings, with the deputy prime minister, treasurer, ministers for Defence and Foreign Affairs and attorney-general attending. The particular benefit of the NSC was that officials attended meetings and could participate in discussions, unlike the full Cabinet, where only ministers participate. NSC became a vehicle to educate ministers on the complexities of defence and security and defined the work agenda of officials.

The first year of Howard's government was tough. Several ministers resigned or were sacked over (by today's standards) relatively minor infractions of the Ministerial Guidelines. It takes time for a new government to find its feet. To my mind a breakthrough moment for Howard came with the 'Sandline' crisis in Papua New Guinea (PNG). Frustrated with the inability of the PNG Defence Force to quell a secessionist movement on Bougainville, Prime Minister Sir Julius Chan signed a contract with British mercenaries to bring some Russian attack helicopters, weapons and mercenaries to the island. By March of 1997 a giant Antonov aircraft was transiting through Kuala Lumpur with the equipment destined for PNG.

Australia had been following developments from around February. The challenge was to stop the weapons arriving and to persuade Chan to consider 'reasonable alternatives' to deliver a settlement on Bougainville. The NSC sat in regular crisis meetings to determine a course of action. Chan came to Sydney for talks with Howard where some tough potential Australian measures including cutting aid funding were set out. Foreign Minister Alexander Downer visited Port Moresby as did senior Australian officials, again presenting reasonable alternative options.

NSC determined to divert the Antonov to the Royal Australian Air Force (RAAF) Base Tindal on 27 March 1997, and considered rules of engagement that might be used to force the aircraft to land if necessary. Over a complex and fast changing situation Howard used the NSC to shape a whole of government response, create new policy options, and persuade PNG's pressured leaders to cooperate. *The Australian's* Greg Sheridan wrote at the time:

> Throughout the past month the crisis with PNG has been handled primarily by the Minister for Foreign Affairs, Alexander Downer, and Howard himself, chairing the Cabinet's National Security Committee. The NSC has become an important institution in the Howard Government. … It meets frequently and has met several times to consider the PNG crisis. Whether because of Howard's threats, his emissaries' persuasiveness or the unravelling situation in the streets of Port Moresby, Chan on Thursday night changed his mind and announced the suspension of the contract with Sandline.[4]

With MacLachlan, I later inspected the two Soviet-era attack and two transport helicopters at RAAF Base Tindal, along with large quantities of ammunition. They were badly dilapidated after years of use in Sierra Leone but still functioning. Had they got to Bougainville a massacre would have ensued. My recollection is that Howard and his ministers were relieved. They had found how to operate the levers of national power in Canberra. The functioning of the NSC was a key to that outcome.

The NSC also had a way of surprising ministers and officials, and not always on the upside. In February 1998 the NSC discussed options for providing military support to a US-led Operation Desert Thunder to provide a military presence in Kuwait, overflying southern Iraq during negotiations between the UN and Baghdad over weapons of mass destruction. I recall Howard's quiet astonishment at being briefed by the Chief of Defence Force that combat aircraft could not be deployed because they lacked the right level of electronic warfare self-protection systems. This was the beginning of Howard's realisation that the ADF was significantly under-equipped for modern warfare. Years of fitting platforms 'for but not with' weapons and sensors had hollowed out the force.

Then it was Defence's turn to be surprised when the NSC agreed to deploy a squadron of the Special Air Service Regiment to act as a rescue force if Iraq shot down a coalition aircraft. This was clearly an 'option' Defence thought would not be taken up. I received a phone call from an angry Deputy Secretary, asking if the [expletive deleted] NSC didn't realise these forces could be killed or wounded. That risk was very much part of the Committee's thinking. A lesson here is that politicians and officials can make assumptions about each other's views that are often incorrect. NSC is an important means to test these assumptions.

The East Timor crisis starting in 1999 best exemplified the role of the NSC as a crisis management mechanism, but a critical precursor to the crisis – a letter from John Howard to Indonesian President BJ Habibie sent in November 1998 – illustrates the limits of even well-managed bureaucratic processes. Howard considered that Habibie's replacement of President Suharto and apparent willingness to consider an autonomy package for East Timor created a possibility to resolve a long-standing conflict between Indonesia and Timorese separatists. A resolution to decades of bloody fighting in East Timor would remove a major impediment to better relations between Canberra and Jakarta and help Indonesia's standing internationally.

Howard's letter to Habibie, described by Deputy Prime Minister Tim Fisher as 'the most important letter ever written during the coalition government's period of office, leading to the creation of East Timor, never went to Cabinet.'[5] The letter proposed to Habibie that he consider 'a review mechanism' providing

> a means of addressing the East Timorese desire for an act of self-determination in a manner which avoids an early and final decision on the future status of the province.[6]

Howard's model was the New Caledonia Matignon Accords, which provided a ten-year preparation for an independence vote. The mercurial Habibie reacted to the letter by instituting steps to a referendum in East Timor on independence in August 1999.

In his autobiography Howard points to an NSC discussion on Timor's status on 1 December 1998 but the contents of the letter, in particular the idea for an act of self-determination, were developed by Howard in discussion with Foreign Minister Alexander Downer. Key departments like Defence were not consulted. Did this amount to a failure of process?

Howard notes that the Canberra consensus firmly supported the status quo, with East Timor remaining incorporated in the Indonesian Republic: 'It was not thought appropriate to question Indonesian sovereignty over East Timor.'[7] Had the letter been part of standard NSC processes it is likely the bureaucracy would have recommended against sending it. It was clearly a major departure in Australian foreign policy and its reception in Jakarta was not without risk, including the possibility of conflict if Indonesia or pro-Indonesian elements in Timor opposed an Australian stabilisation mission. That said, the letter produced better outcomes for an independent Timor Leste, ended the international opprobrium over Jakarta's occupation and has since allowed for generally better bilateral relations between Canberra and Jakarta.

My conclusion is that the NSC, perhaps like all policy clearing houses, works best with incremental policy change. Major shifts in policy tend to come from reactions to strategic shocks or indeed from a prime minister with a small inner circle looking to make formative change.

With Habibie locked on a path to an East Timor referendum in August 1999, the NSC in March that year 'ordered that the 1st Brigade, based in Darwin, be brought to a state of readiness in June', a decision Howard described as 'prescient'.[8] In the build up to, and during the deployment of the INTERFET stabilisation force in September 1999, NSC established a 'battle rhythm' of meeting twice a day, once early in the morning and again in the evening to assess developments. Defence and the wider bureaucracy organised itself around this procedure, servicing the government's information requirements and building the international coalition, securing UN endorsement and Japanese funding for the mission.

Supporting the NSC in crisis management mode was demanding, but a comfortable enough process that government departments could adapt to meet. Government agencies love predictable engagement with ministers. The practices established during the early months of the East Timor crises were repeated for later military operations in the Solomon Islands, Iraq, Afghanistan, redeployments to Timor Leste and many disaster response activities in the Indo-Pacific. The NSC works well to position the prime minister as the 'first among equals' at the table, and therefore the personal work habits, quirks and interests of the prime minister give shape to the success or failure of the NSC's processes. As an orderly person with a calm demeanour and a substantial appetite for work, Howard worked well with the NSC system, and his prime ministership benefited from it.

In Defence crisis management, things can and do go wrong. The ADF chafed at times at the NSC's intent to reach right into the tactical heart of military operations. This is not how the 'operational art' was (indeed still is) taught at Staff College. The military hope is that government will give them a desired end state and then leave the commanders to shape the operation. I doubt that a war has ever been fought that way by democratic states. The reality is that the prime minister and ministers want to know the minute-by-minute action of operations. Managing that relationship and sustaining a rapid flow of accurate information is central to the NSC's success.

Howard's management of the Iraq and Afghanistan deployments following 9/11 enabled the NSC to slip back into a rhythm of meetings and decisions that provided sound management of these operations, particularly in their early years. In his autobiography Howard is unambiguous that the key decision for Australia immediately after 9/11 was the extent to which we would support the United States through the ANZUS alliance. I did not then and still do not think that we had an option not to be militarily involved and still expect Washington to actively support an alliance with Australia.

Howard's aims for the Australian deployments initially set achievable goals which allowed our forces to return to home relatively early in the fighting. A collective failure of the NSC and the wider national security system was not to anticipate that a coalition entering both countries would likely have to face a long and disastrously costly occupation. To my recollection that risk was not seriously contemplated, nor briefed to government by Defence and the intelligence agencies. There was a deep interest in intelligence reporting about Iraq's weapons of mass destruction, which ultimately was not attuned to Saddam Hussein's bizarre choice to deny international verification of what was soon discovered, that there was no significant chemical or biological programs and nothing on nuclear weapons. Why did Saddam refuse to come clean about the absence of such weapons? In my view he was gambling that potentially possessing WMD might deter an attack, not least from

Iran and possibly even from the United States. But the international Coalition's obsession about whether Saddam possessed WMD got in the way of what should have been a more considered assessment of the long-term consequences of occupation.

NSC was also interested in how long it would take to defeat Saddam's military, a question answered in three weeks in March 2003. As for the longer haul, Australia and the wider coalition suffered from a failure of strategic imagination. The NSC needed more access to contrary voices. Here is another lesson about decision-making machinery for military operations: a successfully running machine doesn't function well with discordant inputs. The government wanted to deliver their alliance objectives and Defence wanted to shape a deliverable set of operational activities which could be seen to underpin the government's objectives. These intents shape NSC discussions about the decisions needed for the day – the levers governments can pull. In this context there is little room for dissenting voices arguing for alternate propositions, yet precisely that type of input is needed to, at least, test the risk of groupthink dominating the discussion.

Another weakness of national decision making on Defence operations is that, once forces are deployed, options for sharp departures from current policy lines are very limited. In Afghanistan, for example, and well beyond the life of the Howard Government, NSC struggled to find meaningful strategic purposes for the deployed forces. A primary driver was alliance cohesion and a secondary concern about Afghanistan as an incubator for Islamist terrorism was legitimate. But how did those objectives connect to reconstruction in Oruzgan Province, or counterinsurgency, or counterterrorism? And notwithstanding substantial diplomatic effort, Australia struggled to shape broader coalition strategic objectives in Washington and NATO Headquarters in Brussels.

For all of the evident international failings of the Iraq and Afghanistan conflicts, Howard achieved his key strategic objective, which was to build a closer alliance relationship with the United

States. In 2022 that is an even more critical strategic objective. The NSC was the central mechanism enabling Howard to steer that objective. Nothing can escape the fact that Australia paid a heavy price for these conflicts in terms of lives lost and people injured, but the Australian Defence Force emerged a stronger and more competent military as a result and had become more adept at working with and for governments.

It is briefly worth mentioning the role of the NSC in non-crisis management. Under Howard the Committee became the essential decision-making body for Defence policy development like the 2000 Defence White Paper and for military capability and acquisition decisions. While Howard took major issues, like the White Paper, to full Cabinet for endorsement, NSC was where the detailed work was done to think through strategic issues and make decisions trading off capability and cost.

This was valuable training for Howard, and his senior ministers, many of whom spent years in their portfolios and built a formidable practical expertise that was certainly the equal of the Secretaries, agency heads and senior ADF personnel who attended the NSC. Having worked through the Timor experience and the White Paper development that followed it, Howard never felt the need to produce another Defence White Paper: he had thought through the issues.

Mostly, NSC ministers accepted Defence advice on capability. A notable exception was the decision, led by Defence Minister Brendon Nelson in 2006, to acquire Super Hornet aircraft as a bridging capability to sustain the Air Force fighter capability after the retirement of the F-111 strike bomber and the planned arrival of the F-35 Joint Strike Fighter. That decision, to put it mildly, came as something of a surprise to Defence, which had resolutely been backing the F-35 to arrive on time. Nelson's judgement was that Defence was working with a 'conspiracy of optimism' about the likely time frame for the F-35's arrival:

> From a defence perspective – understandably, I could sense that the Minister was not someone who should be allowed to 'interfere'. He was possibly even an obstacle to be overcome. My advisors and I then took the entire plan apart piece by piece in my office. We looked at every year out to 2018. The risk of an air capability gap was not only real – in my non-expert opinion it was highly likely.

Nelson briefed Howard who told him to 'work up' a proposal for cabinet for a Super Hornet acquisition. Nelson reflected on the moment some years later:

It was lonely at this time. There was no enthusiasm in Defence for moving from the 'plan'. However, I was convinced that the stakes were too high not to do so. The final decision was made in March 2007 to invest $6.6 billion on 24 Super Hornets and infrastructure.[9]

Speaking of the Minister's relationship with the Defence Organisation, Nelson judged that:

> This relationship needs to be a compact of mutual commitment and responsibility. In most cases I took up the cause of the ADF and the department with everything I could muster, accepting their advice and running with it.

But Nelson's time as defence minister will in part be remembered because of his exercise of judgement to press for the Super Hornet capability against the prevailing Defence viewpoint. Like Howard's letter to Habibie the Super Hornet decision was the result of the prime minister working with a small inner circle of ministers and advisers, rather than taking Departmental advice through the NSC.

Under John Howard the NSC became the key instrument for managing Brendon Nelson's 'compact of mutual commitment and responsibility' between the government and the wider national security community. Since 2007 successive prime ministers have chosen the same management structure. NSCs in my view come to reflect the work habits and styles of their Chair, the prime minister. The system is far from flawless, but it enables an effective engagement of political leadership and administrative expertise. Not surprisingly Howard and his ministers grew more effective crisis managers as they gained experience and more shrewd decision makers on Defence strategy and capability acquisition.

Howard's judgement in his autobiography was that

> The consistency and discipline the Howard Government displayed regarding Foreign Policy and Defence was due overwhelmingly to the effective way in which this committee operated.[10]

On balance I share that judgement, reflecting that committees are only as consistent and disciplined as their members.

Reacting to this paper at the John Howard Prime Ministerial Library June 2022 Conference, Howard observed that the NSC in his judgement worked well because it 'held everybody together'. He noted that there were only three or four occasions when he felt the need to hold ministers-only meetings and that it was 'valuable to have high calibre officials' to inform discussions.

The NSC has now operated for more than twenty-five years and has been chaired by seven successive prime ministers. It has clearly become one of the most significant Cabinet Committees and has been used to structure a significant number of military operations and crisis management situations. NSC decisions have shaped Defence White Papers produced in 2000, 2009, 2013 and 2016. The Committee has agreed literally hundreds of billions of dollars in defence equipment projects.

Overwhelmingly, the NSC has been a successful instrument of government. Yet the Howard Government experience is such that innovative and dramatic changes of policy and creative responses to complex geopolitical problems are more often the product of prime ministers working with a small inner circle of advisers. Big policy changes tend not to emerge from standard Cabinet processes. The NSC has been at its best managing the routine of defence equipment decision making or attending to the daily battle rhythm of operational deployments and crisis management. At its worst, the NSC might at times have encouraged policy timidity and group think – often marked by ministers saying they intend to follow military or Defence advice. As a clearing house of steady state policy, the NSC has an enviable reputation, but sweeping policy change is more the provenance of individual leaders taking creative but risky decisions, rather than to be found in the incremental work of government committees.

One NSC moment worth reflecting on was the decision taken on 18 April 2000 to create the Australian Strategic Policy Institute (ASPI). The now-declassified Cabinet Decision sets out the rationale for this decision:

> There are two key reasons to establish an independent institute to study strategic policy. The first is to encourage development of alternative sources of advice to government on key strategic and defence policy issues. The principles of contestability have been central to our government's philosophy and practice of public administration, but these principles have not been effectively implemented in relation to defence and strategic policy, despite the vital national interests and significant sums of money that are at stake. The government has found in relation to the COLLINS Class Submarines project for instance, and more recently in relation to White Paper process, that there are almost no sources of alternative information or analysis on key issues in defence policy, including the critical questions of our capability needs and how they can best be satisfied. The ASPI will be charged with providing an alternative source of expertise on such issues. Second, public debate of defence policy is inhibited by a poor understanding of the choices and issues involved. The ASPI will be tasked to contribute an informed and independent voice to public discussion on these issues.[11]

It is a mature government, confident in its own policy processes, that takes steps to create an independent organisation to provide 'alternative information or analysis' of policy issues. I do not know if John Howard consciously made the connection between the creation of the NSC – an orderly clearing house for national security policy – and ASPI, a public body designed to provide contestability in policy analysis. I think Howard was aware of the risks of too much policy incrementalism and group think in national security policy making. ASPI was his solution: a mechanism to challenge whatever policy settings might be dominating Canberra's imagination. By creating these two bodies Howard was not simply making 'administrative decisions' as he claims in his autobiography. He was also shaping how Australia has debated and thought-through difficult national security issues over the last several decades.

Endnotes

1. John Howard, *Lazarus Rising: A personal and political autobiography* (Harper Collins, 2010) pp. 237-8.
2. Liberal National Coalition, *A Strong Australia: Rebuilding Australia's Defences.* (Canberra, October 1992) pp. 130-2. A PDF is available here: https://parlinfo.aph.gov.au/parlInfo/search/display/display.w3p;query=Id:%22library/partypol/1145624%22.
3. Liberal National Coalition, *Australia's Defence* (1996) p. 4. (Author's collection.)
4. Greg Sheridan, 'Why peace must take priority', *The Weekend Australian*, 22 March 1997, p. 21.
5. Tim Fischer, quoted by the ABC, The Howard Years – Episode 2: Whatever it Takes. Series first aired November-December 2008. Available here: https://www.youtube.com/watch?v=ZhDGvN_JQbs.
6. The letter is available as an appendix in: David Connery, *Crisis Policymaking: Australia and East Timor Crisis of 1999.* (ANU, E-Press, 2010). https://press-files.anu.edu.au/downloads/press/p501/html/appedix.xhtml?referer=&page=13#toc-anchor.
7. Howard, p. 337.
8. Ibid., p. 342.
9. Brendan Nelson, Address to the 2017 Chief of Airforce Sympo-

sium - political perspective. Canberra, 3 March 2017. https://www.awm.gov.au/commemoration/speeches/2017-chief-airforce-symposium.

10. Howard, p. 238.
11. Cabinet memorandum JH00/0131 – Establishment of the Australian Strategic Policy Institute – Decision, 18 April 2000. https://recordsearch.naa.gov.au/SearchNRetrieve/NAAMedia/ShowImage.aspx?B=202981504&T=PDF.

10

The Prime Minister's Office: Anticipation, Coordination, or Spin Doctors?

James Walter

An enduring legacy of John Howard's prime ministerial term (1996-2007) was the elaboration of systematic prime ministerial government. It was founded on, and extended, institutional changes undertaken by earlier prime ministers. The centrality of the Prime Minister's Office (PMO) in policy networks was a feature of this development. After 2007, those who had been involved in the Howard administration spoke admiringly of a 'prime ministerial machine' which, handled appropriately, facilitated anticipation of demands, co-ordinated action on policy objectives, and effective communication. They warned, too, of its capacity to 'chew up' anyone who took command without understanding the history of the machine. In this chapter I explore the prime ministerial machine in relation to Howard's achievements, and the warning signs of flaws that would confound his successors.

Foundations

The development of the Prime Minister's Office as we understand it today stems from the 1970s and initiatives taken by Gough Whitlam and Malcolm Fraser.[1] It was Gough Whitlam who began the trend. In revitalising the Labor Party after years in opposition, and developing a policy agenda related to contemporary challenges, Whitlam recruited advisers with particular expertise while preparing for office.

He took some of them into government when the time came, intending to shake up the Australian Public Service (APS). The architect of this transition – the elaboration of ministerial private offices, and of the PMO, under Whitlam's auspices – was a public servant, Dr Peter Wilenski. When Labor took office in 1972, Wilenski was appointed as Whitlam's principal private secretary in the PMO.

Wilenski at first conceived the PMO as a policy driver, which, along with an associated policy unit, would give a lead to the public service. It soon became clear to him that this was not feasible, that the APS was where change was to be achieved. He later concentrated upon this, urging the establishment of what became the Royal Commission on Australian Government Administration (RCAGA), headed by Nugget Coombs. Nonetheless, the PMO played a conspicuous part in liaison with the APS, in the promotion of the Labor government's objectives, and in some of its notable mishaps.[2]

Malcolm Fraser, though critical of Whitlam's expansion of ministerial staff (which he reduced upon coming to office) was not inclined to abandon the additional resource that the enhanced PMO provided. In conjunction, a Media unit was established to enhance public communication. Fraser's principal private secretary, David Kemp, a Professor of Politics on secondment from Monash University, redesigned the PMO to instil discipline and to differentiate specific policy, media and party liaison functions. Fraser's staffers were arguably less in the news than Whitlam's 'eggheads' had been, but it would be a mistake to underestimate their influence on policy development.[3]

The Hawke and Keating Labor governments adopted the PMO model that Whitlam and Fraser had instituted and beefed up the media unit Fraser had introduced. Notably, it was under Labor that the careers of senior APS officers became dependent on the good will of government as was implicit in Labor's *Public Service Reform Act 1984* (Cth) and later explicit with Keating's introduction of contract appointments and limited tenure. Howard took this further: his government's *Public Service Act 1999* (Cth) gave the prime minister the power to appoint and terminate departmental secretaries.

These changes were paralleled by further enhancement of the PMO. It grew from 17 staff under Hawke to 30 under Keating: Howard would boost it to over 40.[4] Hawke had enormous self-belief, but also a rare gift for distributed leadership, allowing others to get on with their jobs and promoting collective governance.[5] During the Hawke and Keating governments, there was relatively smooth collaboration between the PMO and the APS. Meredith Edwards has analysed their joint input into Labors' reform agenda.[6] Key to this was ensuring that ministerial offices, especially the PMO, were staffed not solely by party insiders and policy activists, but also by able public servants – especially in principal private secretary (PPS) roles.

Consequently, prior to John Howard's ascension to the prime ministership in 1996, there had been steady augmentation of executive power in relation to parliament, the direction of the APS and management of public communication, along with a consolidation of resources in ministerial offices and the PMO. It was a project of both major parties of government. Where balance had been achieved – between independent policy experts, experienced bureaucrats, and party insiders – it had been an effective means of communicating and implementing government objectives. That balance depended upon respect, trust, and collaborative relationships between key agents – departmental secretaries, independent experts, media advisers and ministerial staff – especially as mediated by the principal private secretary to their leader: the minister or prime minister. These were the foundations upon which John Howard's Liberal-National Party Government (1996-2007) relied to achieve an unusually prolonged period of government under a single leader, rivalled only by Robert Menzies (1949-1966).

The build-up of resources around leaders reflected historical changes affecting not only Australia, but most liberal democracies.

The late twentieth century was the age of dealignment, in which class loyalties, party membership and partisan affiliation declined. Parties instead turned to communications professionals and expert advisers rather than party members to sustain their activities. Party leaders and their 'messaging' became more prominent, not only in campaigning, but in everyday politics. Success was '… now seen to revolve around the choice of leaders rather than the choice of policies or programs, while the formation of those policies or programs became the prerogative of the party leadership rather than the party membership'.[7]

The leader's responsibility for the Coalition's fortunes

Howard was eager to take up that prerogative, with a clear set of policies and programs. His political courage in pursuing objectives was soon apparent in his drive for gun law reform, against some resistance within the Coalition, after the Port Arthur massacre of 1996.[8] It was a harbinger of the determination with which he would pursue his agenda. He aimed to ensure balanced budgets and to overturn the prevailing tenets of industrial relations, reducing union power and deregulating the labour market. Labour market flexibility would, he believed, engender productivity, driving growth, prosperity, jobs and choice. He would use all the augmented institutional resources at his command to this end, and demonstrated remarkable policy consistency.[9] He was also acutely aware that campaigning, and leadership, had been accentuated by party change, saying in 1996 that 'for many years now, election campaigns have been very presidential, and I knew from that moment on, most of the responsibility for the Coalition's fortunes would rest with me'.[10]

Howard instituted 'the permanent campaign'.[11] He prefaced each policy announcement with a statement of the values it served and its part in his broader mission. He consolidated the 'government' media units, which had emerged from Whitlam onwards, to ensure PMO oversight of all aspects of publicity. Howard drew on polling advice for insights into mobilising underlying attitudes or shifting opinions, and was well served by Lynton Crosby, from the party organisation, and party pollster and analyst Mark Textor.[12] Finally, like Menzies in distrusting print journalists, Howard focused on radio as a primary medium of dissemination.[13] Not only did this allow direct address to an audience, but also his comments were transcribed and distributed to the Press Gallery. Journalists raising questions were referred by the PMO to those transcripts. This encouraged blanket coverage without the cross-examination of interviews and press conferences, which were indulged increasingly sparingly.[14]

Howard's hands on control of communication had two purposes: to ensure that the public were aware of his agenda and why it served their interests; and to expedite clear direction of the APS and its agencies. In relation to the former, eventually he could rightly claim whether people liked him or not, they knew what he stood for. With respect to the latter, it facilitated anticipation and coordination among those charged with developing and implementing policy. The success of this enterprise depended upon three things: management of the party; Cabinet discipline and coordination of the PMO and the Department of Prime Minister & Cabinet (PM&C).

Management of party, cabinet and government business

Howard knew that philosophical direction was a necessary but not sufficient condition to hold the party together. He ensured that the party machine worked for him by establishing close relationships between the PMO and the federal secretariat of the Liberal Party. Tony Eggleton, long term federal director, had served a succession of Liberal prime ministers, and now Eggleton worked with him. He established similar closeness with Eggleton's successors, Andrew Robb, Lynton Crosby and Brain Loughnane, involving them in strategy and heeding their advice. Robb and Crosby were integral to the communication and refinement of his message, in teaching him how to capture public opinion.

In the parliamentary party, he remained visible and accessible to his backbenchers. He reminded his ministers of the importance of visiting electorates, even marginal seats, as he never ceased to do. It was a way to refresh information. As Paul Kelly observed, 'He is the most domestically travelled Prime Minister in the nation's history, in the regions and in the cities, and is proud of his local knowledge'.[15] This won the loyalty of MPs, demonstrated good faith to the party base, and connected with constituents. Management of party sentiment, ability in working with the party organisation and the generation of loyalty led even his critics to concede that finally he 'owned' the party.[16]

Action of course depended upon Cabinet. Howard was both committed to and respectful of Cabinet government. 'I was determined that the system would function properly and productively', he said. 'The key was to restore a fully functioning and orderly system of cabinet government, with all the major decisions … being made by cabinet or its properly functioning committees'.[17] After his election, Howard established a Cabinet policy unit (CPU), whose head was to be Cabinet secretary. Adjacent to his office, and run initially by his adviser, Michael L'Estrange, it was a transfer of the management of Cabinet business from PM&C to Howard's own strategists. It facilitated two streams of advice – departmental and political – enabling Howard to determine the balance but ensuring political control of policy. L'Estrange's successor, Paul McClintock, said that:

> Howard described at it as the 'link point between the office and the bureaucracy'. Neither totally inside one or the other We certainly didn't see ourselves as part of the PMO … But we weren't part of the bureaucracy either. We were the go-to people from both ends.[18]

Yet decisions went back through Cabinet, where Howard's behaviour ensured a calm deliberative process. In Paul Kelly's view Howard became one of the most effective post-war practitioners of Cabinet government, running ideas though the party room and into Cabinet, insisting on Cabinet debate, focusing presentations, listening to views but then locking his colleagues into Cabinet determinations and achieving a dominance that deterred dissidents and leaks.[19] His Cabinet was the most unified since that of Menzies.

If the CPU was the link-point between the PMO and PM&C, the relationship between the leading figure in the PMO – now designated Chief of Staff (COS) – and PM&C remained integral. Anne Tiernan has stressed the importance of this, noting that the relationship was not initially smooth but that Howard learned quickly from early mistakes:

> … the organisational foundations for the Howard Government's success were laid in the period that followed the 'travel rorts' controversy of September 1997 … Changes instituted by [a] new Chief of Staff (later Senator) Arthur Sinodinos laid the foundations of the unusually stable and highly effective advisory system that supported John Howard for most of his long tenure.[20]

Sinodinos was a partisan loyalist, but also an experienced public servant. He brought to bear political understanding, appreciation of the prime minister's objectives and bureaucratic experience in achieving order in the PMO and facilitating the networks necessary for policy development. The CPU relieved the PMO of responsibility for long term planning to concentrate on political and tactical imperatives, yet policy objectives remained primary.

In this, the stable relationships fostered by Sinodinos were crucial. Dr Peter Shergold, Secretary of PM&C (2002–2007) said:

> There would probably have been no day when I was not in touch with one of the policy advisers in the prime minister's office … And I would have regular contact in person or by telephone with the prime minister … It was a strong relationship. A lot of the relationship was about policy and Arthur … well, I think he was quite exceptional … because he liked policy. And he was interested.

Shergold added that Howard,

> was very clear in understanding the difference between Arthur's role and my role. He would conscientiously remind others in his office, more junior policy advisers or particularly the media advisors of that role.[21]

Ideally, policy development and implementation would be collaborative. But the intention behind the development of the PMO was clear: it was to be an office with the capacity not only to engage with, but to direct the public service, and an unrivalled ability to dictate the government's story.

The PMO and the prime ministerial machine: handle with care

Howard expanded upon the logic of what his predecessors had initiated. In doing so, he clarified the potential of prime ministerial government and the existence of a prime ministerial machine, with the PMO at its core. Those involved were aware of this. Cabinet Secretary McClintock reflected:

> The office amplifies the prime minister. So, if the prime minister is in strife, he amplifies that, makes it worse. If the prime minister is on top of the job, it amplifies it. It makes that control more effective … And the truth is also people's expectations and the media … the leader is assessed and re-assessed all the time … the fortunes of the government rise and fall on that one individual. And the power of the office, to some extent, also reflects the fact that they all know that.[22]

Further, said Alan Rose, after lengthy service in senior APS roles:

> If a prime minister comes in and doesn't understand the history of the machine … they're inheriting, they're at a grave disadvantage and are likely to be chewed up by it … Outside of the government, outside of the prime min-

> ister's office – the media, the lobbies – all have grown to have a particular understanding of what the prime minister is capable of. I don't mean personally but what … his or her machine is capable of, what they're responsible for and what they should be doing. It's not so much the character of the individual but the office and what the office has become that dictates the way it works … Now John Howard commanded it superbly. He knew what he was getting … he commanded it … He took it on in a particular way and ran it in his way.[23]

Yet there were inherent flaws in the ministerial staffing system, and the PMO, which had been there from their inception under Whitlam and Fraser. An enhanced capacity for direction and control was not matched by systematic constraints on, or transparent scrutiny and accountability for ministerial staff. Adverse potential had been held in check because there had been a balance between partisan advisers and bureaucratic professionals: namely, the practice by prime ministers of retaining experienced public servants in key roles within the PMO. Bureaucratic networks were known, the inherent APS concern for a professional ethic was understood, cooperative endeavour and mutual trust could develop. This was evident during the Hawke and Keating administrations and for the most part under Howard.

However, there were telling instances where Howard's pragmatism, capacity to control the prime ministerial machine and acute sense of what the public would accept were interrupted by episodes of crisis management which provoked concern about misinformation, PMO overreach, a reluctance by senior officials to tell the Prime Minister what he needed to hear, and failures of coordination. Two illustrative examples were the 'children overboard' affair of 2001, and the closeted decision-making leading to the Australian commitment to the war in Iraq in 2003.

In 2001, to manage what it saw as a crisis in maintaining 'sovereign borders' in the face of sea-borne incursions by asylum seekers avoiding controlled entry, the government developed the 'Pacific solution': provision for the navy to intercept sea-faring asylum seekers and to transport them to offshore centres where they would be held until their claims were processed. Two months later, shortly before the 2001 election, ministers Phillip Ruddock (Immigration), Peter Reith (Defence) and Howard, acting on incomplete information and images, announced that asylum seekers whose boat was intercepted by the navy, had thrown their children into the sea in the hope that rescue would secure passage to Australia. In reality, as the boat was sinking, navy personnel had leapt into the sea to rescue children and others. Yet the difficulty of reconciling contradictory accounts of who knew what and when in the heat of a campaign ensured that a more accurate picture did not emerge until after the election. Some believed this to be deliberate obfuscation.[24]

Equally contentious, was Howard's solo post 9/11 pledge, in a time of geopolitical turmoil, to stand with America against its enemies. Hence the government's subsequent commitment to the Iraq war, despite adverse public opinion and insufficient intelligence as to the alleged trigger for invasion: Saddam Hussein's supposed possession of weapons of mass destruction (WMD). There was a lack of forward thinking, with no serious anticipation about the restoration of functioning institutions after the invasion. Decisions were restricted to an inner circle, though later strongly supported by Cabinet. It was apparent that countervailing advice was not welcome, and that neither the Department of Foreign Affairs and Trade (DFAT) nor Defence conveyed reservations about the available intelligence or the Iraq strategy to government.[25]

The extensive discussion provoked by each of these examples revealed a common pattern.[26] There were serial failures of senior public servants to tell Howard and his ministers when they were wrong, influenced by the PMO and other ministerial staff. Senior officials' efforts to find evidence to support the government's story in relation to 'children overboard' and Iraq's alleged WMD capacities, for example, were identified. This persistence convinced observers that public service 'responsiveness' had gone so far as to inhibit officials from telling government other than what it wanted to hear.[27] Ministerial staff were significant influencers, not simply cooperating with officials, but improperly attempting to direct them and to control or 'spin' the dissemination of information. Anne Tiernan's and Patrick Weller's studies of 'children overboard' showed staffers to have intervened in departmental processes and mediated between the political and administrative domains. They demanded information directly from departmental officers. Their emphasis on what ministers wanted stifled due attention to the public interest or the integrity of processes. Then they suppressed inconvenient detail in communicating with the media, and possibly with their political masters.[28]

Howard and his ministers took refuge in 'plausible deniability' – when inconvenient details emerged, they maintained that advisers (both public servants and personal staffers) did not pass on crucial information. Such incidents did not of themselves precipitate the defeat of the Howard Government. But they did serve to highlight the incipient flaws in the prime ministerial machine that Howard had, in other respects, controlled remarkably effectively. Would others prove equally able in managing the machine, or would they be 'chewed up' by it?

Revolving door prime ministerships: From Kevin Rudd to Scott Morrison

Howard's success hinged upon six factors, but the key to their productive articulation was an identifiable mission, consistency and the web of connections between his PMO and PM&C in enabling command of the prime ministerial machine. These factors, and the points where PMO and PM&C leverage was predictable, were:

- A sense of purpose; clarity of objectives (key ideas were developed in opposition, but advisers and then the PMO and the APS/PM&C were key to their practical application).

- Translation of the above into realistic policy projects, capable of implementation subject to proficient administration (both personal advisers and APS officials refined and co-ordinated policy development, and administrative efficiency depended on productive relationships between leading figures in the PMO and PM&C: the potential flaw, disputation between political and policy streams).
- Determination, and political courage when necessary (witness gun law reform and, later, the fraught introduction of the Goods and Services Tax).
- Effective communication, to staff, public servants, stakeholders and through the media to the electorate (Howard's own ability and media savvy was much enhanced by specialists in the PMO, the party organisation and polling agencies: the potential flaws, PMO control of the dissemination of information, partial, misleading data and 'spin', loyalists telling their principal what they think he wants rather than what he needs to know).
- Unifying and carrying the party (parliamentary, and extra-parliamentary) with you (Howard exercised Cabinet discipline, kept his backbench happy, worked closely with party officials, and ceaselessly visited party branches to spread the message and hear their concerns).
- Winning the vote (here the APS is factored out, but staffers and their media networks are essential in the 'permanent campaign', are core players in the campaign proper, and continually scrutinise polling data: precipitate drops in indicators of electoral support threaten a leader's survival).

After 2007, Australia entered an era of 'disposable leaders'.[29] Until 2019, there was little synchronisation between the tenure of prime ministers and the rise and fall of Labor and Coalition governments. Instead, incumbents were serially removed from office by their colleagues. The national and international contingencies of our historical moment – financial crises, energy turmoil and the pandemic – played their part. Yet in facing these challenges, I argue that each failed on one or more elements in managing what were now the expectations of prime ministerial government, elements that had a history stretching back to the 1970s but that were clarified by Howard's prime ministerial machine.

Rudd, Gillard, Rudd

Kevin Rudd won a commanding victory for the Labor Party in 2007. He had gained advancement in his party by demonstrating his capacity in media performance, which promised delivery of the vote, and now it had paid off. He assumed office with popularity ratings that matched those of Bob Hawke. Rudd spoke of big ideas, moral challenges, and new beginnings, but reassured voters anxious about change by representing himself as even more economically responsible than Howard. He conveyed a sense of purpose and was manifestly a master of effective communication. He and a small team of senior ministers and public servants were credited with saving Australia from the worst effects of the Global Financial Crisis (GFC). Then, after little more than two years, he was overthrown by his party Caucus.

What cruelled his leadership was 'a string of dysfunctional relationships within the PMO and between the wider government and bureaucracy, and between the prime minister and the Labor Party, Cabinet and, fatally, Caucus as a whole. A common source of these failed relationships was Rudd's refusal to devolve power'.[30] When, having designated climate change a great moral challenge, Rudd walked away from the battle to gain support for his legislation, his popularity plummeted. Opponents, convinced that he no longer had the capacity to win the impending 2010 election, successfully mobilised against him, generating a spill of the leadership, which installed Julia Gillard as party leader and prime minister. Effective communication, big ideas and a sense of purpose were not enough when initiatives did not generate policy resolution, Rudd had been increasingly immured in the PMO and estranged from PM&C; political courage failed, him destroying his strongest card (capacity to win the vote); and he had alienated the party.

Gillard won the 2010 election, after negotiating support from the Greens to sustain a minority government. In some respects, she showed considerable capacity for leadership. She was a proficient administrator, a policy realist and the closer on many of the initiatives that Rudd had failed to complete, including an emissions trading scheme. She was disciplined, maintained self-control under enormous pressure, had the confidence of her staff and was highly regarded by her departmental secretary, Terry Moran. Her PMO did not overstep boundaries, and she was attentive to policy briefs from the APS. She was an adept negotiator and managed the successful passage of more legislation than any of her successors to date have done. Her tragedy was that Labor was not in office long enough for this to be bedded down, allowing the succeeding Coalition government to dismantle much of it. Though her Caucus was riven by supporters of Rudd, she maintained majority support despite a series of internal challenges until near the end of her elected term. But then, as the 2013 election loomed, and the polls ran strongly against Labor (while Rudd's popularity revived), Caucus deposed Gillard and turned back to Rudd to 'save the furniture'. It was to no avail.

Gillard carried the baggage of the coup against Rudd, 'Nice girls don't carry knives.'[31] Despite a small bounce in the polls when she assumed leadership and scraped back to power (in minority government), there was a residual scepticism that benefited the opposition. Moreover, she faced, in then Liberal leader Tony Abbott, a tribal warrior who allowed no quarter, and unremitting antagonism from some elements of the media, which compounded Abbott's assault. Few could doubt her political courage given the adversity she confronted, but she faced a storm that prevented her gaining political capital despite achievement against the odds.[32] Her chief failing was that she could not meet the expectation that a prime minister is spokesperson in chief for her government. Stoicism counted for little when she could not muster the rhetoric to counter what was thrown against her, could not demolish the proposition that her carbon trading scheme was a tax, and could not explain why the inevitability of negotiation and compromise necessary to sustaining minority government did not amount to sacrificing principles.

Abbott, Turnbull, Morrison

Tony Abbott led the Coalition back into government in 2013. He benefited from constantly referencing Labor's civil war, and campaigned on Coalition staples – security, capping immigration, stopping asylum seeker boats, ending Labor's economic irresponsibility – but especially on ending the 'carbon tax'. He was regarded as having almost single-handedly destroyed the Labor government, but his speciality was three-word slogans of denunciation rather than a purposeful direction for his administration. He had produced a manifesto in *Battlelines* (2009), but no coherent program followed.[33] He entered office with a low popularity rating.

Once in power, Abbott demolished Labor's initiatives, introduced a poorly received austerity budget, dithered about reduced immigration and federal reform, proved politically timid on issues that he had advanced in his book, and made idiosyncratic 'Captain's calls' that bemused many. Socially conservative, he regarded the right-wing among his supporters as the party base. This pushed him to positions at odds with majority opinion. His poll ratings continued to slide. Within the party, there was the habitual worry: could he deliver the vote? Dissatisfaction was exacerbated by the degree to which Abbott relied upon his PMO for support and direction, and especially his reliance on his chief of staff, Peta Credlin. Eventually, in 2015, Malcolm Turnbull, a more moderate Liberal with high popularity ratings, challenged Abbott and won. Abbott provides, alongside Rudd, a case study of how retreat into the PMO can destroy an administration.[34]

Turnbull becoming prime minister was a telling reversal. Abbott had displaced him as party leader in 2009 when Turnbull began negotiating with Rudd on an emissions trading scheme. His return seemed the restoration of a small 'l' liberal order. But his party was more interested in a restoration of its electoral fortunes. The paradox was that such popularity relied upon Turnbull's effective communication of promises that were more progressive than those of Abbott and hence closer to majority opinion. Yet some in the Coalition could not stomach such an agenda. Consequently, Turnbull could not carry the party with him. Intra-party impediments to delivering much that he had undertaken eroded that crucial vote winning capacity. Eventually, when a signature policy ambition – the National Energy Guarantee – collapsed in discord, he was challenged by Peter Dutton. Yet in the ensuing spill of positions, Scott Morrison managed to manoeuvre through the middle to snatch the leadership, becoming prime minister in August 2018.[35]

In the ensuing election of 2019, Morrison seemed the answer to the Coalition's problems. He proved a formidable one-man-band in campaigning, able to overturn Labor's apparent polling lead by representing its ambitious policy agenda as economically irresponsible and to capitalise on public ambivalence about its leader, Bill Shorten, by representing him as 'the Bill you can't afford'. It was an exercise honed through focus-group and polling research – an extraordinarily effective negative campaign.[36] That it was so centred on Morrison himself rather than a government team (just as Rudd's 2007 campaign had been) was indicative of problems that soon became acute.

That Morrison was outcomes driven, hard-working and had committed allies and supporters within his party was undeniable. Yet his success in earlier portfolios depended on application to a particular brief; he was unable to adapt to the team building and collective management demanded of a prime minister. Obsessed with controlling the daily theatre of politics, managing perceptions rather than considering what must be done, Morrison failed to anticipate the big challenges. When they arrived, there was hesitancy, inadequate planning and backlash from a disheartened public.

Yet Morrison was conscious of the potential of the prime ministerial machine. He installed as Secretary of PM&C, Philip Gaetjens – a distinguished public servant, but one inevitably seen as a partisan appointment given previous lengthy employment by Peter Costello and Morrison himself. In parallel, staff in the PMO, obliged to cater to his penchant for secrecy and spin, increased. Having ensured both an APS and a PMO geared to respond to his wishes, Morrison's enterprise was undermined by the lack of any guiding purpose for government. Even John Howard finally, ruefully, conceded that, 'The absence of a program for the future … the absence of some kind of manifesto, hurt us very badly'.[38]

The public soured. The Coalition lost the 2022 election. Soon after, the startling revelation of Morrison's adoption of ministerial powers in five additional portfolios, of which, in four cases, neither Cabinet, the serving minister nor the relevant department was made aware, underlined Morrison's preoccupation with power and raised serious questions of propriety. A press conference in which he claimed to have assumed emergency powers needed as a back-up during the pandemic persuaded few. Morrison implicated his staff, saying 'people in the department and the people in my office … were directly responsible for managing these specific things'.[39] The Solicitor General concluded that Morrison's self-appointments were not illegal, but that their secrecy precluded transparent accountability and so was not consistent with the principle of responsible government.[40] By now, the rage in the Liberal Party against Morrison was palpable, and even senior figures, including Howard and the new party leader Dutton, conceded his action was wrong. It was a defining instance of McClintock's observation a decade earlier that if the prime minister is not on top of the job, '[the office] amplifies that, makes it worse'.[41]

Conclusion

John Howard, along with Bob Hawke, was one of the most effective prime ministers since Robert Menzies. Both benefited from the augmentation of executive resources initiated by Gough Whitlam and Malcolm Fraser. Where Hawke encouraged distributed leadership allowing diverse talents to flourish within his ministry, Howard perfected the art of prime ministerial government, using his Prime Minister's Office (PMO), command of the Department of Prime Minister and Cabinet (PM&C) and Cabinet discipline to pursue a reform agenda. Both Hawke and Howard conveyed determination and a shared sense of purpose, with effective communication.

Successors have struggled with their inheritance. Kevin Rudd had lofty ambitions and was a masterful communicator, initially generating great popularity. But he was a persistent centraliser who operated with a small inner circle, remained over-reliant on his PMO, alienated the Australian Public Service (APS) and finally lost the confidence of his colleagues. Julia Gillard was an effective administrator, won the loyalty of her staff and the confidence of the APS, demonstrated considerable talent as a negotiator, and achieved legislative success. In better circumstances, she may have succeeded in establishing distributed leadership. But she failed as communicator-in-chief for her government.

Tony Abbott was a political warrior who thrived in opposition but failed in government. Insufficiently engaged with the APS, immured in his PMO, seen as over-reliant on his Chief of Staff (COS), Peta Credlin, insufficiently consultative and eccentric in his choices, the prime ministerial machine stuttered until Malcolm Turnbull was installed in his stead. Turnbull, like Rudd, was full of ideas, established a credible PMO and began to build effective relations with the APS, especially in co-operative development of policy. But he was incapable of unifying the party behind his agenda.

Scott Morrison was, as were they all, a person ambitious to exercise power. But for him, this seemed to be all. His agenda was piecemeal and inconsequential until the pandemic demanded a more applied discipline and deference to expertise. Even then, there were failures of planning and coordination that provoked public backlash. His department was seen as politicised, the APS as hobbled, and his PMO as defensive, secretive and addicted to spin. The startling revelation of Morrison's 'secret ministries', especially if facilitated by the PMO and PM&C as Morrison indicated, convinces me that here, despite its potential to amplify a good leader, Morrison's misunderstanding of how to harness the prime ministerial machine to a cause allowed its inherent flaws to flourish. The 2022 election result suggests that many people share such impressions, but also hope that Labor's promise of transparent, consensual leadership will be realised. That remains to be seen.

Endnotes

1. In describing here the development of the Prime Ministers' office between the 1970s and the mid-1990s, I draw on my previous works, *The Ministers' Minders: personal advisers in national government*, Oxford University Press, Melbourne, 1986; 'Ministers, minders and public servants: changing parameters of responsibility in Australia', *Australian Journal of Public Administration*, vol. 65, no. 3, 2006, pp. 22-7; and 'Whitlam's transformation of the prime ministerial office, its precursors and all that followed' in Jenny Hocking (ed.) *Making Modern Australia: The Whitlam Government's 21st Century Agenda*, Monash University Publishing, Melbourne, pp. 242-69.
2. See Paul Strangio, Paul 't Hart and James Walter, *The Pivot of Power: Australian Prime Ministers and Political Leadership, 1949-2016*, Miegunyah Press, Melbourne, 2017, pp.109-14.
3. See Strangio et al., pp. 135-40.
4. R.A.W. Rhodes and Anne Tiernan, *Lessons in Governing: Profiles of Prime Ministers' Chiefs of Staff*, Melbourne, Melbourne University Press, 2014, p. 69.
5. Strangio et al., pp. 146-74.
6. See Meredith Edwards with Cosmo Howard and Robin Miller, *Social Policy, Public Policy: From Problem to Practice*, Allen & Unwin, Sydney, 2001.
7. Richard Katz and Peter Mair, 'Changing models of party organiza-

tion and party democracy: the emergence of the cartel party', *Party Politics,* vol. 1, no. 1, 1995, p. 7.

8. Philip Alpers and Zareh Ghazarian, 'The "perfect storm" of gun control: From policy inertia to world leader', in Joannah Luetjens, Michael Mintrom and Paul 't Hart, eds, *Successful Public Policy: Lessons from Australia and New Zealand,* Canberra, ANU Press, 2019, pp. 207-34.
9. See M. L. Murray, *John Howard: A Study in Policy Consistency*, PhD Thesis, Discipline of Politics, University of Adelaide, 2010.
10. John Howard, *Lazarus Rising: A Personal and Political Autobiography,* HarperCollins, Sydney, 2010, p. 222.
11. Peter van Onselen and Wayne Errington, 'The democratic state as a marketing tool: the permanent campaign in Australia, *Commonwealth & Comparative Politics,* vol. 45, no.1, 2007, pp. 78-94.
12. In 2001, Lynton Crosby and Mark Textor established a commercial consultancy but continued to work for the party throughout Howard's term and beyond.
13. Strangio, et al., pp. 209-13.
14. Helen Ester, 'The media', in Clive Hamilton and Sarah Maddison (eds), *Silencing Dissent: How the Australian government is controlling opinion and stifling debate,* Allen & Unwin, Sydney, 2007, pp. 118-22.
15. Paul Kelly, *Re-thinking Australian Governance: The Howard Legacy,* Cunningham Lecture 2005, Academy of the Social Sciences in Australia, Canberra, 2005, p. 10.
16. Guy Rundle, *The Opportunist: John Howard and the Triumph of Reaction*, Quarterly Essay No. 3, Black Inc., Melbourne, 2001.
17. Howard, p. 237.
18. Paul McClintock, interview with James Walter, 2 February 2012.
19. Kelly, pp. 3-4
20. Anne Tiernan, 'Staffing the the PM's office – a key to national leadership', in Tom Frame, ed., *Back From the Brink, 1997–2001: The Howard Government, Vol II*, Sydney, UNSW Press, Sydney, 2019, p. 64.
21. Both remarks from Dr Peter Shergold, interview with James Walter, 22 February 2012.

22. McLintock interview, 2 February 2012.
23. Alan Rose, interview with James Walter, 3 February 2012.
24. See Patrick Weller, *Don't Tell the Prime Minister*, Melbourne, Scribe Books, 2002.
25. Parliamentary Joint Committee on ASIO, ASIS and DSD, *Intelligence on Iraq's weapons of mass destruction,* Canberra, Parliament of the Commonwealth of Australia, 2003; P. Flood, *Report of the Inquiry into Australian Intelligence Agencies*, Canberra, Australian Government, 2004; Paul Kelly, *The March of the Patriots: The Struggle for Modern Australia*, Melbourne, Melbourne University Press, 2009, pp. 260-2.
26. See Weller, for a detailed exposition of the pattern.
27. Kelly, *Re-thinking Australian* Governance, pp. 5-7; Andrew Podger, 'What Really Happens: Department Secretary Appointments, Contracts and Performance Pay in the Australian Public Service', *Australian Journal of Public Administration*, vol. 66, no. 2, 2007, pp. 143-6; Michael Keating, 'In the Wake of "A Certain Maritime Incident": Ministerial Advisers, Departments and Accountability', *Australian Journal of Public Administration*, 2003, vol. 62, no 3, pp. 92-7.
28. Anne Tiernan, *Power Without Responsibility,* UNSW Press, Sydney, pp. 171-208; Weller, *Don't Tell the Prime Minister.*
29. Rod Tiffen, *Disposable Leaders: Media and Leadership Coups from Menzies to Abbott,* NewSouth, Sydney, 2017, pp. 18-69.
30. Strangio et al., p. 249.
31. The opening, and since much cited, sentence in Michelle Grattan, 'Finessing a flagrant backflip', *Sydney Morning Herald*, 26 June, 2010, Finessing a flagrant backflip (smh.com.au), accessed 26 August 2022.
32. See James Walter, 'No loans for ladies: Julia Gillard and capital denied', in Mark Bennister, Ben Worthy and Paul 't Hart, eds, *The Leadership Capital Index: A New Perspective of Political Leadership,* Oxford University Press, Oxford, 2017, pp. 45-62.
33. See Tony Abbott, *Battlelines*, Melbourne: Melbourne University Press, 2009.
34. See Aaron Patrick, *Credlin & Co.: How the Abbott Government*

Destroyed Itself, Black Inc., Melbourne, 2016; Watne Errington and Peter van Onselen, *Battleground: Why the Liberal Party Shirtfronted Tony Abbott,* Melbourne University Press, Melbourne, 2015.

35. Sean Kelly, *The Game: A Portrait of Scott Morrison,* Black Inc., Melbourne, 2021, pp. 25-35; Anika Smethurst, *The Accidental Prime Minister,* Hachette, Melbourne, 2021, pp. 215-43.

36. Paul Strangio and James Walter, 'The personalization of the campaign', in Anika Gauja, Marian Sawer and Marian Simms, eds, *Morrison's Miracle: The 2019 Australian Federal Election,* ANU Press, 2020, pp. 107-24.

37. James Walter, 'Power without purpose', *Inside Story,* 24 September 2021, https://insidestory.org.au/power-without-purpose/, accessed 24 September 2021.

38. Brian Hevesi, 'John Howard reflects on the Liberals defeat at the Federal Election under Scott Morrison', *Sky News,* 13 August 2022, https://www.skynews.com.au/australia-news/politics/john-howard-reflects-on-the-liberals-defeat-at-the-federal-election-under-scott-morrison/news-story/942fff69d43e64438bbd4b8dba4a447a accessed 20 August 2022.

39. Morrison is quoted in Lisa Visentin, 'Prime ministerial staff face calls to explain what they knew about Morrison's secret ministries', *The Age,* 24 August 2022, https://www.theage.com.au/politics/federal/prime-ministerial-staff-face-calls-to-explain-what-they-knew-about-morrison-s-secret-ministries-20220824-p5bcc8.html?btis, accessed 24 August 2022.

40. Scott Morrison's secret ministries – what we learned from the Solicitor General's advice', *ABC News,* 23 August 2022, https://www.abc.net.au/news/2022–08-23/scott-morrison-secret-ministries-solicitor-general-investigation/101360028, accessed 23 August 2022.

41. See full quotation above, note 22.

11

LIVE EXPORT: THE GIFT THAT KEEPS ON GIVING

This paper was not presented at the conference but was kindly submitted and subsequently accepted as an addition to this series.

Fiona Wade

John Howard made no secret he believed in less red tape and industry adopting self-regulation. His unwavering commitment to business operating as efficient and streamlined as possible worked for many industries and businesses alike. I would suggest, however, that leaving the regulation of the animal live export industry in the hands of the export companies was a disaster waiting to happen. Not least because, waiting in the wings, was a very effective animal welfare lobby that understood the value the community places on the lives and welfare of animals and who enthusiastically embraced the social media revolution.

The ability to influence government policy agenda is considered one of the most important sources of political power by both politicians and advocates.

> Governments at both state and federal levels are forced to make concessions to certain interest groups ... because they [the interest groups] have it in their power to promote or frustrate the achievement of the government's objectives.[1]

If the above statement is true, little wonder that advocating on behalf of interest groups, has become a multimillion-dollar industry. There are countless social movements worldwide that attract like-minded supporters to speak as one voice, with the singular aim of influencing policy decision-makers. There is also no doubt media is a useful tool for social movements to build support.

The animal welfare lobby has had a profound effect on media discourse – by defining and framing their grievances to attract media attention. Using the images of distressed animals as a backdrop to change government policy, is an example, and one the live export trade seems happy to accommodate.

In June 2011, the Gillard Government was faced with a hard choice: ban completely Australia's multi-billion-dollar live export of cattle trade *or* suspend it (pending the implementing of a regulatory system that would assure compliance with welfare standards). Doing nothing was not an option. The government chose to place a six-month ban on Australia's live cattle exports to Indonesia until the Exporter Supply Chain Assurance System (ESCAS) was in place. This occurred following an Australian Broadcasting Corporation (ABC) *Four Corners* investigation, in collaboration with the animal welfare lobby, featuring disturbing and gruesome footage of the treatment of Australian cattle in Indonesian abattoirs. The footage was so shocking it initiated an intense public outcry, demanding the government act. The timing of the 2011 ban, could not have been more poorly received by cattle producers, coming during the thick of the crucial cattle mustering period – with thousands of cattle stranded in depots south of Darwin or enroute to ports. Northern cattle began flooding southern markets placing further pressure on prices while devastating farmers and regional economies. The ban had a multiplying impact on helicopter pilots, hay producers, and other industries that relied directly or indirectly on the live cattle trade, and on the value of land.

2011 was not the first-time live export had come under the microscope, nor the first time it had featured prominently in daily media. Since the 1970s, when Australia first began investing heavily in the live export of animals to Asia and the Middle East, there has been a parallel rise in the public's concern for the welfare of animals often fuelled by sporadic public reports of mistreatment. There have been several watershed moments for the live export trade, two of which occurred during the Howard Government: the first in 2003, involving stranded sheep in the Middle East, and the second in 2006 involving the inhumane slaughter of cattle in Egypt. On both occasions, while trade was suspended and inquiries held, there were limited long-term repercussions for exporters. This response leaves us to contemplate whether events that occurred in 2011 could have been prevented had the Howard Government acted differently.

2003: MV *Cormo Express*

On 6 August 2003, the MV *Cormo Express* embarked from Fremantle, Western Australia with some 57,000 sheep on board, bound for the Middle East. Two weeks later, on arrival in Saudi Arabia, officials denied permission for the sheep to be offloaded, claiming diseased stock. What ensued was nothing short of a nightmare for the livestock. The ship was to spend the next two and a half months (80 days) sailing in scorching heat around the Middle East in search of a port willing to take the animals. First, the ship sailed to Jordan, then onto the United Arab Emirates, and Kuwait, taking onboard extra feed and other supplies at the ports of the latter two countries. Reports suggest that some 30 nations were approached by the Australian Government. After the government committed $10 million and employed three months of round-the-clock diplomacy, the sheep were donated to the northeast African country of Eritrea. The toll was significant: some six-thousand sheep had perished, the livestock industry lost $125 million in revenue, two live export firms closed, and Australia's international reputation had been damaged.

Legislation

The livestock export industry is unique and inherently risky. The industry deals with live animals along an extended production chain. Animal welfare issues arise including loading, voyage, transportation, and arrival at their destination. Notwithstanding these inherent risks, there was little by way of regulation concerning welfare aspects of trade – although live animals had been included in the provision of the *Export Control Act 1982 (Cth)* and the *Australian Meat and Industry LiveStock Act 1997* permitted industry self-regulation.

The *Cormo Express* provided harsh lessons for both the government and industry. The 'Keniry Review', led by Dr John Keniry AM (company director and chemical engineer) concluded its report highlighting the existing legislative and administrative framework was no longer adequate for such a high-risk trade. Keniry recommended that, 'Government must be solely responsible in the relevant legislation for granting export licenses and permits and enforcing compliance by exporters against the national standard'.[2] Self-regulation by industry had failed.

With the regulatory shift from industry to the Commonwealth Government – and the creation of the 'Australian Standards for the Export of Livestock' (AESL) – the Howard Government claimed it was taking significant strides in 'cleaning up' the live export trade. Critics argue the review was flawed; that it was created without parliamentary debate, there was an absence of a working definition of 'animal welfare,' and the terms of reference were restrictive. The government had its back to the wall.

Response

Channel Nine's flagship current affairs program, *60 Minutes* aired 'Ship of Shame' on 21 September with veteran journalist Richard Carleton declaring

> Somewhere in the Middle East tonight, there's a ship of shame, a ship packed with more than 50,000 Australian sheep that no-one wants. Now, it should have been only a 16-day voyage, but these poor animals have now been at sea for 47 days and a large number are known to have died. Now, this is yet another animal-welfare disaster, compounding the case against the Australian live-animal export trade, a trade we first highlighted two months

> ago. Now, that story is still attracting mail from outraged viewers and tonight's will no doubt cause more anger, as some scenes are quite distressing.[3]

The scene was set.

During the program, Carleton spoke to an on-board veterinary doctor, a stockman with experience of the voyage *and* the ship, an animal welfare lobbyist, and the Minister. The ship's plight drew media attention throughout Australia and internationally, including French actress and animal rights campaigner, Brigitte Bardot. Following the airing of the investigative program, the parliamentary gallery took hold of the story. Reporting on the government's progress, or lack thereof, in finding a solution, parliamentary gallery doyen, Michelle Grattan did not hold back: 'The MV *Cormo Express* has [had] become the *Tampa* of the live sheep export trade.'[4] Grattan and members of the press gallery could smell blood. The government's initial reluctance to disclose the location of the ship and its stricken cargo was ill-advised with Agriculture Minister Warren Truss MP defying a Senate order to publicly release information. When the Australian media disclosed the ship's location as being ten nautical miles from Dubai, a spokesman for Minister Truss refused to confirm its accuracy. Secrecy was the order of the day. Truss, who was leading the government's response to the crisis, was on the defensive, most days; keeping the location secret was in the best interest of the animals, he claimed.

> For commentators, reporters, or animal liberation activists to paint the situation in any way that is likely to undermine the confidence of potential buyers is not helpful to the welfare of the sheep.[5]

The public and animal welfare lobby saw the decision to hide the location of the ship as an attempted cover-up. The government's hesitation in releasing sheep mortality rates aboard the *Cormo Express* was concerning. A wave of discontent swept over the government, best illustrated by Carleton when questioning Truss:

> Minister, may I suggest to you it's not very helpful talking to you if you won't reveal the number of dead when the owners of the ship have posted a figure on their website, and yet you're trying to keep it secret.[6]

Truss was on the ropes. When the Minister attempted to quell concerns regarding the health of the sheep, by quoting an on-board vet as saying, 'that apart from the 3800 that have died, the rest have put on weight', Carleton did not hold back. Truss was lambasted for his insensitive remark making it sound like the sheep were enjoying 'some Mediterranean Cruise'.[7] The severity of the issue was not lost on Howard. On entering the debate, Howard agreed with the public's feeling of distress, reassuring it that the animals were being looked after in the best way possible, while also pleading for a sense of balance.

> My latest advice is that fresh supplies of food continue to be taken on board and that the condition of the sheep – according to the veterinary advice we've had – is good. But I do share the distress of many people about this and it worries me, but we have to have a sense of proportion.[8]

Howard continued

> I deplore cruelty, any ordinary human being would and does. But we have to keep these things in perspective, we have to remember that you are talking about a very valuable economic asset … it's just not as easy as you suggest to dismiss the importance of an industry that provides a livelihood to tens of thousands.[9]

As the days and weeks passed reports surfaced of the ship running out of food and the sheep being in distress. The opposition seized on these reports fuelling the perception the prime minister (and his minister) were reluctant to get their hands dirty. Calling on Howard to intervene and secure a suitable port in the Middle East, then Leader of the Opposition, Simon Crean MP argued

> '[i]t's about time the agriculture minister stopped making excuses; the prime minister has to involve himself and make some representations to the Saudis to get the sheep landed.[10]

The opposition were taking the fight to the government.

Fifty-five days into the debacle, and after using taxpayers' money to purchase the sheep from the exporter, the prime minister raised the idea of bringing the sheep home. This caused an instant backlash from the agricultural sector with farming organisations and the livestock industry recoiling from the idea. Senior industry representatives vehemently protested the return of the sheep to Australia fearing 'they may have contracted exotic diseases during their long sea voyage that could ravage this island nation's huge livestock industry'.[11]

Howard acknowledged the sheep could pose a danger to the country's livestock herds, but the situation left him perplexed, saying 'I understand that people are nervous, you're damned if you do and you're damned if you don't'.[12] The idea of slaughtering the remaining sheep at sea was dismissed.

What would be required to slaughter them at sea would not only be graphic but also raise very serious environmental considerations and it would take a very long time, in fact 40 to 50 days.[13]

In the end, Australia gifted the sheep, along with a million dollars' worth of feed, to the State of Eritrea. Given the Kingdom of Saudi Arabia rejected the sheep on 28 August, and the sheep were finally unloaded some eight weeks later (on 24 October), it is easy to see why Labor's shadow minister for primary industries, Kerry O'Brien, referred to the situation as 'a fiasco' – a claim refuted by the government. Liberal Senator Judith Troeth (Victoria), telling a Senate hearing

> The government does not accept that it is a fiasco, and I wish to point out to you that, after the sheep were rejected, the government took charge of this situation, and we

> managed the situation. It may have taken some time and a degree of negotiation, but ultimately the situation was resolved, and government and industry are very happy at the outcome. We totally reject your word.[14]

From the outset of this 'incident', the government apportioned no blame on the industry, despite this being an industry with a reputation of acting like 'cowboys' seemingly resistant to improving welfare standards.[15] That may be why the initial response by the Howard Government on 28 August 2003 appeared lackluster. While the government did not issue a public statement following Saudi Arabia's rejection of the sheep, it could not be said they sat on their hands. The government did place an immediate suspension on trade of live export to Saudi Arabia and simultaneously announced a review (the 'Keniry Review') into the livestock export industry, leading to $11.3 million set aside to implement the report's recommendations in the following year's Federal budget.

The calling of an inquiry and a suspension of trade had – after all – worked for earlier scenarios. The government had hoped their response would make the problem disappear, and it very well may have, but for the *60 Minutes* report. *Cormo Express* was now in the public domain.

Almost one month after the *Cormo Express* had been ordered to leave the Saudi port, the government found it needing to step up its rhetoric regarding live export. The situation was damaging the government. The media and subsequent public outcry, including the tabling of a petition in the Senate by the Australian Democrats (with more than 20,000 signatures) forced the hand of the government. As reported by *The Age*,

> The Howard Government refused to take the welfare of the animals on board seriously until the Prime Minister was attacked on talkback radio over the Minister's handling of the crisis and that it took a backbench rebellion

> inside the Coalition before Warren Truss took seriously his task.[16]

The government had no option but to find a suitable outcome. The unrelenting public outcry now threatened the entire billion-dollar trade. As a former LiveCorp executive recalls

> During the *Cormo Express* episode in the early 2000s, Prime Minister John Howard wanted to shut the industry down, but we managed to convince him that it was in the best interest of everyone to keep it going. The deal we cut with him was 'fix it up', but don't give me any more shocks.[17]

The industry's failure to sign an agreement with Saudi Arabia in 2000 (providing overarching governance of the trade) was a serious misstep. Prior to 2000, Australia had ceased the exporting of live animals to Saudi Arabia for close to a decade due to animal welfare concerns. Surely LiveCorp (as the industry body responsible for regulating the trade) could see recommencing trade with little to no governance in place was as an unacceptable risk for exporters? It was of no surprise the suspension of trade with Saudi Arabia lasted until the release of the 'Keniry Review' and a new policy (ASEL) was realised. Better late than never.

The Coalition government placed a value on the live export trade and was not inclined to adhere to calls by the live animal lobby to cease trading. As Truss argued

> Government and industry need agreed contingency plans such as an alternative destination or use for the cargo in the unlikely event of a similar unforeseen rejection arising with industry.[18]

While Howard let his minister take the lead, by his own admission, he gave strong direction for a resolution. With an election to be held in the coming year (9 October 2004), the thought of live export trade being a barnacle during the election campaign, was intolerable. Although Howard's actions were suggested as a 'failure in leadership' by his political opponents, he illustrated confidence in his senior leadership team to act in the national interest. This did not mean Howard shirked from media engagement. On the contrary, he willingly addressed the media in the hope of assuaging his colleagues, the public, and industry representatives. His stock in trade throughout his time in office.

2006: Cattle in Egypt

Three years later, the live export industry was again front and centre of a negative media campaign: this time it was cattle, and the country was Egypt. On Monday 27 February 2006, Agriculture Minister Peter McGauran MP (Nationals, Victoria), announced the banning of exporting live animals to Egypt pending an inquiry into reports of maltreatment of cattle in Egyptian abattoirs. This response came after another *60 Minutes* program, 'A Cruel Trade', aired the evening before.

The footage, secretly filmed by Animals Australia (an Australian animal protection organisation), showed cattle stabbed in the eye before having their rear leg tendons cut by a knife. While the cattle were not homegrown in Australia, the footage was filmed at an abattoir where Australian cattle were routinely slaughtered – an abattoir where Australian farmers and industry had invested equipment and manpower to ensure humane processes. From the footage aired it was clear the equipment was not being used humanely *and* advice was clearly ignored. McGauran found the vision '[g]ut wrenching ... you won't see worse examples of animal cruelty than that'.[19] While the subsequent inquiry established the animals captured in the footage had not come from Australia, the animal welfare lobby claimed the government was failing in its responsibilities and charged it with complicity. Richard Carleton was equally blunt:

> Richard Carleton: You're responsible?
>
> Peter McGauran: No.

> Richard Carleton: Yes.
>
> Peter McGauran: How so?
>
> Richard Carleton: Because you were told about this at least three years ago. You set about doing something about it, which was quite futile. You've got men in the Middle East who know this is going on. They answer to you.[20]

McGauran was snookered. Consequently, the parliamentary week was dominated with questions targeting (again) the government's track record on live exports. Howard would sit uneasy throughout Question Time.

In 2003 and 2006, the apparent failure of the government to act on behalf of the welfare of animals left the government wrongfooted and looking besieged. Labor's shadow agriculture spokesman Gavan O'Connor MP argued the government had known about welfare concerns at the abattoir for the past six years. He stressed the government's delays and inaction placed the future of Australia's live exports to Egypt (and other countries) at risk. In difference to the *Cormo Express* – where the animals involved originated from Australia – the Egyptian cattle saga spoke more to the brutality of the trade, intimating improvements introduced by Australian industry were insufficient. The public rhetoric suggesting that if the government could not stop these events from occurring then live export trade should cease altogether. The damage done to Australia's farming reputation was potentially irreversible.

When the animal activists and elements of the media were not driving the narrative, the government showed itself capable of mitigating a crisis. I doubt many people knew of the 3000 cattle temporarily stranded in the Red Sea in late 2004 due to a shortage of space at the Israeli holding facilities. As a result of a flurry of backroom diplomacy with the government of Israel, the cattle were saved from being stranded on board for any length of time, preventing another potentially embarrassing international incident for the Government. One that would have played into the hands of opponents of live export trade.

Lessons learned

Lyn White, a former South Australian police officer, joined the animal welfare group Animals Australia in 2003. White, a proponent of covert filming, had conducted numerous investigations into the trade was now partnering with a major media outlet. White's arrival on the scene and the heightened furor over trade is not a coincidence. White understood that to release footage via a national media outlet (like the ABC or Nine) meant a potentially wider audience that what would normally resonate with a fringe group, potentially placing an issue on both political and public agendas. This tactical approach was evident in her work with *60 Minutes* in 2003 (and 2006) and later with the ABC in 2011.[21]

Putting White's actions aside, a pertinent question is whether Howard (or his ministers) could have foreseen what unfolded in 2011. There was enough history of media attention and public opinion surrounding the trade for any government to see that further negative press would seriously harm the lucrative business. I question whether even Howard would have been able to predict the 'perfect storm' that existed in 2011: when the ABC ran the live export expose causing a devastating effect on the cattle trade, combined with the precarious nature of the 'hung' parliament with the Gillard Government holding onto power with the support of independent Members of Parliament. In 2011, miscalculations of values placed on the live export trade were in part to blame for what has been referred to as a 'kneejerk' reaction by Minister Joe Ludwig (action later to be found unlawful by the Federal Court) in attempting to address an animal welfare issue. The government chose to cripple an entire industry, rather than working with industry to fix problems inside the supply chain.

As highlighted in a report tabled by the Senate Rural Affairs and Transport Committee

> The program was so hard-hitting that it panicked sections of the community and the Australian government into thinking that the only solution was to immediately suspend the live cattle trade, without consideration of the devastating and far-reaching impact this action would have on the many families and communities that depend on the trade for their livelihood.[22]

The Howard Government had been criticised for not being tough enough on the live export industry following the 'Keniry Review'. For one former Western Australian Labor backbencher and prominent anti-live export campaigner

> They [the Howard Government] just didn't go far enough. A ban is one thing but making sure the industry cleans up its act could have been done before we got to 2011. Howard missed the boat on that one. The industry hadn't done anything to develop the tools the government needed to deal with any future incident. And Howard could have stepped in, way back in 2006, and made the industry far more accountable. Don't forget it was the animal activists as well [as 2011] that put the trade on the agenda. Banning was great but Howard could have put stringent and appropriate measures in place. But either couldn't or wouldn't.[23]

As indicated in statements made by Howard in 2003, he and his government clearly understood the lucrative nature of the trade. A former Liberal National Party backbencher whose electorate relied heavily on cattle production for income contends

> Howard did what he could but knew the value of the relationship with the rural heart landers, and we [the Nationals] weren't going to let him punish the whole trade for a few who wanted to cut corners.[24]

The junior member of the Coalition was flexing its muscles. The *Cormo Express* placed Howard in a tricky position. Keeping the Nationals happy while acknowledging the voices of suburban voters was no easy task. Truss, a future Nationals leader, provided Howard some buffer against criticism from other rural leaders – but not entirely. Joint party room discussions throughout the crisis were said to be unusually robust, with divisions emerging between rural and urban Members of Parliament. Howard did well to shield internal disagreements from the media and public.

If we compare the three animal welfare incidents: the death of thousands of sheep aboard MV *Cormo Express* did not create much public uproar, in difference to the treatment of cattle in 2011. As one farmer said wryly, perhaps the public cared less about the livestock on *Cormo Express* as they were only 'maggots on legs'[25] simply not resonating in the same way as big-eyed cattle.

I suggest there is a far more logical reason as to why the public response was far less effusive than what occurred in 2011. It has to do with the evolution of social media and its relationship with the mainstream press.

Social media

In 2003 (and 2006), the public was informed of the *Cormo Express* via traditional media sources: television, radio, and newspapers. Political responses were driven by what was seen and heard. For Senator Ian MacDonald (during a heated exchange in Senate Estimates in later 2003), members of the Cabinet, '... can read the papers and read the letters to the editor. They can listen to the news and the airwaves.'[26] In 2003, talkback radio was the more immediate public temperature gauge available. As Howard readily acknowledged about the situation, 'I know there's a lot of concern expressed on talkback, and I understand that and I'm very sensitive to it.'[27]

The reliance on traditional media was to change by 2011. The advent of social media offered a new means of political access for ordinary Australians: providing an efficient and effective way to contact politicians demanding immediate action. By 2011, social media was embraced by the animal welfare lobby (and others) changing the participatory landscape. Political activist group GetUp! in partnership with Animals Australia and the Royal Society for the Protection of Cruelty against Animals (Australia), used social media to great effect. Coordinating an army of protesters to target the email inboxes of politicians, the digital era had landed on the doorstep of Australian politics.

Last thoughts

Julia Gillard was Australia's first prime minister to feel the force of the 24-hour news cycle. While this new competition for audience share emerged during the first Rudd Government (2007–2010), it was not until Gillard the full suite of social media platforms was put to effect. I contest the impact of social media would have been negligible had the story in 2011 not been picked up by mainstream media nor the events occur within an unstable political environment. I contend further that had John Howard been confronted by a barrage of online dissent and subjected to the pressure of a relentless and targeted email campaign in either 2003 or 2006 (such as what was organised by the animal welfare lobby in 2011) then perhaps this may have resulted in stricter controls over exporters. Such a response may have gone some way to reducing the mistreatment of animals while protecting Australia's valuable export trade. We shall never know.

Endnotes

1. J. Quiggin, *Australian Economic Growth: The Role of Special Interest Groups and Political Factors*, Discussion Paper 161, Canberra, Australia: Australian National University, 1987, p. 2.
2. J. Keniry, *Livestock Export Review, Final Report: A Report to the Minister for Agriculture, Fisheries and Forestry*, 23 December 2003. Retrieved from http://www.agriculture.gov.au/SiteCollectionDocuments/animalplant/animalwelfare/tradeexport-transport-review/keniry_review_jan_04.pdf, p. 6 cited.

3. 'Ship of Shame', *60 Minutes*, 21 September 2003 http://www.liveexportshame.com/60_minutes2.htm.
4. Michelle Grattan, *The Age*, 'Sheep onboard a national shame', 24 September 2003. https://www.theage.com.au/opinion/sheep-onboard-a-national-shame-20030924-gdwe89.html.
5. Andrew Webster, *The Age* 'Secret deal gives sheep to Baghdad', 26 September 2003, https://www.theage.com.au/national/secret-deal-gives-sheep-to-baghdad-20030926-gdwewe.html.
6. Richard Carleton interview, 'Ship of Shame', *60 Minutes*, 21 September 2003 http://www.liveexportshame.com/60_minutes2.htm.
7. Ibid.
8. John Howard, Radio interview with Jeremy Cordeaux, Radio 5DN, 1 October 2003, https://pmtranscripts.pmc.gov.au/release/transcript-20933.
9. Ibid.
10. Interview, Honourable Simon Crean MP, Leader of the Opposition, 23 September 2003.
11. News24, 'Sheep sail to island pasture', 17 October 2003, https://www.news24.com/news24/sheep-sail-to-island-pasture-20031017.
12. John Howard, Radio interview with Jeremy Cordeaux, https://pmtranscripts.pmc.gov.au/release/transcript-20933.
13. Ibid.
14. Senate Rural Affairs and Transport Legislation Committee (2003), 3 November 2003, https://parlinfo.aph.gov.au/parlInfo/search/display/display.w3p;adv=yes;orderBy=customrank;page=0;query=cormo%20SearchCategory_Phrase%3A%22committees%22%20Decade%3A%222000s%22%20Year%3A%222003%22;rec=2;resCount=Default.
15. Interview for doctorate with a WA National Party MP and feedlot owner October 2014.
16. AAP, 'RSPCA accuses government of sheep cover-up', 23 September 2003, https://www.theage.com.au/national/rspca-accuses-government-of-sheep-cover-up-20030923-gdwdyg.html.
17. LiveCorp was the industry body responsible for the trade. This comment was made during a conversation by a LiveCorp executive with the author in Perth in 2014.

18. *AAP*, Australia vows changes in livestock exports after 'Ship of Death fiasco', 15 October 2003, http://web.lexis-nexis.com/ universe/document?_mbc19ffced7be66c2ec2ec2031b9e1f3cf8&_docnum = 2&.
19. 'A Cruel Trade', *60 Minutes*, 26 February 2006, http://www.liveexportshame.com/60_minutes_2006.htm.
20. Ibid.
21. *60 Minutes* refused to take the footage from Lyn White on the grounds it was too gruesome to show on 'mainstream' television.
22. Rural Affairs and Transport References Committee https://www.vale.org.au/uploads/1/0/4/3/10438895/senate_enquiry_2011.pdf, p. 89 cited.
23. Interview with former Labor MP with the author as part of doctorate research, September 2014.
24. Interview with former Queensland National Party MP with the author as part of doctorate research, September 2014.
25. In conversation with author and a Queensland farmer, Perth, November 2014.
26. Rural and Regional Affairs and Transport Legislation committee Estimates, 3 November 2003, https://www.aph.gov.au/binaries/hansard/senate/commttee/s7050.pdf p. 52 cited.
27. John Howard, radio interview with Jeremy Cordeaux, https://pmtranscripts.pmc.gov.au/release/transcript-20933.

12

Communication: Cornerstone of the Howard Government

David Marshall[1]

Introduction

The communication skills exhibited by prime ministers during their time in office vary in both comprehension and articulation. In this chapter, I focus on how the Howard Government communicated with the Australian community, particularly during crises. I argue that John Howard possessed specific characteristics and approaches that made him an outstanding communicator. However, this was not always the case. During his tenure as Leader of the Opposition (1985-1989), Howard experienced a period marked by undermining, self-doubt, and often bruising encounters with the media. It is often said that experience is the best teacher. Through a forced period of reflection and personal growth, Howard became better prepared for the prime ministership, ultimately making communication the cornerstone of his government.

Howard's Media Management Philosophy

Howard understood the importance of a mutually beneficial relationship with the Australian media. He did so as he wanted to engage directly with the Australian public. Immersing himself in waves of media coverage, Howard would flood the airways on a daily occurrence talking directly to people listening in their cars, at home or on construction sites. Paul Kelly, a doyen of the Federal Parliamentary press gallery once remarked, that 'Howard operates in a 24-hour media cycle for the 1000 days of each three-year term'.[2] Kelly's colleague, political author and media commentator, George Megalogenis agreed: 'John Howard used talkback as a form of electronic focus group'.[3] Mike Steketee, columnist, and national affairs editor described Howard as 'arguably the most media-active prime minister Australia has ever seen'.[4] Melbourne radio personality, Neil Mitchell declared Howard 'deliberately increased' his use of talkback radio 'as a way of directly communicating with people'.[5] Howard's use of the media was a masterstroke.

Talking directly to large audiences, in both major cities and regional areas, and often over the heads of journalists and commentators, was a valuable communications strategy for Howard. He knew the importance of media management and stressed this point to colleagues.

Peter Costello, Australia's longest serving treasurer remarked on the value Howard placed on media relations: 'The big things at the leadership group meetings would be how to handle the media of the day, how to handle question time'.[6]

Howard's media appearances were never left to chance: 'I would have a brainstorming session with senior staff before major news interviews' to be prepared for any line of question. Drawing on his wife Janette's passion for Shakespeare, Howard believed 'every successful politician has to have some thespian qualities … you need a certain sense that you are on a stage'.[7] There was no bigger stage for Howard than the Prime Minister's Courtyard for a press conference. Sky News presenter David Speers observed 'it was very rare that he (Howard) would be caught out'. [8] Political biographers Peter Van Onselen and Wayne Errington suggest Howard 'is a media manager's dream'.[9] Howard's senior media advisor, David Luff was equally resolute: 'You don't spin John Howard'. [10] The Liberal Party's official website confirms Howard made 2,657 media appearances during his term as prime minister.

According to Clive Hamilton and Sarah Maddison[11] 'Howard ushered in a decade of unprecedented executive control over political communication'. Howard said, 'A prime minister can always shape the agenda if he or she is talking sense and is producing good policy'.[12] Brian McNair, a political communication expert, believed 'there was an intensity of his (Howard's) battle to maintain control over the news agenda'.[13]

With Howard's focus on consistent communication with the public, social researcher Hugh Mackay reflected on the Australian electorate's feelings towards the prime minister: 'No challenger, on either side of politics, comes close to Howard in terms of the respect he enjoys in the Australian electorate.'[14]

A change in the media environment emerged in the mid-2000s, as Howard approached his fifth election campaign in the second half of 2007. Megalogenis stated 'You could probably have Howard as the first multimedia Prime Minister that we had'.[15] It was also reported by academic, Jim Macnamara, that 'the election campaign in 2007 was described as the *YouTube election*'.[16] While Howard was to embrace social media platforms he was never as comfortable as he was with talkback radio.

Amidst the changing media landscape, there were many times Howard was called on to navigate complex and challenging issues during his eleven and a half years as prime minister. Many notable events would, however, colour the Coalition's time in office. This included: nine ministers resigning for various acts of impropriety - seven in less than a year (October 1996-September 1997); the 'Children Overboard' affair with government ministers alleging asylum seekers had thrown their children overboard (north of Christmas Island) to be rescued and given safe passage to Australia; the detaining of South Australian David Hicks (captured in Afghanistan in December 2001 and released from Guantanamo Bay detention camp in December 2007); the unlawful detention of Australian resident Cornelia Rau (2004-2005); the cancelling of the visa of Indian doctor Mohamed Haneef in 2007; and, the government's politically charged workplace law, *WorkChoices*.

Troy Bramston reporting on 'Howard's stinging critique of the Morrison era' noted:

> Memories fade. The Howard government could be chronicled by the protests against it: over guns, reconciliation, refugees, Hansonite racism, workplace relations, climate change and the Iraq war' ... 'Howard became consoler-in-chief in response to tragedies and disasters such as the Bali bombings. Yet critics will question his call for balance in politics given his government's confrontation with unions on the waterfront and WorkChoices laws, limiting Native Title, joining the invasion of Iraq, and divisions and scandals over asylum-seeker policies.[17]

Howard's legacy

There were many political and policy challenges faced by the Howard Government which tested the prime minister's capacity to effectively manage these events. In the following sections, I will explore key events and consider how they demonstrate strengths and limitations in the Howard Government's approach.

Gun buyback scheme

On 28 April 1996, six weeks after the Howard Government was sworn into office, a gunman murdered 35 innocent people (and injuring many others) sightseeing at the Port Arthur Historic Site in Tasmania. This tragic event shook the nation. The government was determined to act. Weeks later and standing before a public rally in the Victorian town of Sale on 16 June 1996, Howard spoke of the Liberal-National Coalition Government's nationwide plan to ban self-loading rifles and self-loading and pump-action shotguns. A gun buy-back scheme was central to this strategy.[18]

The government's response led to an outpouring of support from the public but also a backlash from some farmers and farming groups. Addressing an at times hostile audience, Howard was adamant that 'a dramatic reduction in the number of automatic and semi-automatic weapons in the Australian community was in the national interest'.[19]

Howard's appearance was marred in controversy when he fronted the community in a vest, a decision he later regretted. As Howard shared with columnist Janet Albrechtsen:

> … because the Commonwealth police told me the local police had spoken to somebody who had rung up and wandered into the local police station and said I'm going to shoot the so-and-so. I foolishly in my view, it's my responsibility and nobody else's, I wore it and I felt afterwards I shouldn't have … I felt quite stupid, and it was stupid because I never actually felt frightened, it was just the wrong signal.[20]

The impact of Howard's approach to gun control is still debated today, including overseas. The almost weekly occurrence of a mass shooting in the United States has media outlets reaching out to Howard for answers. On occasion, however, his forthright response can be a step too far for some Americans. As a guest on the *American CBS Sunday Morning program* in 2016, Howard left the interviewer in no doubt he was right in taking necessary steps to protect Australian citizens from harm. As reported:

Former Australian Prime Minister John Howard has re-entered the US gun debate, declaring it is "incontestable" gun-related homicides fell significantly after he introduced strict laws following the Port Arthur massacre. Speaking on CBS *Sunday Morning* TV news program, Mr Howard said he was compelled to act after 35 people were gunned down at the Tasmanian historical site [Port Arthur] in 1996. "And you had a 74 per cent fall in the gun-related suicide rates, isn't that evidence? Or are we expected to believe that that was all magically going to happen? Come on".[21]

This tragic event highlights Howard's ability to handle a contentious and highly emotionally charged issue with calmness and composure.

Goods and Services Tax (GST)

Howard's communication skills were on full display throughout the 'selling' of the goods and services tax (GST) reform prior to the 1998 Federal election.[22] The introduction of a new consumption tax (replacing wholesales sales tax) was felt by some political insiders to be a potential policy crisis for the government. After all, the Coalition, led by former leader John Hewson, lost the 1993 election promising to implement a GST. The introduction of a new tax system, however, was a risk worth taking for Howard. He was not to die wondering. Howard had seen previous governments baulk at major policy reform; he was to pursue taxation reform with alacrity.

The strategic approach adopted by Howard and his long-serving treasurer, Peter Costello was one of careful and methodical communication with the public. Daily talkback radio interviews were held explaining the need for reform. Howard knew from experience the media would pounce on any mistake or omissions of detail. While the Coalition lost the two-party preferred vote at the 1998 election, it was able to hold a majority of seats in the House of Representatives and the GST was introduced on July 1, 2000.

The impact of this communication strategy remains relevant in Australian politics today. Summarised best by Ken Henry, then Secretary of the Treasury, when implying why the Turnbull Government's attempt at taxation reform (in 2015) had failed:

> As the Howard and Costello Government demonstrated with the GST, there needs to be 12 to 18 months spent in preparing the ground for the tax reform package, in genuine conversation or at least consultation with the Australian community, and all sectors of the Australian community. That hasn't happened. We're going to need at least that for this tax reform package.[23]

Openness to explaining policy change was a longstanding trait of Howard. He viewed as essential achieving 'a balance of what made sense in policy terms' and placing an onus on gaining 'sufficient public support'.[24] Interviewed on the 25th anniversary of his 1996 election win, Howard stated:

> I always thought you could sell a big reform provided you could satisfy people on two things: first, it was good for Australia and second it was fundamentally fair to the more vulnerable in the community.[25]

Notably, this trait has been left wanting in prime ministers who have succeeded Howard.

Charter of Budget Honesty

After an election victory, the prime minister and treasurer sit down (often the next morning) to receive a briefing from Treasury officials. It is customary to follow up this staged media event with a press conference condemning the previous government for a budgetary situation worse than the government (and electorate) was led to believe. Howard was no stranger to this.

Howard and Costello described the inherited financial situation from the Keating Government as a 'Budget Black Hole' and later using the 'parlous state' of Australia's finances to redefine pre-election promises as 'core commitments' (leading the public to infer everything else as being 'non-core').[26] The opposition made much of Howard's attempt to wriggle out of his commitments with this phrase living on in Australian political folk lore.[27]

In 1998, the Howard Government introduced the *Charter of Budget Honesty Act* to provide an independent pre-election financial update. The aim was to avoid post-election surprises. This is still required today; however, it has not prevented new administrations from using the time-honoured statement that the 'finances are worse than we were told' rhetoric on being elected to government.

September 11, 2001

John Howard was in Washington on 11 September 2001, when four United States airliners were hijacked by Islamic extremists. Their murderous actions resulted in the deaths of 2,977 people, including 10 Australians. These attacks transformed the world forever, with heightened security in virtually every country across the world including Australia, with the focus on the transforming of air travel. Howard told Channel 10 News Stela Todorovic on the twentieth anniversary of the attacks (in September 2021), that

> when it happened it was so unexpected and so audacious, a lot of us thought well is the next attack going to occur in America, or it is going to be London, is it going to be Tokyo, or is it going to be Sydney.

Howard also had Australia join the United States led international military coalitions in Afghanistan and Iraq. On 17 September 2001, Members of the House of Representatives and Senate passed a resolution stating the Australian Parliament 'fully endorses the commitment of the Australian Government to support within Australia's capabilities United States-led action against those responsible for these tragic attacks'.[28] The 'War on Terror' morphed into a 20-year conflict in Afghanistan and a decade of combat in Iraq. Howard reflected on this decision when speaking about leadership at a *Sydney Writers Festival* event promoting his book, *The Menzies Era* in 2015. For Howard, '[t]he hardest thing is to send young men and women to war'.[29]

Airport security now impacts travellers worldwide, with Australia maintaining some of the strictest pre-border checks introduced during the Howard Government. In an address to a forum hosted by the *Australian Strategic Policy Institute* then-Minister for Home Affairs Karen Andrews MP outlined Australia's position:

> The Commonwealth immediately spearheaded an initiative to join with the Premiers and Chief Ministers of the States and Territories to establish new counter -terrorism arrangements. Through an intergovernmental agreement, the National Counter-Terrorism Committee was launched. This new structure ensured cooperation between the Commonwealth, State and Territory governments and their respective operational agencies, in-

> cluding police and Commonwealth intelligence services … the architecture was sound – and so successful that a decade later, it reached across the Tasman to become the Australia-New Zealand Counter-Terrorism Committee, known as the 'ANZCTC'. This structure of seamless cooperation across jurisdictions has proven to be a key component of Australia's counter terrorism response.[30]

Tampa

In late August 2001, the Royal Australian Navy ('Navy') intercepted the Norwegian freighter MV *Tampa*, carrying 433 rescued refugees (mainly Hazaras from Afghanistan) who had been rescued from a distressed fishing vessel in international waters off Christmas Island (an Australian territory in the Indian Ocean), along with five crew. The Howard Government had refused permission for the Tampa to enter Australian waters.

The '*Tampa* Crisis' became the catalyst for Australia's new 'border protection' policy. It also became a pivotal issue in the 2001 federal election campaign. By 2 September the government had hastily secured agreements with the governments of Nauru and New Zealand. The Navy transported the *Tampa*'s asylum-seekers to Nauru from where 131 were sent to New Zealand. The remaining 302 asylum-seekers were processed in Nauru over coming months (though a handful remained for three years). In the aftermath of the '*Tampa* Crisis' the government passed a series of laws creating a new legislative framework for handling asylum-seekers: the 'Pacific Solution'. This framework included the excision of many of Australia's offshore islands, including Christmas Island, from Australia's migration zone.

The Australian Government's handling of the *Tampa* Crisis - and subsequent implementation of the Pacific Solution - attracted criticism both in Australia and overseas. One of the more memorable lines spoken by Howard during his prime ministership was uttered at the Liberal Party campaign launch in Sydney in October 2001 declaring: 'We will decide who comes to this country and the circumstances in which they come'.[31] The Howard Government would win the election confounding its critics and opponents. Notably, in the six years from 2002, only 23 boats arrived in Australia compared to 43 carrying more than 5000 asylum-seekers in 2001 alone.[32]

This policy continued under the Morrison Government, which used a similar defence during the contentious Novak Djokovic-Australian Open tennis saga in January 2022. Djokovic's exemption to compete in the Grand Slam tournament in Melbourne was initially approved by the Victorian Government and Tennis Australia. On arriving, Djokovic's visa was revoked by the Commonwealth Government then later reinstated. Djokovic won a legal battle to stay in the country. Alex Hawke MP, then Immigration Minister cancelled Djokovic's visa. Djokovic lost his appeal against the Minister's decision and was deported.

Political website, *Crikey* ran a story titled, 'When playing God is far easier than winning an election', stating 'Nothing says there's an election coming like tough talk on borders. John Howard did it in 2001. Scott Morrison hopes it'll work for him in 2022'.[33]

The question is how would the Howard Government have handled this series of disastrous events?

Howard's ability to read public opinion shaped his approach to these events. At the launch of the 2001 Cabinet papers, Howard told *The Guardian's* Anne Davies that he 'remains unapologetic about his tough policies on asylum seekers,' stating these policies had 'saved lives.'

Howard explained his reasoning:

> The Australian public's position on migration has always been supportive, provided it's properly controlled. But once they think it's getting out of control, their support diminishes. When control is restored, support returns.[34]

Howard must have been surprised that a future government

would dilute his strong border protection stance, which had wide public support in 2001. Howard's legacy continues to influence Australia's border protection policies today.

Northern Territory Intervention

Howard responded to the 2007 'Little Children Are Sacred' report by launching an immediate emergency intervention in the Northern Territory. This response was justified as a measure to protect Aboriginal children from sexual abuse and family violence, which had reached crisis levels. However, there was no consultation with the 73 Indigenous communities affected by this decision. The government's intervention powers were extensive, including the right to acquire Aboriginal land for five years, bans on alcohol and pornography, compulsory health checks for all Aboriginal children, and the quarantining of half of all Australian welfare payments for use on basic items only. In August 2012 the Intervention formally ended. Many components however continued under the '*Building Stronger Futures*' policy. This policy remained effective until 2022. The new Albanese Government promised to abolish the Cashless Debit Card Scheme and all forms of compulsory income management, which still exists in other federal legislation.

A report published on *The Conversation* website in 2017, stated:

> Many different bodies have evaluated the Intervention over the past decade. Most of the policy measures were not evidence-based – and outcomes have been generally very poor. The cautious hopes for increased resources flowing into remote communities in terms of health, education and housing services have turned to disappointment.[35]

An *Arena Online* article published online in 2021 referred to a presentation made at a conference titled 'The Endless Intervention: First Nations Speak Out', convened by the Intervention Rollback Action Group (IRAG) in Mparntwe (Alice Springs) and Stop the

Intervention Collective Sydney (STICS) in Sydney. The conference paper analysed the impact of the Intervention:

> All the available official statistics tell us that the behavioural Intervention to assimilate, develop and close the gaps is failing: unemployment is higher than ever, school attendance is lower than ever, poverty rates are higher than ever (more than 50 per cent of people live below the poverty line), overcrowding in public housing is everywhere and – most damning of all – more than 40 per cent of households report running out of food, many living in rich Australia are going hungry, and people are dying prematurely because of poverty.[36]

Michael Park, reporting for *NITV News* in 2022 on Human Rights Law Centre director and Arrernte man Nick Espie description of the intervention as: 'a shameful chapter in the treatment of First Nations people in the Territory, which began in 2007. During these fifteen years, we have seen the demonising of Aboriginal people and culture and the erosion of self-determination'.[37]

Howard's continuing influence

In February 2019 the *Sydney Morning Herald* reported that: '*Morrison is modelling John Howard, but it's a risky move.*'[38] Following that revelation and two weeks before Christmas 2021 Scott Morrison was asked by *2GB* radio host Ben Fordham whether he leaned on Malcolm Turnbull for advice. He said 'no' - then volunteered that he did however speak to John Howard quite a bit. 'How often?', Fordham asked: 'every week or two', said Morrison, 'but sometimes it happens just a bit more often than others.' Every prime minister speaks to their predecessors occasionally, but every fortnight appears to be quite frequent.

In an article published by *The Australian* on 18 August 2022, Howard delivered a stinging critique of the Morrison era. Howard criticised Scott Morrison's 'egregious' attack on Christine Holgate and discussed the expulsion of Malcolm Turnbull and Peter Dutton, along with other failures of the former government. Bramston notes that Howard did not hold back in expressing his views on these issues. For Bramston:

> Peter Dutton has talked with Howard several times since becoming Liberal leader. “Peter and I have always got on well,” Howard says. “I was very grateful that he won a seat in 2001 and I made him a minister early in the piece. I was impressed with him. He was a common-sense Queensland copper”.

In addition, Bramston asked Howard about his proudest achievements during his time in office:

> Looking back, Howard names economic and budget management as important achievements and rates gun law reform following the 1996 Port Arthur massacre as an especially proud moment. Pressed to identify things he might have done differently, Howard names the decision to take the *no-disadvantage test* out of the *Workplace Relations Act*. ‘That was a mistake,’ he admits. While Howard regrets his speech to the 1997 Australian Reconciliation Convention (where he lost his temper as some in the audience turned their backs), he does not regret not attending Kevin Rudd’s apology to the Stolen Generations in 2008. ‘That would have been hypocritical,’ he says. ‘I had expressly eschewed delivering an apology.’[39]

Lessons from the Howard era

Former Prime Minister Tony Abbott wrote an opinion piece in the *Daily Telegraph* on 3 March 2021 arguing: ‘John Howard’s government didn’t just win elections, it got things done. It doesn’t just respond to events, it shaped them’. Then there was the Albanese statement that ‘I’ll be more like a Bob Hawke or John Howard’ This was the headline in *The Australian* on 8 March 2022. The article went on to state: ‘Anthony Albanese is pledging to end Labor’s class and climate wars, govern in the style of Bob Hawke and John Howard if elected’.

This is an extraordinary statement for a Labor leader to make. It highlights the esteem and respect Howard is held in today after leading the nation for eleven and a half years and becoming the second longest serving prime minister in Australia's history.

This contrasts with the somewhat haphazard approach of the Morrison Government when Morrison took on additional ministerial responsibilities without informing the public or Cabinet colleagues.[40]

This matter was a crisis of great significance, one created by the former prime minister himself. It was revealed on 15 August 2022 that Prime Minister Scott Morrison had secretly appointed himself as Minister for health, finance, treasury, home affairs and industry, science and resources portfolios between 2020 and 2021.

Initially Morrison had claimed he held three ministerial portfolios and had no recollection of any other ministries aside from health, finance and resources. He believes the move had been 'prudent and responsible'.

Sky News reported on 16 August about Prime Minister Anthony Albanese's media conference, where he stated that Scott Morrison's decision to secretly swear himself into five ministerial portfolios was an "unprecedented trashing of our democracy." The reaction from other members of Parliament was swift.

Phil Coorey reported that former Home Affairs Minister Karen Andrews demanded Scott Morrison quit politics after learning he had taken on her Home Affairs ministry in the lead-up to the May federal election.[41] Latika Bourke quoted former Prime Minister Tony Abbott in *The Age*, stating that Morrison's secret decision to swear himself into five ministries and conceal it from most of those ministers was 'unusual, unorthodox, and strange.[42] Former Prime Minister Malcolm Turnbull tweeted his criticism, emphasising the breach of trust and transparency:

> we should be very concerned that a PM, an AG, the GG and apparently their officials thought Morrison's sinister

> secret state appointments were legitimate. Did anyone object? Resign in protest? All showed a grave lack of respect for and understanding of democratic governance.[43]

Mark Kenny, former press gallery reporter and currently a professor of practice in Australian Studies at the Australian National University (ANU) writing in *The Canberra Times* states the reason Morrison appointed himself as joint minister 'was in case their decisions presented "some threat to the national interest as a result of unilateral action by an individual"'. Kenny posits 'this staggering admission will go down in infamy as among the most ill-judged and revealing remarks of any Australian leader'.[44]

John Howard was as diplomatic as ever. Interviewed on ABC's *7.30*, Howard stated:

> I don't think it's something that is so reeking with principle as to require an unwanted, expensive, unnecessary by-election … Mr Morrison had 'contextualised' his reasons for doing so.[45]

Howard was to later reflect that the pandemic did not justify Morrison's actions, suggesting he could not imagine any circumstances in which he would have sworn himself in as a duplicate minister.[46]

Last, a lesson from the Howard era: communication is key, and trust is paramount to your success as a prime minister and to protecting your legacy. Morrison failed on all accounts.

Howard's legacies are numerous and diverse. He was a prime minister for his time, well respected and often criticised, but people always knew where he stood. Howard is now an elder statesman with a reputation for political astuteness that endures to this day. His tenure as prime minister for eleven and a half years may never be repeated. His clear communication, consistent policies, and ability to maintain public trust were crucial to his enduring impact on Australian politics.

Endnotes

1. Parts of this paper draw on my doctoral thesis, D. Marshall, 'Political discourse in a media saturated environment: the Howard Government's approach to communicating with the Australian electorate', University of Canberra, 2015.
2. Paul Kelly, 'Re-thinking Australian Governance: The Howard Legacy', Cunningham Lecture, as published in *Australian Journal of Public Administration, 65*(1), 2006, pp. 7-24.
3. David Marshall, 'Political discourse in a media saturated environment: the Howard Government's approach to communicating with the Australian electorate', p. 223.
4. Mike Steketee, 'Canberra in Control', *The Australian*, 8 March 2001.
5. Marshall, p. 223.
6. Ibid., p. 167.
7. Ibid., p. 222.
8. Ibid., p. 222.
9. Paul Van Onselen & Wayne Errington, 'John Howard the Great Communicator: No, Really', paper presented at Australia and New Zealand Communication Association, University of Adelaide, 2006.
10. Marshall, p. 111.
11. C. Hamilton & S. Maddison, *Silencing Dissent*, Sydney: Allen & Unwin, 2007.
12. Marshall, p. 175.
13. B. McNair, *An Introduction to Political Communication* (Fifth ed.). Abingdon, Oxon: Routledge, 2011.
14. Hugh Mackay, 'Howard: an ordinary bloke who feeds a nation's prejudices', *The Age*, 21 February 2006.
15. Marshall, p. 227.
16. J. Macnamara, *E-Electioneering: Use of New Media in the 2007 Australian Federal Election*, Australian Centre for Public Communication University of Technology, Sydney, 2008.
17. Troy Bramston, *The Australian*, 18 August 2022.
18. Australian National Audit Office (ANAO) reports the gun buyback scheme secured the surrender of some 640 000 prohibited

firearms nationwide, https://www.anao.gov.au/sites/default/files/anao_report_1997-98_25.pdf?acsf_files_redirect

19. John Howard, Address to a public rally, Sale, Victoria, 16 June 1996, https://pmtranscripts.pmc.gov.au/release/transcript-10030
20. Janet Albrechtsen, Channel 7's *Sunday Night*, aired 21 September 2014.
21. See *Sydney Morning Herald* report, 14 March 2016.
22. https://treasury.gov.au/sites/default/files/2019-03/Whitepaper.pdf
23. Ken Henry, ABC *7.30* interview, 22 September 2015.
24. Marshall, p. 104.
25. 'Sky News celebrates 25 years since John Howard's first election win', https://www.skynews.com.au/australia-news/politics/sky-news-celebrates-25-years-since-john-howards-first-election-win/video/d367b1e29f863d112d5cfcc8d1557a87
26. John Howard interview with John Laws, 21 August 1996, https://pmtranscripts.pmc.gov.au/release/transcript-10078
27. https://theconversation.com/1996-1997-cabinet-papers-show-how-howard-and-costello-faced-a-budget-black-hole-107273
28. House of Representatives, *Debates,* 17 September 2001, p. 30739.
29. John Howard, *Sydney Writers Festival*, 18 May 2015.
30. Hon. Karen Andrews address to *Australian Strategic Policy Institute* forum '*The Road from 9/11*', 13 September 2021.
31. John Howard, 2001 election campaign launch, Sydney, 28 October 2001, https://electionspeeches.moadoph.gov.au/speeches/2001-john-howard
32. 'Tampa affair', National Museum of Australia, https://www.nma.gov.au/defining-moments/resources/tampa-affair
33. Amelia Lester, *Crikey,* 17 January 2022, https://www.crikey.com.au/2022/01/17/djokovic-morrison-tough-borders/
34. Anne Davies, "'It stopped the boats': John Howard on Tampa, Siev X, and the Pacific Solution", *The Guardian*, 1 January 2022, https://www.theguardian.com/australia-news/2022/jan/01/it-stopped-the-boats-john-howard-on-tampa-siev-x-and-the-pacific-solution
35. Article in *The Conversation*, 'Ten years on, it's time we learned the lessons from the failed Northern Territory Intervention', 26 June 2017,

https://theconversation.com/ten-years-on-its-time-we-learned-the-lessons-from-the-failed-northern-territory-intervention-79198

36. Jon Altman, 'Lest we forget the harmful policy legacies of the Northern Territory Intervention', *Arena Online*, posted on 24 June 2021, https://arena.org.au/lest-we-forget-the-harmful-policy-legacies-of-the-northern-territory-intervention/
37. Michael Park, *NITV News* report 18 July 2022.
38. Sean Kelly, *Sydney Morning Herald*, 18 February 2019.
39. Troy Bramston, *The Australian*, 18 August 2022.
40. https://www.themandarin.com.au/197242-the-five-hats-of-scott-morrison-the-secret-ministerial-every-man/
41. Phil Coorey. *The Australian Financial Review*, 16 August 2022.
42. Latika Bourke, *The Age*, 17 August 2022.
43. Malcolm Turnbull, Twitter message posted on 16 August 2022.
44. Mark Kenny, 'Howard has not ended yet', *Canberra Times*, 21 August 2022.
45. Sarah Ferguson, *7.30* interview, 16 August 2022.
46. John Howard, appearance at the National Press Club, Canberra Thursday 18 August 2022.

13

Policy and political learning: The Howard Government's legacy on contemporary Australian government

Zareh Ghazarian, Laura Woodbridge,
Jacqueline Laughland-Booÿ

Introduction

As Australia's second longest serving prime minister, John Howard led the Coalition to four election victories between 1996 and 2007. During this time, the government introduced major policy changes that still impact contemporary Australian society. These included firearms reforms in 1996, as well as the introduction of a new Goods and Services Tax (GST) following the 1998 election. The Howard Government also committed Australia's armed forces to join the United States of America and other allies in Iraq in 2003, as well as increased the first home-owners grant in 2000, and introduced the so-called 'baby bonus' in 2004.

The chapters of this book consider many elements of Howard's time in office. A key theme, however, is the spectre of crisis and the way in which the Howard Government responded to policy and political challenges as they arose. This is timely as the world moves out of the COVID-19 pandemic and faces concerns about the health of the economy and the climate. With the Howard Government now having been out of office for nearly two decades, it is timely to reflect on its performance as well as how it compares with more modern Australian governments. In this chapter, we look back on the previous chapters in this volume in considering John Howard's approach to leadership, as well as how his government responded to crises. We also examine the issues of foreign affairs and security to see what lessons we may take from the Coalition's time in office at the start of the 21st century. In doing so, we seek to understand how governments after Howard have learnt from the experiences of these years.

Legacies and learnings

In the context of government, learning can take place in policy or political matters. Policy learning focuses on learning about how to design and deliver targeted policy outcomes, while political learning focuses on how best to advance policy decisions using political tools.[1] It is generally accepted that, in the political sphere, individuals, groups, organisations, and entire governments may continue to learn and these learnings may inform and influence their future actions and decisions.[2] Typically, governments can learn by translating individual lessons into organisational and systemic-level changes in behaviour.[3] Learning in government can encompass concepts such as evidence-based policy-making,[4] evaluation as a step in the policy process,[5] and policy transfer from concurrent governments in other jurisdictions.[6]

Similarly, experiences of political events or policy outcomes may also impact on how political leaders and governments respond to new challenges. Those involved in policy making build 'shared ideas, norms and symbols' which are often informed by previous experiences.[7] The development of such knowledge constitutes 'policy memory'; a subcategory of cultural memory, which bears similarities to policy learning and the use of historical analogies.[8] As a counterpart to policy memory, policy amnesia entails a failure to learn from the past which may contribute to policy failure.[9]

Within this context, we will now explore the contribution of preceding chapters on three key themes concerning the Howard Government. Leadership, the first theme, considers Howard's role as leader of the government and leader of the Liberal party. The second examines 'crises' and how governments may respond to them. The third theme is foreign affairs and security. By considering these three themes, we highlight the impact of the Howard Government on contemporary Australian government and Howard's continuing legacy.

Leadership

The experiences of the Howard Government provide a valuable source of learning when it comes to leadership. Patrick Weller, for example, regards Howard as one of the most successful prime ministers in the world since 1980, measured on the factors of his longevity, control over the government, and ability to introduce his preferred policy programme.[10] Howard is also ranked highly amongst Australian academics, making the top ten of all Australian prime ministers and scoring particularly well on his management of the Cabinet and the Liberal party and Coalition, as well as his 'relationship with the electorate'.[11] Howard's story has been remarked upon as a story of survival.[12] While both his successors and predecessors struggled to maintain their role of the Liberal party leadership, Howard was able to hold on from the time he assumed the role in 1995 until his defeat in 2007.

This did not mean that Howard did not face internal competition for the prime ministership. There was persistent speculation that then-Treasurer Peter Costello was positioning himself to take the leadership from Howard. This intensified after the 2004 election when media reports circulated that Howard had made an agreement with Costello in the mid-1990s about a handover of the leadership in his second term as prime minister.[13] This came to a head at a press conference in July 2006 when Howard acknowledged that the treasurer 'would obviously like to see a leadership change in his favour before the election'.[14] Howard explained that his decision to remain was in response to 'the will of the party and interests of the party'.[15] Howard later wrote to Liberal parliamentarians clarifying his position to remain as prime minister and lead the party to the 2007 election. As Howard reminded members, he considered leadership of the Liberal party to be 'the unique gift of the party room'.[16] Days earlier, Howard had reportedly argued that Costello's moves towards the Liberal party leadership were fuelled by 'hubris and arrogance'.[17]

While this episode derailed the government's approach in the short term, and ultimately allowed Labor to argue that it was just a matter of time until Costello became prime minister, it also demonstrated a model through which leadership tensions could be defused. Rather than cede his position, Howard goaded Costello and his supporters for a challenge that never eventuated. Howard's deep conviction that the leadership was indeed a 'gift of the party room' ultimately diminished Costello's run for the prime ministership. In essence, Howard was calling for Costello to show he had support from members, which Costello failed to do.

This episode also contrasts sharply with how prime ministers since Howard have dealt with internal party cohesion. Between 2007 and 2018, Australia went through six prime ministers which led to some commentators labelling the country the 'coup capital of the democratic world'.[18] Others lamented a crisis of leadership and were concerned about the implications for governing during a period typified as the 'revolving door' of prime ministership.[19] This period of churning through prime ministers contrasted with the relative stability of the preceding decades. Bob Hawke, for example, was prime minister for eight years, Paul Keating remained in the role for five years, while John Howard was prime minister for 11 years.

This raises the question of whether the chopping and changing of prime ministers in subsequent years was because contemporary prime ministers failed to exercise leadership. Former senator Richard Alston discusses how Howard learned lessons about successful leadership from previous prime ministers, such as Menzies and Keating. His own leadership style was marked by a commitment to communicating with the public. Alston describes Howard's personal vision, but also his dedication to 'taking people with you'. Howard's management and communication skills are explored further by James Walter in the context of the Prime Minister's Office and its development. While Walter notes that Whitlam instigated the trend towards expansion of the office, Howard built upon it exponentially. Even as ministerial staff proliferated and a 'permanent campaign' approach to governing was adopted, Howard maintained a high level of hands-on control over government messaging, as well as overall management of the party and Cabinet.

Within this context, Walter invites us to speculate about how subsequent governments have, or have not, learned from and been able to replicate Howard's success in this area. He concludes that Howard's '[s]uccessors have struggled with their inheritance', resulting in an era of disposable leaders. While Rudd took a similar approach to Howard in centralising control, he was also over-reliant on the Prime Minister's Office, and his small inner circle limited his ability to maintain good relationships with the wider government and party room. Rudd was also criticised for being a 'micro-manager' which contributed to his eventual removal as prime minister.[20] In contrast, Walter sees Gillard as more effective in this area, evidenced by legislative successes. On the other hand, according to Walter, Abbott was over-reliant on a small circle of ministerial advisors, in particular his chief of staff, which led to dysfunction. Turnbull was then more successful at building relationships with the public service, but failed to effectively lead the party room. Morrison, meanwhile, was overly 'secretive and addicted to spin', attracting criticism for making clandestine ministerial appointments. This is a mixed record, and no subsequent government appears to have approached Howard's level of confidence and success in management and communication.

Did subsequent governments and prime ministers, then, fail to learn from Howard's lessons about management and communication for leadership success? Indeed, Rudd and Morrison sought to use organisational arrangements to stop their respective parties from changing leaders so easily. In 2013, upon his return as prime minister, Rudd changed the party rules so that removing a Labor prime minister would be very difficult. Rather than simply rely on the numbers in Caucus, Rudd's new rules meant that a ballot of the parliamentary team and ordinary Labor party members would determine the party's leadership. Similarly Morrison, when he defeated Turnbull to become prime minister in 2018, changed the rules so that a leader could only be removed if at least two-thirds of the parliamentary wing voted to do so. The impact of this was significant as Morrison became the only prime minister since Howard to lead for a full term after winning an election.

It is also important to note the significant changes in the media that have occurred in the years after the Howard Government which may have played a role in making the prime ministership more fragile. Social media, in particular, was in its formative years during the Howard prime ministership. For example, Facebook was launched in 2004, YouTube appeared in 2005, Twitter emerged in 2006, and the now-ubiquitous iPhone debuted in 2007. Today, millions of Australians use smart devices to access social media platforms as part of their daily lives.[21] These platforms have made an impact on the communication approaches, and coverage of, of Australian political actors.[22] This has hastened the 24-hour news cycle, and provides politicians with the ability to engage with the community constantly and directly.

This, however, is a double-edged sword. Digital media platforms also can foster the distribution of 'fake news' which may impact the policy debate. Recent examples of the so-called 'Mediscare' campaign against the Coalition in 2016 and the misinformation about Labor's 'death tax' in 2019 highlight the potential challenges of policy and political communication in contemporary Australian politics. Additionally, media outlets and social media platforms increasingly prefer content that can be presented in shortened and 'more visual and more emotive' ways.[23] This also provides opportunities for prime ministers to present themselves through an unfiltered lens. For example, Scott Morrison's attempts at positioning himself as a 'daggy dad' were highlighted by photos released by the prime minister on social media, especially in one instance where he was wearing boardshorts during COVID-19 isolation.[24] In doing so, prime ministers may seek to build rapport with the electorate but, as Walter in this collection hints, may also lead to imagery and spin overshadowing policy and substance.

It is also important to note the significant shifts and changing political landscape in which prime ministers since Howard have found themselves. In the 2007 election, for example, the Labor Party's primary vote was 43.4 per cent, while the Coalition's was 42.1 per cent (including the Country Liberal Party result). Combined, the primary vote for the major parties at the 2007 election was approximately 85.5 per cent. This contrasts sharply with the most recent election in 2022 where the combined primary vote of the Labor and Coalition parties had fallen to just 68.3 per cent. Furthermore, at the 2007 election just two seats were won by candidates not from a major party. In comparison, the 2022 election resulted in 16 seats being won by minor parties and independents. These results show that there has been a significant shift in the voting choices of Australians which is impacting on the support on the major parties. Within this context, prime ministers and governments seemingly must communicate with an electorate comprising a more diverse range of interests and views than in previous years.

Crisis and opportunity

Another key leadership skill emphasised by authors in this volume is that of navigating policy challenges. David Lovell's chapter finds the record of the Howard Government 'instructive' in its handling of adversity. Lovell recommends learning from both Howard's perceived successes – such as the response to the Port Arthur massacre – and from more fraught examples, like the military intervention in Timor-Leste. Paul Kelly goes further, and views the Howard Government 'as a transition point in relation to crisis', noting that the nature and scale of challenges facing governments has since changed. Kelly characterises Howard as a figure who not just responded to, but precipitated major challenges. In several examples, such as the GST, the waterfront campaign, and *WorkChoices*, Howard 'was prepared to provoke major upheavals to pursue his reform agenda', in Kelly's words.

One of the first crises that the Howard Government faced was in April 1996 when 35 people were killed by a gunman in Port Arthur, Tasmania. This, just weeks after the Coalition had won the 1996 election, presented the Howard Government with an opportunity to make a lasting impact on public policy in Australia. Trying to bring about change in firearms policy was complicated by the constitutional arrangements in Australia. While the Commonwealth had responsibility for customs, states had responsibility for law and order. The Port Arthur murders, however, provided the national government with a window of opportunity to bring about long-lasting reforms.

Within twelve days, the government had introduced a new national firearms policy. This was an incredibly fast outcome, especially since it involved cross-jurisdictional cooperation between national and sub-national governments. The speed in which this policy outcome was reached, however, was due to the fact that much of the work on creating a national firearms policy had been done by the bureaucracy over the preceding decade, and was ready for implementation at the time of a government's choosing.[25] Reflecting on the speed in implementing these reforms, Howard noted, 'You never let a good crisis go to waste … you do have to recognise that sometimes a crisis forces people to focus on something'.[26] The way in which the Howard Government responded to gun violence was significant and had an influence over the government's future policy and political approach. In particular, the perception of Howard as a leader with deep convictions was strengthened. In an interview some eleven years after leaving office he said that 'I often used to joke that I encountered a lot of people who would say I can't stand you, but I know what you stand for'.[27]

Chapters in this volume also reflect upon specific crisis events during the Howard Government and note their connection to perceived successful leadership. They also draw out questions about what cause crises, what kinds of events may be regarded as crises, and who shapes these narratives. Many authors used the term 'crisis' as a touchstone for their discussion of political events and policy problems. The very use of this word tells us something about how we may view policy making in the modern era – as reactionary, emergent, and critical. The 'crisis' label is often applied to construct a sense of urgency around both external events and internal policy failures.[28] The authors in this volume generally view that the ability to manage and respond to crises is a key leadership quality that is in consistent demand and was possessed by Howard.

Mal Brough, for example, reflects upon his experience as Minister for Indigenous Affairs in Howard's Cabinet, but particularly in relation to allegations of child abuse in isolated communities in the Northern Territory late in the Howard Government's final term. Brough describes this as a crisis, and the speed and intended impact of the Howard Government's so-called Northern Territory 'intervention' suggests it was treated as one. Despite the significance of the policy, Brough questions whether the right lessons have been learned in the years since the intervention.

Similarly, Shaun Carney reflects on the Howard Government's record on industrial relations, most notably the waterfront dispute. According to Carney, an important characteristic of this episode was that it was a crisis 'generated by the Howard Government' itself. John Howard was keen to pursue reforms to industrial relations and reduce the impact of unions in Australian workplaces. This was arguably an explicit ideological decision by the Howard Government, and Howard's determination on this issue ultimately strengthened the sense that, even though voters may not have agreed with his policies, they had a clear sense of what he stood for.[29] Subsequent governments appear to have struggled to show this level of policy consistency. As Carney reminds us, more recent governments have appeared to step away from commitments in policy areas like climate change and energy, ostensibly to maintain cohesion within the party as well as electoral support.

Meanwhile, Stephen Martin argues that there has been a distinct lack of learning by governments in relation to crises in the financial sector. He traces the revelations of the recent Royal Commission into Misconduct in the Banking, Superannuation and Financial Services Industry back to the Howard years, arguing that '[c]urrent issues confronting Australian banks bring to light failures of government policy in the financial sector whilst on Howard's watch'.

Live exports are another contentious policy area that reached crisis points both during the Howard years and in the time since, as discussed by Fiona Wade. Two high-profile events occurring in 2003 and 2006 prompted the Howard Government to institute a shift of regulatory onus from the industry and onto the government. The Gillard Government in 2011 was also confronted by a media-driven exposé of animal mistreatment in the trade, prompting public outrage to which the government responded by temporarily banning live exports. This parallel highlights the significance of bringing about long-lasting policy change when the opportunity presents itself. The issue of live animal exports lay dormant until another crisis hit, and reactionary measures had to be taken. Wade observes in her chapter, however, that social media had a big impact on the story in 2011 during Gillard's time as prime minister. As we have noted, social media was not as well developed during the Howard years, while a significantly expanded media landscape confronts contemporary national governments that may disrupt their ability to apply lessons from history.

Arguably, of all crises that occurred during the Howard years, the outbreak of communicable diseases resonates most strongly with many Australians today. In the chapter by Peter Collignon, we are challenged to consider how Australia's response to COVID-19 may exhibit or promote lesson-learning. During the Howard years, Australia faced two notable outbreaks of contagious disease, though on a much smaller scale. A border control policy was instituted in response to Severe Acute Respiratory Syndrome (SARS), and accordingly no spread occurred in Australia. After the avian flu in 2005, the Howard Government released a new Australian Management Plan for Pandemic Influenza. This plan presented an overview of how an influenza pandemic could be managed in Australia.

When COVID-19 emerged in 2020, however, the Morrison Government implemented a suite of far more significant and disruptive policies – such as complete border closures, emergency income support, and a shut-down of non-essential activity. Many of these measures aligned with what state and territory leaders were also doing in their jurisdictions and the speed in which these policies were being implemented reflected the approaches of many governments around the world. In this case, the path of the Morrison Government was not seemingly informed by the Howard Government's approach but were instead seen at the time as highly novel and unprecedented. Indeed, the lengthy lockdowns which governments introduced to try and manage COVID-19 were controversial and disruptive.[30]

Foreign policy and security

Several chapters in this volume take another view of crisis, using the term to emphasise the significance of broader security issues during the Howard Government. These include terrorism and military intervention, the alliance with the United States of America, and asylum seeker policy which all stand out as key issues confronted by the Howard Government. For example, Paul Kelly delves into security issues as part of his broader discussion of Howard's crisis management – including the Tampa events, Timor Leste, the war on terror, and the Bali bombings. Similarly, Peter Jennings reflects on the capacity of the National Security Committee of Cabinet, established for the first time by Howard, to respond to these events – particularly Afghanistan, Iraq, and East Timor. Jennings notes that subsequent governments have retained the Committee, such that it has become 'a successful instrument of government' in military and crisis scenarios. Kelly, in his chapter on Howard's crisis management, goes further to speculate that the National Security Committee was part of a broader trend towards the centralisation of power around the prime minister – a trend that subsequent governments have followed.

David Kilcullen also notes the 'terrorism crisis' during the Howard years, but particularly focuses on Australia's alliance with the United States. He argues that Australia was not simply act as 'deputy sheriff' to the United States of America, but was acting independently and strategically to provide regional leadership. Howard's shaping of the United States alliance forms a significant part of his legacy, and Kilcullen posits that 'the direction set by Howard on the morning of 9/11 has endured until today'. Recent decisions by governments to have even closer relations with the USA and UK through the AUKUS security pact and nuclear submarine arrangements remind us of the enduring links Australia has with the USA and UK. While the Howard Government was not the first to build close links with these countries, the actions of more recent governments highlights that they are generally following the same path when it comes to international relations and security.

Meanwhile, Pene Mathew takes on one of the most fraught issues for recent governments – the refugee crisis. The events surrounding the Tampa vessel in 2001 prompted Howard to develop the Pacific Solution, which has involved transporting asylum seeker arrivals to detention centres on islands such as Nauru and Manus Island. While the Rudd Government watered down this policy, it was later renewed by Gillard and again by the second Rudd Government. Subsequent Coalition governments began to close down the island detention centres, but retained the strict border control and boat turnbacks policy.

Mathew views the Howard Government's approach to Australia's international refugee obligations as a failure, and suggests that while subsequent governments have replicated that approach – exhibiting a form of learning – it has not been for the better, as a 'crisis of nondecision' has persisted in the twenty years since Tampa. Reflecting a debate in the literature on government learning, we may ask whether learning necessarily involves lessons learned for success – can failure be learned, too?

Conclusion

Themes of leadership, crisis management, and security have defined reflections on Howard as undertaken by the contributors to this volume. They present an overview of some of Howard's greatest successes, as well as failures, and invite us to learn from both. It is difficult, if not impossible, to effectively determine whether subsequent governments have learned from Howard's experiences. Answering such a question with regard to just one of the issues or events discussed in this volume would require a significantly more space than we have here. However, the authors of this volume gathered together ideas in the development of leadership, crisis management, prime ministerial communication and office management, asylum seeker policy, and decision making on matters of security to allow us to begin to understand the impact of the Howard era on modern Australian politics.

The question of whether governments learn is informed by an examination of what governments are learning *from*. What is the political and policy memory, what does it encompass, how is it constructed, and by whom? Understanding how the public, commentators, policy makers and leaders of the present day understand Howard's legacy, and tell the narrative of his time in office, is vital in understanding how government learning takes place. When prompted to reflect on one of Australia's longest serving prime ministers, what do we remember? This volume goes some way towards assembling a picture of Howard's legacy from which current and future governments may learn.

Endnotes

1. P. J. May, 'Policy learning and failure', *Journal of Public Policy*, vol. 12, no. 4, 1992, pp. 331-54.
2. S. Moyson, P. Scholten & C. M. Weible, 'Policy learning and policy change: theorizing their relations from different perspectives', *Policy and Society*, vol. 36, no. 2, 2017, pp. 161-77; B. Levitt and J. G. March, 'Organizational Learning,' *Annual Review of Sociology*, vol. 14, 1988 pp. 324-34.
3. J. S. Levy, 'Learning and foreign policy: Sweeping a conceptual minefield', *International Organization*, vol. 48, no. 2, 1994, pp. 279-312; CA Dunlop & CM Radaelli, 'Learning in the bath-tub: the micro and macro dimensions of the causal relationship between learning and policy change', *Policy and Society*, vol. 36, no. 2, 2017, pp. 304-19; see also T. Heikkila and A. K. Gerlak, 'Building a conceptual approach to collective learning: Lessons for public policy scholars', *Policy Studies Journal*, vol. 41, no. 3, 2013, pp. 484-512.
4. A. Witting, 'Insights from 'policy learning' on how to enhance the use of evidence by policymakers', *Palgrave Communications*, vol. 3, no. 49, 2017.
5. I. Sanderson, 'Evaluation, policy learning and evidence-based policy making'. *Public Administration*, vol. 80, no. 1, 2002, pp. 1-22.
6. Moyson, Scholten & Weible 2017; E Page, 'Future governance and the literature on policy transfer and lesson drawing' *ESRC Future Governance Papers*, 2000; D. P. Dolowitz & D. Marsh, 'Who learns what from whom: A review of the policy transfer literature', *Political Studies*, vol. 44, no. 2, 1996, pp. 343-7; D. P. Dolowitz & D. Marsh, 'Learning from abroad: The role of policy transfer in contemporary policy-making', *Governance*, vol. 13, no. 1, 2000, pp. 5-23; R. Rose, 'What is lesson-drawing?' *Journal of Public Policy*, vol. 11, no. 1, 1991, pp. 3-30; R. Rose, *Learning from Comparative Public Policy: A Practical Guide*, Routledge, London, 2005.
7. J. Batteau, S. Princen & A. Rigney, 'Lessons from the past? Cultural memory in Dutch integration policy', *European Journal of Political Research*, vol. 57, no. 3, 2018, p. 741.
8. Batteau, Princen & Rigney, 2018, p. 741.

9. See R. Hulme & M. Hulme, 'Policy learning? Crisis, evidence and reinvention in the making of public policy', *Policy and Politics*, vol. 40, no. 4, 2012, pp. 473-89; A. Stark & B. Head, 'Institutional amnesia and public policy', *Journal of European Public Policy*, vol. 26, no. 10, 2019, pp. 1521-39.
10. P. Weller, *The Prime Ministers' Craft: Why Some Succeed and Others Fail in Westminster Systems*, Oxford University Press, Oxford, 2018.
11. P. Strangio, 'Prime-ministerial leadership rankings: the Australian experience', *Australian Journal of Political Science*, vol. 5, no. 2, 2022, p. 189.
12. P. Strangio, P 't Hart & J Walter, *The Pivot of Power : Australian Prime Ministers and Political Leadership, 1949-2016*, Melbourne University Publishing, Carlton, 2017.
13. L Tingle, 'Howard refuses Costello handover', *Australian Financial Review*, 12 July 2006, https://www.afr.com/politics/howard-refuses-costello-handover-20060712-jfbkq
14. Cited in Tingle 2006.
15. Ibid.
16. AAP, 'John Howard's letter', *The Age*, 31 July 2006, https://www.smh.com.au/national/john-howards-letter-20060731-gdo2s4.html
17. Cited in Tingle 2006.
18. See N. Bryant, 'Australia: Coup capital of the democratic world', *BBC News*, 14 December 2015, https://www.bbc.com/news/world-australia-34249214
19. See M. Walsh, 'The revolving door of Australian prime ministers', in M. Evans, M. Grattan & B. McCaffrie (eds), *From Turnbull to Morrison: Understanding the Trust Divide*, Melbourne University Press, Melbourne, 2019, pp. 332-8.
20. See 'The micromanager's downfall', *The Sydney Morning Herald*, 25 June 2010, https://www.smh.com.au/business/small-business/the-micromanagers-downfall-20100625-z3xe.html/
21. Australian Communications and Media Authority, *Trends in online behaviour and technology usage: ACMA consumer survey 2020*, September 2020.
22. See G. Jericho, *The Rise of the Fifth Estate: Social Media and Blogging in Australian Politics*, Scribe Publications, Brunswick, 2012.

23. D. Wilding et al., *The Impact of Digital Platforms on News and Journalistic Content*, University of Technology Sydney, 2018, p. 36.
24. See N. Zhou, "'Daggy dad' or 'propaganda'? The media's growing use of official Scott Morrison pictures', *The Guardian*, 25 November 2020, https://www.theguardian.com/australia-news/2020/nov/25/daggy-dad-or-propaganda-the-medias-growing-use-of-official-scott-morrison-pictures.
25. P. Alpers & Z. Ghazarian, 'The 'perfect storm' of gun control: From policy inertia to world leader', in J. Luetjens, M. Mintrom & P. 't Hart (eds), *Successful Public Policy: Lessons from Australia and New Zealand*, ANU Press, Acton, 2019.
26. Cited in Alpers & Ghazarian 2019, p. 218.
27. M. Gordon, 'John Howard on leadership: 'People would say I can't stand you but I know what you stand for'', *The Sydney Morning Herald*, 22 January 2018, https://www.smh.com.au/politics/federal/john-howard-on-leadership-people-would-say-i-cant-stand-you-but-i-know-what-you-stand-for-20180122-h0m1lb.html
28. B. Spector, 'Even in a global pandemic, there's no such thing as crisis', *Leadership*, vol. 16, no. 3, 2020, pp. 303-13.
29. See Gordon 2018.
30. See C. Le Grand, "Long lockdowns a 'failure of policy', says WHO envoy on COVID', *The Sydney Morning Herald*, 18 August 2022, https://www.smh.com.au/national/long-lockdowns-a-failure-of-policy-says-who-envoy-on-covid-20220816-p5ba6t.html

Closing Remarks

The Hon. John Howard OM, AC

Ladies and Gentlemen.

One reason my Government was reasonably successful is that I had a talented team of men and women who brought a lot of passion to their roles. Mal Brough exemplified this passion, particularly in dealing with issues that have long challenged governments and people of goodwill from both political parties. From my days in opposition, I remember working with various ministers responsible for Indigenous affairs. While I profoundly disagreed with some approaches and found others more agreeable, I never doubted their genuine concern for the challenges and their commitment to addressing them.

Throughout the conference, I reflected with former colleagues on the time after the Northern Territory Intervention began in June 2007. We had a dinner at the Lodge, with Mal Brough, Sue Gordon, a wonderfully talented woman who led the intervention group, and Noel Pearson. We talked about the nitty-gritty of the challenge: the terrible circumstances in which children were not raised but just existed in parts of the Northern Territory. We did not pretend it was the only problem of child neglect or abuse, but it was a discussion I have never forgotten. Sue brought a hands-on understanding, being a highly regarded Indigenous woman with a successful family. She had a practical approach, not neglectful of the rights equation, but she said, "You've got to give people a bit of hope for the future."

I thank Paul Kelly for his wonderful overview. During my years in politics, the two great chroniclers of Australian politics have been Alan Reid and Paul Kelly. Each brought unique talents suited to their respective eras, but both have a remarkable ability to use language that is relatable and understandable. They provide valuable perspectives on the politics of their times. Just as I remember Reid's *The Power Struggle*, *The Whitlam Venture*, and *The Gorton Experiment*, I remember Kelly's *The End of Certainty*, *The March of Patriots*, and others. Both have been unparalleled chroniclers of Australian politics.

The presentations have been fair. I do not take violent exception to anything that has been said. It would be churlish of me to do so. We live in an era where free expression should be the order of the day, and every government must be subjected to scrutiny. My government had plenty of failures. I think we had several major successes, but one of our strengths was stability. It is the only time since Federation three people occupied the prime ministership, the Treasury, and the Department of Foreign Affairs for the whole time. It is also important to point out it went beyond those three positions. Relations between the Liberal Party and the National Party were fundamental to the Howard Government's success. The capacity of many senior figures in the government to argue the case in the media was very important.

I was disappointed that the recently defeated Morrison Government did not see full participation from all its ministers. Far too much responsibility fell on a small number of individuals, and at times it felt like only the prime minister, the treasurer, and the defence minister were speaking for the government. In his own area, Greg Hunt (Health) did an excellent job.

I had many ministers keen to do the media. Alexander Downer was a wonderful, enthusiastic media performer. On several occasions, he would do an interview and a news conference on some foreign policy issue, and I would be doing a news conference on something else. I would get a question about foreign affairs, and he complained to me later that night, "You knocked me off the seven o'clock news tonight." They always ran me instead of him. It was a metaphor for his enthusiasm. You cannot overestimate the importance of continuous communication.

I have reflected on the communication styles of past and present prime ministers. Menzies was an outstanding communicator, the greatest political orator I have ever heard. We remember him from great public meetings, like when a constituent said, "I wouldn't vote for you if you were the Archangel Gabriel," and he famously replied, "Madam, if I were the Archangel Gabriel, you wouldn't be in my constituency." Bob Hawke used television brilliantly, excelling in one-on-one interviews. Paul Keating was known for his powerful parliamentary speeches, which received rave reviews from the gallery, though the public might have felt differently. I focused on talkback radio, as it seemed the most effective way to communicate, though I did not exclude other media. Every prime minister must make their own judgment about which media to prioritise. David Marshall effectively highlighted that different forms of communication suit different eras and times.

The relationship between the Prime Minister's Office and the public service is fundamental to any successful government. We are not returning to the pre-1972 era when only public servants worked in prime ministerial offices. Those days are gone, but the need for a respectful relationship between the Prime Minister's Office and the public service remains crucial. Problems arise when this relationship breaks down, as seen in the "children overboard affair," which stemmed from a communication failure between the minister's office and the Department of Defence.

The relationship Arthur Sinodinos (Chief of Staff to Prime Minister Howard) had with Max Moore-Wilton (Secretary of the Department of Prime Minister and Cabinet) and later with Peter Shergold was crucial. I share Professor Walter's high opinion of Peter Shergold as an adviser; he was an outstanding policy enthusiast. While traveling overseas, I asked him what he was reading, and he replied, "I'm reading this study about the reaction of native-born Englishmen to welfare benefits given to recently arrived Bangladeshis." This was relevant to the welfare review we were conducting and exemplified his attention to policy detail.

Respecting the public service and listening to their advice is essential. While you may not always take their advice, it is your responsibility to explain why if you do not. There is nothing more demoralising for public servants than submitting papers to ministers and hearing nothing in return for months.

Peter Jennings' assessment of the National Security Committee (NSC) was fair and accurate. I am very proud of the NSC; it operated extremely well and never leaked. It included senior ministers—prime minister, treasurer, foreign minister, defence minister—and defence leaders like Peter Cosgrove, along with public servants like Ric Smith and Dennis Richardson, who were outstanding advisers to both sides of politics.

The NSC functioned effectively and cohesively. Having people like Richardson and Cosgrove involved in all discussions was invaluable. I only called for ministers-only discussions on three or four occasions. Decisions on Timor, Iraq, the Solomon Islands, and Afghanistan were made with the full benefit of advice from senior public servants.

I am indebted to all who have contributed. It is very humbling that so many people of such calibre are willing to contribute their time and intellectual effort to a very effective retrospective. All governments must be scrutinised, and mine is no exception. It is important to have someone offering critical views of some received strengths of the Howard Government in controversial areas. The participation of former senior Labor figures like Stephen Martin and Simon Crean has enriched the contest of ideas.

Finally, as we witness the seventh change of government in Australia since World War II, it is heartening to see the seamless transfer of power. I expressed this sentiment in a letter to the new Prime Minister, congratulating him on our country's tradition of peaceful transitions. Even in the great arsenal of democracy (the United States), the last transfer of power there was far from seamless. This is something we should take pride in within Australian democracy.

I sincerely thank Professor David Lovell, Professor Tom Frame AM, Andrew Blyth and staff at the Howard Library for their exceptional stewardship and guidance in organising these retrospective conferences.

Thank you.

Acknowledgements

The journey of bringing *The Art of Crisis Management: The Howard Government Experience, 1996-2007* to life has been both rewarding and enlightening, and it would not have been possible without the support and contributions of many individuals and institutions.

First and foremost, I would like to extend my deepest gratitude to former Prime Minister John Howard, whose willingness to share his insights and experiences has been invaluable to this and other works analysing his four governments.

I acknowledge the support of my former colleagues at UNSW Canberra, UNSW Canberra Special Collections and the John Howard Prime Ministerial Library at Old Parliament House. Their encouragement and intellectual insights were a constant source of motivation. I am especially grateful to Professor Tom Frame AM, the inaugural director of the Howard Library, and Professor David W. Lovell. Both are giants in their respective fields, and their mentorship and friendship have been invaluable to me. I extend my gratitude to Erin Wishart and Laura Woodbridge for their meticulous attention to detail.

I am also grateful to Tom Switzer and my colleagues at the Centre for Independent Studies. Thank you for your encouragement and for creating an environment that fosters rigorous and thoughtful analysis.

Our cultural institutions have also played a pivotal role in the development of this book. I thank sincerely the staff at the National Archives of Australia and the National Library of Australia for their patience and forbearance.

This book would not have been possible without the unwavering support of Anthony Cappello, founder of Connor Court Publishing. His dedication and belief in this project have been instrumental in bringing it to fruition. I also extend my thanks to Michael Gilchrist for his exceptional work in designing such an impressive book.

Finally, I thank the readers who will engage with this book. It is my hope that *The Art of Crisis Management: The Howard Government Experience, 1996-2007* will provide valuable insights and foster a deeper understanding of a pivotal period in Australian political history.

Andrew Blyth

www.ingramcontent.com/pod-product-compliance
Lightning Source LLC
Chambersburg PA
CBHW052058300426
44117CB00013B/2186
* 9 7 8 1 9 2 3 2 2 4 2 6 1 *